ANDREA L. WEISS, Ph. D. (2004) in Near Eastern Languages and
Civilizations, University of Pennsylvania, is Assistant Professor of
Bible at the Hebrew Union College-Jewish Institute of Religion in
New York.

Figurative Language in
Biblical Prose Narrative

Supplements

to

Vetus Testamentum

VOLUME 107

Figurative Language in Biblical Prose Narrative

Metaphor in the Book of Samuel

by

Andrea L. Weiss

BRILL

LEIDEN • BOSTON

2006

This book is printed on acid-free paper.

Library of Congress Cataloging-in-Publication Data

Weiss, Andrea L.
  Figurative language in biblical prose narrative : metaphor in the book of Samuel / by Andrea Weiss.
    p. cm. — (Supplements to Vetus Testamentum, ISSN 0083-5889 ; v. 107)
  Includes bibliographical references and index.
  ISBN 90-04-14837-X (alk. paper)
  1. Bible. O.T. Samuel—Language, style. 2. Metaphor in the Bible. I. Title. II. Series.

  BS410.V452 vol. 107
  [BS1325.52]
  221 s—dc22
  [222/.40   2005058250

ISSN 0083-5889
ISBN 90 04 14837X

To my parents,
Martin and Ruth Weiss

CONTENTS

ACKNOWLEDGEMENTS

This project has taken shape over a number of years, evolving from a doctoral dissertation presented to the department of Near Eastern Languages and Civilizations at the University of Pennsylvania to the current book. In a conversation in the fall of 1997, Adele Berlin advocated the need for a thorough exploration of metaphor in the Bible. After I accepted her challenge and began researching this subject, I struggled to find an approach to metaphor that would significantly enhance the present understanding of biblical metaphors and the texts in which they operate. Then, in the fall of 1999, I enrolled in a course on metaphor and tropes taught by Asif Agha in the Anthropology department of the University of Pennsylvania. Dr. Agha provided tremendous insight into this topic, and he proposed a means of identifying and interpreting metaphors that proved to be pertinent to the Bible and promising in its exegetical outcomes. I am grateful for the guidance given by all four members of my dissertation committee: my advisor, Jeffrey Tigay, Adele Berlin, Asif Agha, and David Stern. Their profound contributions to my thinking about figurative language and my analysis of the Bible is evident throughout.

In addition, I am thankful for the tremendous support provided by my colleagues at the Hebrew Union College-Jewish Institute of Religion in New York. I owe a special debt of gratitude to David Sperling, who closely read a draft of this manuscript, and to my dear friend, Carole Balin. While working on the early stages of this project, I received generous financial assistance as a University of Pennsylvania William Penn Fellow and as Scholar-in-Residence at Har Zion Temple in Penn Valley, Pennsylvania.

Finally, I lovingly thank my husband, Alan Tauber, and our children, Rebecca and Ilan, for encouraging my work and enriching my life. I dedicate this book to my parents, Martin and Ruth Weiss, in gratitude for a lifetime of love and support.

ABBREVIATIONS

CAD	*Assyrian Dictionary of the Oriental Institute of the University of Chicago*
CBQ	*Catholic Biblical Quarterly*
conj.	conjunction
c.p.	common plural
DCH	*The Dictionary of Classical Hebrew*
def. art.	definite article
demon. pro.	demonstrative pronoun
dir. obj.	direct object
EA	El-Amarna tablets
emd	emendation
f.s.	feminine singular
imperf.	imperfect
indir. obj.	indirect object
JAAR	*Journal of the American Academy of Religion*
JANES	*Journal of the Ancient Near Eastern Society of Columbia University*
JAOS	*Journal of the American Oriental Society*
JBL	*Journal of Biblical Literature*
JNSL	*Journal of Northwest Semitic Languages*
JPS	*Jewish Publication Society Tanakh*
JSOT	*Journal for the Study of the Old Testament*
KJV	*King James Version*
m.s.	masculine singular
m.p.	masculine plural
N	noun
NAB	*New American Bible*
neg. part.	negative particle
NJB	*New Jerusalem Bible*
NRS	*New Revised Standard Version*
perf.	perfect
PP	prepositional phrase
prep.	preposition
REB	*Revised English Bible*
subj.	subject

suf.	suffix
TDOT	*Theological Dictionary of the Old Testament*
TLOT	*Theological Lexicon of the Old Testament*
UF	*Ugarit-Forschungen*
V	Verb
VT	*Vetus Testamentum*
ZAW	*Zeitschrift für die alttestamentliche Wissenschaf*
ZAH	*Zeitschrift für Althebraistik*

CHAPTER ONE

AN INTRODUCTION TO THE STUDY OF METAPHOR

I. Introduction

When the Tekoite woman appears before King David, she states: "They would quench my last remaining ember" (2 Sam 14:7). In this narrative context, the utterance describes her kinsmen's purported desire to kill her sole living son. In another setting, the very same words might refer to an attempt to extinguish a fire. Elsewhere, they might indicate the satisfaction of a long held desire. A single lexeme, when situated in different linguistic contexts, can convey different meanings and nuances. Depending on the components of the surrounding text segments, the interpretation of the lexeme and its effects may vary. In the example at hand, how does one determine the referents of the verb and object and the implications of the utterance as a whole? What marks a sentence like this as a metaphor? What distinguishes this statement from other forms of figurative language? This book seeks to answer these questions, thus gaining greater insight into the way metaphor and other tropes operate in biblical prose narrative.

This chapter surveys the extant research on metaphor and highlights the works that have proven most influential to the developing understanding of metaphor. The review of the relevant literature traces the history of metaphor research, exploring why this topic has been the subject of such enduring, expanding interest in a range of fields and analyzing how it has been treated by biblical scholars.

II. Aristotle's Treatment of Metaphor and Its Implications

The word "metaphor" comes from the Greek *metaphora*, derived from *meta* meaning "over" and *pherein*, meaning "to carry." The study of metaphor customarily begins with Aristotle and his statement in *The Poetics* that "metaphor is the transference of a term from one thing to another: whether from genus to species, species to genus, species to species, or by analogy."[1] Aristotle uses the term metaphor in an expansive manner, encompassing four varieties of "transference" under the rubric of metaphor. The first three forms of transference, "genus to species, species to genus, species to species," fit the basic definition of metonymy. Only transference by analogy, which Aristotle heralds as "the most celebrated" of the four types of metaphor,[2] properly qualifies as a metaphor in the more restricted sense of the term. Aristotle's expansive use of the term "metaphor" has influenced subsequent applications of the term, for the word sometimes refers to various forms of figurative language or to figurative language in general, and at other times it designates one specific trope. The tendency to employ the term in a variety of ways compounds the difficulties involved in understanding this trope and contributes to a lack of consensus as to what exactly constitutes a metaphor. In the present study, "metaphor" will be used in the more restricted sense, as the designation of one particular rhetorical device.

In *The Poetics* and other writings, Aristotle conceives of metaphor as a word-long phenomenon, a distinct word that can be extracted from a sentence and replaced with a related word. He explains how this process takes place:

> Metaphor 'by analogy' is a case where the relation of *b* to *a* is the same as that of *d* to *c*: the poet will use d instead of *b*, or the reverse. Sometimes they add to the metaphor something to which it is related: for instance, the wine cup is to Dionysus what the shield is to Ares, so the poet will call the wine cup 'Dionysus' shield' and the shield 'Ares' wine cup'. Again, old age is to life what the evening is to the day: so the poet will call evening 'day's old age', or, like Empedocles, call old age 'the evening of life' or 'the dusk of life'.[3]

Only toward the latter part of the twentieth century, over two thousand years after Aristotle's day, did scholars begin to question the established notion that a metaphor involves the transference or substitution of specific words. Rejecting the long-held "word-based" conception of metaphor, Roger White asserts:

---

[1] Aristotle, *The Poetics*, trans. Stephen Halliwell (London: Gerald Duckworth and Co. Ltd., 1987), 55. Marjo Korpel dates the first usage of the word "metaphor" back to the Greek grammarians of the fifth century B.C.E. (*A Rift in the Clouds* [Munster: Ugarit-Verlag, 1990], 35).

[2] Aristotle, *The Art of Rhetoric*, trans. H. C. Lawson-Tancred (New York: Penguin Books, 1991), 236.

[3] Aristotle, *Poetics*, 55–56.

The idea of the metaphorical *word* is a largely self-perpetuating idea. Despite the fact that the theories of writers like Black and Ricoeur are far more complicated than the account of metaphor we encounter in the *Poetics*, the idea that in every metaphor there is an insoluble word or phrase which is the word or phrase being used metaphorically is never questioned. It is never questioned, because the theories not only take their origin in examples where it is plausible to talk in terms of such an idea, but no subsequent attempt is made to explain their application to those examples where at least apparently such an idea has no application.[4]

White argues that when one examines metaphors of greater complexity than, say, the oft-cited example, "Man is a wolf,"[5] Aristotle's notion of the transference of isolated words can no longer explain the workings of a metaphor. Instead, he insists: "*The* key to understanding the way metaphor works is to understand the way words have been combined in the metaphorical sentence."[6]

Asif Agha also criticizes Aristotle's word-based conception of metaphor, noting that problems arise as a result of Aristotle's simplistic theory of language.[7] He explains that for Aristotle, the metaphor is found in the word; however, there is nothing metaphoric about a particular word in and of itself. When Empedocles calls old age "the evening of life," the word "evening" remains an ordinary word, the same as in a phrase like "seven o'clock in the evening." The term becomes a metaphor when used in conjunction with the word "life." The study of figurative language in biblical narrative confirms that understanding a metaphor requires one to consider more than just an isolated lexeme; one must examine the relationship between words and their surrounding context.

In chapter 21 of *The Poetics*, Aristotle situates metaphor within eight different types of words, explaining that "all nouns can be

---

[4] Roger White, *The Structure of Metaphor* (Cambridge, MA: Blackwell Publishers Inc., 1996), 57. Similarly, Eva Kittay insists "that metaphors are sentences, not isolated words" (*Metaphor: Its Cognitive Force and Linguistic Structure* [Oxford: Clarendon Press, 1987], 23).

[5] Max Black, "Metaphor," in *Philosophical Perspectives on Metaphor*, ed. Mark Johnson (Minneapolis: University of Minnesota Press, 1981), 73. Reprinted from *Proceedings from the Aristotelian Society*. N. S. 55 (1954–55) 273–294.

[6] White, 4. Italics here and in all subsequent quotations reflect the printing of the original texts.

[7] Asif Agha is a linguist and Associate Professor of Anthropology and South Asia Studies at the University of Pennsylvania. He shared his insights about metaphor in a course entitled "Metaphor and Tropes" taught in the fall of 1999 and in numerous private conversations. He has reviewed all quotations cited in this work.

distributed into the following categories: standard terms, foreign terms, metaphors, ornaments, neologisms, lengthened terms, abbreviated terms, altered terms."[8] While here he defines a "standard term" rather vaguely as a term "in the usage of a particular group,"[9] he elaborates on the notion of standard versus nonstandard speech in chapter 22, when he writes:

> Excellence of style consists in clarity without banality. Now, the greatest clarity comes from the use of standard terms, but this involves banality . . . Grandeur and avoidance of the ordinary, by contrast, can be achieved by the use of alien language (by which I mean foreign terms, metaphor, lengthened terms, and everything which goes beyond the standard) . . . No small contribution is made to both clarity of style and the avoidance of the ordinary by lengthenings, abbreviations and alterations of words: the divergence from standard and usual usage will produce a heightened effect.[10]

In other words, the seven types of nouns listed after, and implicitly contrasted with, "standard terms" in chapter 21 provide a means of producing some sort of "heightened effect" and thereby avoiding banality; yet the speaker risks a loss of clarity if the words are not employed with skill and moderation. In his commentary on *The Poetics*, Stephen Halliwell notes that Aristotle's conception of style implies "a clear model of speech registers." The vocabulary of standard speech is located at the center of this system, and "all other registers are conceived, explicitly or implicitly, as divergences from standard speech, particularly through the choice of individual words which depart from normal usage."[11] Two aspects of metaphor discussed by Aristotle in chapters 21 and 22 prove particularly noteworthy: his view of metaphor as a divergence from standard speech and his observation that metaphor produces a "heightened effect."

To learn more from Aristotle about the effects of metaphor, one must turn to *The Art of Rhetoric*, where Aristotle again extols the value of clarity. He writes that "if one handles things well, there will be something unfamiliar and it will be able to be concealed and the meaning will be clear—and this we found to be the virtue of rhetorical speech."[12] He points to metaphor as a means of achieving these

[8] Aristotle, *Poetics*, 55.
[9] Aristotle, *Poetics*, 55.
[10] Aristotle, *Poetics*, 56–57.
[11] Halliwell, commentary on *The Poetics*, 160.
[12] Aristotle, *Rhetoric*, 219.

goals, for "metaphor also preeminently involves clarity, pleasantness and unfamiliarity."[13] Aristotle highlights various rhetorical benefits of metaphor, including the ability to ornament a subject,[14] to contribute to stylistic amplitude,[15] or to produce vividness.[16] In addition, he warns his audience of some of the perils of metaphors, such as the potential for inappropriate metaphors to produce "frigidity" and flatness instead of clarity. He cautions:

> There are also inappropriate metaphors, some through their absurdity . . . and some through their being too solemn or tragic. They are also unclear if they are drawn from too far afield. . . . All these are unpersuasive.[17]

Reflecting on Aristotle's interest in the rhetorical, practical side of metaphor, Agha maintains that Aristotle took an interest in language as "technology," as an instrumentality of action. He claims that the rhetorical context in which Aristotle first formulated the problem of metaphor has been largely forgotten in most twentieth century discussions of metaphor. Instead, those interested in metaphor have focused primarily on Aristotle's definition in *The Poetics* and largely ignored his comments in *The Art of Rhetoric*. A full appreciation of how metaphor operates in biblical narrative necessitates attention to the "technology" of metaphor and its rhetorical effects.

III. Historical Survey of the Study of Metaphor

A. *The Progressive Depreciation of Metaphor:*
Aristotle to the Mid-Twentieth Century

In the introductory chapter of a collection of articles entitled *Philosophical Perspectives on Metaphor*, the editor Mark Johnson traces the development, or, more appropriately, the demise of metaphor from Aristotle to the mid-twentieth century. His history of "the troubled life of metaphor" begins with what he sees as the four aspects of Aristotle's view of metaphor that have "had unhappy influences on the tradition."[18]

---

[13] Aristotle, *Rhetoric*, 219.
[14] Aristotle, *Rhetoric*, 220.
[15] Aristotle, *Rhetoric*, 227.
[16] Aristotle, *Rhetoric*, 238–239.
[17] Aristotle, *Rhetoric*, 223.
[18] Mark Johnson, "Introduction: Metaphor in the Philosophical Tradition," in *Philosophical Perspectives on Metaphor*, ed. Mark Johnson (Minneapolis: University of Minnesota Press, 1981), 5–7.

First, like White and others, Johnson points out that Aristotle restricts his attention to words as the basic semantic unit. As a result, a metaphor is restricted to the level of words, rather than sentences. Second, he notes that Aristotle understood metaphor as a deviance from literal usage. Although he acknowledges that Aristotle sees an appropriate, and potentially beneficial, place for the deviance from ordinary usage, Johnson argues that by differentiating standard and nonstandard usages of language, he created a "fatal separation" between figurative and literal language. According to Johnson, the third influential aspect of Aristotle's writing is that he perceives metaphor as being based on similarities between two entities, with some underlying resemblance allowing for the transference to take place. He concludes:

> Thus the future of metaphor is prefigured in terms of these three basic components: (i) focus on single words that are (ii) deviations from literal language, to produce a change of meaning that is (iii) based on similarities between things.[19]

To this list, Johnson adds a fourth influential aspect of Aristotle's treatment of metaphor: his comments on the relationship between metaphor and simile. In *The Art of Rhetoric*, Aristotle writes: "The simile is also a metaphor, only it is slightly different."[20] Further on, he repeats this point, explaining that similes are "in a way metaphors; for they are always produced from two things, like the metaphor by analogy."[21] In spite of their similarities, Aristotle implies that metaphors are superior to similes: "The simile is . . . a metaphor differing in one addition only; hence is it less pleasant, as it is more drawn out, and it does not say that this is that, and so the mind does not think out the resemblance either."[22] Johnson claims that Aristotle's comments have been misconstrued over the centuries and misused to support a view of metaphor as an elliptical simile which "can always be reduced to literal statements of similarities between objects."[23] He asserts that Aristotle's remarks were reshaped into the notion of metaphor that remained dominant for the next twenty-three hundred

---

[19] Johnson, 6.
[20] Aristotle, *Rhetoric*, 224.
[21] Aristotle, *Rhetoric*, 240.
[22] Aristotle, *Rhetoric*, 235.
[23] Johnson, 7.

years: the view that "a metaphor is an elliptical simile useful for stylistic, rhetorical, and didactic purposes, but which can be translated into a literal paraphrase without any loss of cognitive content."[24]

Stage by stage, Johnson reviews the development of this prevailing view of metaphor, starting with the classical Latin rhetoricians. Cicero, the first century B.C.E. Roman orator, characterizes metaphor as "a brief similitude contracted into a single word" which "conveys, if the resemblance be acknowledged, delight" but "if there is no resemblance, it is condemned."[25] Like Aristotle, Cicero focuses on the potential rhetorical effects of metaphor: "There is no mode of embellishment more effective as regards single words, nor any that throws greater lustre upon language."[26] Cicero differs from Aristotle, however, in one notable respect: he considers metaphor to be a subordinate form of a comparison, as does Quintilian. Quintilian, the first century C.E. teacher of rhetoric, describes metaphor as a "shorter form of simile" in which the "object is actually substituted for the thing" to which it is compared.[27] Explaining the significance of the shift in the value of simile over metaphor, Johnson writes:

> This reversal of dominance, placing simile over metaphor, helps to explain why Cicero, Quintilian, and other Latin rhetoricians give metaphor a less important place in persuasive speech than Aristotle did. If metaphor is only a brief form of comparison, it has no unique function in proof. It is valued chiefly as ornamentation that gives force, clarity, and charm to language.[28]

In the medieval period, the importance of metaphor continued to diminish. In a treatise on tropes, the late sixth, early seventh century rhetorician Bede proclaims that rhetoric should be distinguished from logic and reduced to a manual of style. The devaluation of rhetoric resulted in the further devaluation of metaphor, for metaphor was viewed simply as a stylistic device, not a tool for serious philosophical argumentation. In addition, medieval theologians attacked the embellishment of language in general. Johnson explains:

> More overt and hostile criticisms of figurative language grew out of the monastic emphasis on the inward and spiritual over the outward

---

[24] Johnson, 4.
[25] Cicero (106–43 B.C.E.), *De Oratore*, 3.38.156–39.157; quoted in Johnson, 8.
[26] Cicero, *De Oratore*, 3.38.156–39.15 and 3.41; quoted in Johnson, 8–9.
[27] Quintilian (c. 35–c. 100), *Institutio Oratoria*, book VIII, vi. 8–9; quoted in Johnson, 8.
[28] Johnson, 9.

and physical. Words are outward signs for expressing our inner truths. But they can be misused, as by those who clothe falsehoods in pleasing language and style.[29]

Nevertheless, contrary to this predominantly negative position on metaphor, a more favorable view of figurative language arose from the attempt to account for the profusion of metaphors in the Bible. For instance, Aquinas argues that Holy Scripture "makes use of metaphors as both necessary and useful."[30] Summarizing this period, Johnson states that the medieval view has two aspects:

> Metaphors are good when used in Scripture and bad when used (or misused) to mask untruths with seductive figures. The same underlying conception remains in both cases: metaphor is a *deviant* use of a *word* to point up *similarities*.[31]

Likewise, a bifurcated perspective on metaphor emerges from studies of medieval Jewish exegetes. Moses Maimonides and Moses Ibn Ezra follow an Arabicized Aristotelian model that views metaphor as a linguistic "borrowing" or "transfer" of a word that normally belongs to one thing to designate something else. Mordechai Cohen situates this approach to metaphor within a Jewish interpretive tradition that stems from Saadia Gaon and was influenced by Qur'anic exegetes, one that considers metaphor "a type of *majāz*, i.e., improper, figurative language, as opposed to a *ḥaqiqa* (lit. truth), i.e., literal language."[32] He observes:

> Despite its poetic sophistication, the Andalusian peshat tradition treated metaphor as an exegetical obstacle, an elegant veneer that disguises Scripture's essential meaning. The otherwise profound peshat tradition culminating with Ibn Ezra and Maimonides was reluctant to explore metaphor's special suggestive power.[33]

However, a different perspective on metaphor appears in the work of David Kimhi, who "manifests greater sensitivity to the expressive potential of metaphor" and formulates "a new literary conception of

---

[29] Johnson, 9–10.

[30] Aquinas, *Summa Theologiae*, I, 1, 9ad.1; quoted in Johnson, 10.

[31] Johnson, 11.

[32] Mordechai Cohen, "Moses Ibn Ezra vs. Maimonides: Argument for a Poetic Definition of Metaphor (*Istiʿāra*)," in *Edebiyât: Journal of Middle Eastern and Comparative Literature* 11 (2000) 13–14; also see Cohen's remarks about Ibn Ezra's classification of metaphor as *majāz* in footnote 54, pp. 23–24.

[33] Mordechai Cohen, *Three Approaches to Biblical Metaphor: From Ibn Ezra and Maimonides to David Kimhi* (Leiden: Brill, 2003), 5.

metaphor as an expressive tool that the biblical authors used to convey subtle overtones."[34] Ibn Ezra also expresses a more positive conception of metaphor, not in his exegetical work, but in his hand-book for the composition of Hebrew poetry according to the rules of Arabic poetics. There, he departs from the Aristotelian model embraced by the Arabic logical tradition and adopts an approach to metaphor shaped by the Arabic poetic tradition, one that highlights "the imaginative capacity of metaphor."[35]

Post-medieval philosophers continued to perpetuate a negative atti-tude toward metaphor. For example, in the seventeenth century, the empiricist Thomas Hobbes asserted that if we express our thoughts in order to communicate our knowledge, "this function is frustrated and impeded whenever we 'use words metaphorically . . . and thereby deceive others.'"[36] Hobbes considers literal language ("words proper") the only adequate vehicle for expressing meaning precisely and making truth claims. According to this line of thinking, a metaphor consti-tutes a deviant use of words and results in a tendency to confuse and deceive. Subsequent philosophers, such as Locke and Hegel, echo the disparaging view of rhetoric and figurative language expressed by prior thinkers. Others dismiss the topic altogether. Johnson observes:

> Toward the end of the eighteenth century, mention of metaphor in philosophical writing diminished considerably. Philosophers tended either to ignore the subject or to repeat the stock views and criticisms car-ried over from earlier thinkers and preserved in manuals of rhetoric.[37]

In spite of this trend, some exceptions can be found in the early modern period, in the writings of Kant, Rousseau, Nietzsche, and the Romantic poets who praised poetic metaphor and exhibited an interest in figurative language.[38] However, these minority voices did not transform the prevailing, negative view of metaphor.

---

[34] Cohen, *Three Approaches*, 5.

[35] Cohen, "Moses Ibn Ezra vs. Maimonides," 1. Cohen's article focuses on the conception of metaphor found in Ibn Ezra's handbook, *Kitāb al-Muḥāḍara wa-al-Mudhākara* (*Book of Discussion and Conversation*), which he labels "imaginary ascription" (8). He contrasts this view with the treatment of metaphor found in Maimonides' writings and in Ibn Ezra's work on biblical exegesis, *Maqālat al-Ḥadīqa fī Maʿnā al-Majāz wa-al-Ḥaqīqa* ("The Treatise of the Garden on Figurative and Literal Language"); see his concluding remarks (17) and his comments in note 54, pp. 23–24.

[36] Hobbes, *Leviathan*, pt. I, chap. 4; quoted in Johnson, 11.

[37] Johnson, 15.

[38] Johnson, 14–16.

In the early twentieth century, the pervasive philosophy of logical positivism maintained a perception of metaphor as unimportant, deviant, and vague, an appropriate tool for politicians or poets, but not for scientists attempting to accurately describe physical reality. In an introductory article in the collection, *Metaphor and Thought*, Anthony Ortony explains:

> A basic notion of positivism was that reality could be precisely described through the medium of language in a manner that was clear, unambiguous, and, in principle, testable—reality could, and should, be literally describable. Other uses of language were meaningless for they violated the empiricist criteria of meaning. During the heyday of logical positivism, literal language reigned supreme.[39]

Johnson outlines the two suppositions that shaped the positivist criticism of metaphor:

> (1) the distinction between the alleged 'cognitive' and 'emotive' functions of language, and (2) the attendant belief that scientific knowledge could be reduced to a system of literal and verifiable sentences.[40]

During this period, philosophers either ignored metaphor completely, or they translated figurative expressions into literal paraphrase so as to capture any underlying truth claims. According to Johnson, although the two foundations of the positivist condemnation of metaphor had been demolished by the mid-twentieth century, the positivist view of metaphor—"that a metaphor is a comparison reducible without cognitive loss to a literal statement of similarities between two compared things or events"—remained dominant for many years.[41]

B. *A Renewed Appreciation of Metaphor*

Only with the spread of a new philosophical perspective, relativism, did the view of metaphor that had persisted for over two thousand years begin to change. Ortony summarizes the key components of relativism:

> The central idea of this approach is that cognition is the result of mental *construction*. Knowledge of reality, whether occasioned by perception, language, or memory, necessitates going beyond the information

---

[39] Anthony Ortony, "Metaphor, Language, and Thought," in *Metaphor and Thought*, ed. Andrew Ortony, 2d ed. (Cambridge: Cambridge University Press, 1993), 1.
[40] Johnson, 17.
[41] Johnson, 18.

given. It arises through the interaction of that information with the context in which it is presented and with the knower's preexisting knowledge. This general orientation is the hallmark of the relativist view . . . that the objective world is not directly accessible but is constructed on the basis of the constraining influences of human knowledge and language. In this kind of view—which provides no basis for a rigid differentiation between scientific language and other kinds—language, perception, and knowledge are inextricably intertwined.[42]

Unlike the traditional approach which devalues metaphor "as deviant and parasitic upon normal use," relativism celebrates metaphor "as an essential characteristic of the creativity of language."[43] As a result, during the second half of the twentieth century, philosophers, linguists, psychologists, literary critics, and scholars in a wide range of disciplines started to reassess the established, ornamental view of figurative language and to appreciate metaphor as a vital component of language and thought.

Prior to this period of burgeoning interest in metaphor, I. A. Richards made a radical break with the established assumption that "metaphor is something special and exceptional in the use of language, a deviation from its normal mode of working."[44] In his 1936 work, *The Philosophy of Rhetoric*, he rejects the long-held notion that metaphor is "a sort of happy extra trick with words" or "a grace or ornament or *added* power of language, not its constitutive form."[45] Instead, he asserts that "metaphor is the omnipresent principle of language."[46] Cognizant of the pervasiveness of metaphor in speech, Richards cautions that "our pretence to do without metaphor is never more than a bluff waiting to be called."[47] In formulating a principle of metaphor, he turns to Samuel Johnson, who declared: "As to metaphorical expression, that is a great excellence in style, when it is used with propriety, for it gives you two ideas for one."[48] Although Richards recognizes that Johnson's statement reflects elements of a limited, traditional conception of metaphor, he expands upon Johnson's notion of metaphor involving "two ideas for one." Richards states:

---

[42] Ortony, 1–2.
[43] Ortony, 2.
[44] I. A. Richards, *The Philosophy of Rhetoric* (Oxford: Oxford University Press, 1936), 90.
[45] Richards, 90.
[46] Richards, 92.
[47] Richards, 92.
[48] Richards, 93.

> In the simplest formulation, when we use a metaphor we have two
> thoughts of different things active together and supported by a single
> word, or phrase, whose meaning is a resultant of their interaction.[49]

In considering not only words, but also thought, Richards pioneered
a new direction in metaphor research. Emphasizing the difference
between his theory and those of his predecessors, he explains:

> The traditional theory . . . made metaphor seem to be a verbal matter,
> a shifting and displacement of words, whereas fundamentally it is a
> borrowing between and intercourse of *thoughts*, a transaction between
> contexts. *Thought* is metaphoric, and proceeds by comparison, and the
> metaphors of language derive therefrom.[50]

Another influential aspect of Richards work stems from his attempt
to invent terminology to label the various aspects of a metaphor, for
he observes that "one of the oddest of the many odd things about
the whole topic is that we have no agreed distinguishing terms for
these two halves of a metaphor."[51] Rejecting the existing "clumsy
descriptive phrases," he proposes that the word "metaphor" be
restricted to "the whole double unit" and the technical terms "tenor"
and "vehicle" be used for the two thoughts active in a metaphor.
"Tenor" refers to the underlying topic addressed by the metaphor
and "vehicle" designates the means by which this subject us understood.[52] For example, in the quotation "A stubborn and uncon-
querable flame creeps in his veins," he considers the flame the vehicle
and a fever, the tenor.[53] Richards also introduces the phrase "the
ground of the metaphor" to talk about the common characteristics
of the vehicle and the tenor.[54] Using this terminology, he articulates
a new vision of metaphor, "a modern theory" in which the meaning of the metaphor results from the interaction of two co-present
thoughts. He asserts:

> The vehicle is not normally a mere embellishment of a tenor which is
> otherwise unchanged by it but . . . vehicle and tenor in co-operation
> give a meaning of more varied powers than can be ascribed to either.[55]

---

[49] Richards, 93.
[50] Richards, 94
[51] Richards, 96.
[52] Richards, 96–97.
[53] Richards, 102.
[54] Richards, 117.
[55] Richards, 100.

In spite of his numerous insights and innovations, philosophers initially paid little attention to Richards' work. Johnson notes:

> In 1936 it was not prudent to insist that thought is essentially metaphoric, that metaphors are cognitively irreducible and indispensable, and that any adequate account of meaning and truth must give a central place to metaphor. . . . It took another twenty years and many failures of the positivist position before a respected philosopher, Max Black, finally succeeded in getting a few adventuresome souls to take metaphor seriously. Black's essay, "Metaphor," is perhaps *the* landmark by which we may orient ourselves in attempting to understand recent work on the subject.[56]

In this 1954–1955 essay, Black sets out "to dispel the mystery that invests the topic" of metaphor and to answer a number of basic questions about a subject neglected by philosophers who "assume that metaphor is incompatible with serious thought."[57] After drawing up a list of what he considers clear cases of metaphor, he proposes a rough definition:

> In general, when we speak of a relatively simple metaphor, we are referring to a sentence or another expression, in which *some* words are used metaphorically, while the remainder are used non-metaphorically.[58]

Like Richards, Black develops terminology to use in speaking about the various aspects of a metaphor. As he analyzes the example, "The chairman ploughed through the discussion," he concludes:

> In calling this sentence a case of metaphor, we are implying that at least one word (here, the word "ploughed") is being used metaphorically in the sentence, and that at least one of the remaining words is being used literally. Let us call the word "ploughed" the *focus* of the metaphor, and the remainder of the sentence in which the word occurs the *frame*.[59]

---

[56] Johnson, 19.

[57] Black, 63.

[58] Black, 65.

[59] Black, 65–66. While the language of "frame" and "focus" has been adopted by many subsequent scholars, others have criticized Black's conception of a metaphor containing one isolatable focus. White, for one, raises a number of questions about Black's notion of frame and focus: "(i) Given a metaphor, how are we supposed to pick out *which* are the words within it that are being used metaphorically? . . . (ii) If a sentence contains two or more words used metaphorically, what does it mean to say that it contains a single *focus*, rather than two or more *foci*? . . . (iii) If there are two or more metaphorical words, what exactly is the *focus* of the metaphor meant to be? The idea is only explained for the case of a single word" (11). Because

An even more influential aspect of Black's work concerns his "inter-action view of metaphor." Building on Richards' notion that a metaphor forces a reader to connect two ideas, Black asserts: "In this 'connexion' resides the secret and the mystery of metaphor."[60] As he presents an account of what transpires when this connection takes place, Black introduces his concept of "associated commonplaces":

> Consider the statement, "Man is wolf". Here, we may say, are two subjects—the *principal subject*, Man (or: men) and the *subsidiary subject*, Wolf (or: wolves). Now the metaphorical sentence in question will not convey its intended meaning to a reader sufficiently ignorant about wolves. What is needed is not so much that the reader shall know the standard dictionary meaning of "wolf"—or be able to use that word in literal senses—as that he shall know what I will call the *system of associated commonplaces*. . . . The important thing for the metaphor's effectiveness is not that the commonplaces shall be true, but that they should be readily and freely evoked.[61]

Next, he elaborates on how a hearer processes a given metaphor:

> The effect, then, of (metaphorically) calling a man a "wolf" is to evoke the wolf-system of related commonplaces. If the man is a wolf, he preys upon other animals, is fierce, hungry, engaged in constant struggle, a scavenger, and so on. Each of these implied assertions has now to be made to fit the principal subject (the man) either in normal or in abnormal senses. . . . Any human traits that can without undue strain be talked about in "wolf-language" will be rendered prominent, and any that cannot will be pushed into the background. The wolf-metaphor suppresses some details, emphasizes other—in short, *organizes* our view of man.[62]

Black repeats this final point in a summary of the basic claims of the "interaction view": "The metaphor selects, emphasizes, suppresses, and organizes features of the principal subject by *implying* statements about it that normally apply to the subsidiary subject."[63] The impact of Black's "interaction view" of metaphor, built in part on Richards' ideas, becomes apparent as one examines subsequent stages of

---

Black's account of metaphor does not apply to metaphors of linguistic complexity, White insists: "My fundamental objection to him will not be that he gives a wrong theory of metaphor, but that, for a huge number of metaphors, he gives us no theory at all" (16).

[60] Black, 73.
[61] Black, 73–74. He adds that, for this reason, "a metaphor that works in one society may seem preposterous in another" (74).
[62] Black, 74–75.
[63] Black, 78.

metaphor research. Utilizing a metaphor of his own, Johnson claims that Black's essay "represented the start of a trickle of philosophical interest in metaphor that has now swelled to flood proportions."[64]

C. *Current Trends in Metaphor Research*

1. *The "Cognitive Turn" in Metaphorology*

During the fifty years since the publication of Black's essay, the study of metaphor has expanded remarkably, both in terms of the quantity of literature written and the diversity of academic fields interested in this topic. In a 1978 lecture on "Metaphor as Rhetoric," Wayne Booth marvels at the explosion of interest in metaphor. He speculates:

> I'll wager a good deal that the year 1977 produced more titles than the entire history of thought before 1940. . . . I have in fact extrapolated with my pocket calculator to the year 2039; at that point there will be more students of metaphor than people.[65]

Jean-Pierre van Noppen and Edith Hols' bibliography, *Metaphor II, A Classified Bibliography of Publications 1985–1990*,[66] provides another indicator of the immense amount of recent research on metaphor. This work lists over three thousand, four hundred and eighty books and articles on the topic of metaphor published during the five-year period from 1985 to 1990. An index in the back of the book categorizes the publications according to disciplines. Scholars in nearly every field seem to be writing on metaphor, from aesthetics, anthropology, architecture, art, artificial intelligence, and axiology to technology, theolinguistics, theology, translation, women's studies, and writing.

Gerard Steen provides insight into the growing and changing nature of the research on metaphor in his book, *Understanding Metaphor in Literature*. He explains that until fairly recently, many linguists, philosophers, and other scholars avoided the study of metaphor, viewing metaphor as a linguistic oddity better left to literary critics. In the late 1970's, however, a number of "landmark publications" such as Ortony's 1979 collection, *Metaphor and Thought*, and George

---

[64] Johnson, 20.
[65] Wayne Booth, "Metaphor as Rhetoric: The Problem of Evaluation," in *On Metaphor*, ed. Sheldon Sacks, (Chicago: University or Chicago Press, 1979), 47.
[66] Jean-Pierre van Noppen and Edith Hols, *Metaphor II: A Classified Bibliography of Publications 1985 to 1990* (Amsterdam/Philadelphia: John Benjamins Publishing Company, 1990).

Lakoff and Mark Johnson's 1980 book, *Metaphors We Live By*, signaled what Steen characterizes as "the 'cognitive turn' in metaphorology."[67] Instead of perceiving metaphor "as a purely linguistic phenomenon" or "as a more general, communication phenomenon," scholars started to study metaphor "as a phenomenon of thought and mental representation."[68] Lakoff and Johnson distinguish this new approach from what, at the time, constituted the prevailing view of metaphor. They explain:

> Metaphor is for most people a device of the poetic imagination and the rhetorical flourish—a matter of extraordinary rather than ordinary language. Moreover, metaphor is typically viewed as characteristic of language alone, a matter of words rather than thought or action.... We have found, on the contrary, that metaphor is pervasive in every-day life, not just in language but in thought and action. Our ordinary conceptual system, in terms of which we both think and act, is fundamentally metaphorical in nature.[69]

According to Steen, as a result of this "cognitive turn," metaphor "has become the thing to be expected in cognition instead of the thing to be avoided in language."[70]

The cognitive approach treats metaphor primarily as a figure of thought, as opposed to a figure of speech, and it examines the mental processes involved in the creation and interpretation of metaphor. Lakoff, a leader in this approach, asserts that "the locus of metaphor is not in language at all, but in the way we conceptualize one mental domain in terms of another."[71] He claims that what constitutes a metaphor "is not any particular word or expression. It is the ontological mapping across conceptual domains." As a result, he maintains that metaphor is not simply a matter of language, but also of thought. He insists that "language is secondary."[72]

---

[67] Gerard Steen, *Understanding Metaphor in Literature* (London: Longman Group Limited, 1994), 3.

[68] Ortony, 11. As noted above, Richards first recognized the metaphoric aspects of thought (93–94).

[69] George Lakoff and Mark Johnson, *Metaphors We Live By* (Chicago: The University of Chicago Press, 1980), 3.

[70] Steen, 4.

[71] George Lakoff, "The Contemporary Theory of Metaphor," in *Metaphor and Thought*, ed. Andrew Ortony, 2d ed. (Cambridge: Cambridge University Press, 1993), 203.

[72] Lakoff, 208. Numerous scholars have criticized the work of Lakoff and his collaborators. David Aaron provides a cogent critique in *Biblical Ambiguities* (Leiden: Brill, 2001), 101–111. Also see Ray Jackendoff and David Aaron, Review of *More Than Cool Reason* by George Lakoff and Mark Turner in *Language* 67 (1991) 320–338,

In this study, however, language is primary; the goal is to understand how certain figures of speech operate in a particular literary text. While such a stance does not deny the conceptual aspects of metaphor, it simply does not focus on the cognitive functioning that takes place when a person processes a metaphor.[73] As a result, this project focuses less on those interested in the cognitive facets of metaphor[74] and more on those primarily concerned with the linguistic aspects of figurative language.

---

as well as Steen (9–27), Kittay (185–186), and White (300–301), among others. A frequent criticism concerns their exceedingly broad notion of metaphor, which classifies as a metaphor an utterance like "He shot down all of my arguments" (from the conceptual metaphor ARGUMENT IS WAR), as well as statements like "Thank you for your time" (from the conceptual metaphor TIME IS MONEY) or "What's coming up this week" (from the conceptual metaphor FORESEEABLE FUTURE EVENTS ARE UP [and AHEAD]) (examples from Lakoff and Johnson, 4, 8, 16). As Jackendoff and Aaron point out, "their overall characterization enlarges the scope of the term 'metaphor' well beyond the standard use of the term" and "stretches the notion 'metaphor' to a number of cases that should be understood in other terms" (325). Reflecting on Lakoff and Turner's statement that "it could be the case that every word or phrase in language is defined at least in part metaphorically," Aaron writes: "Despite the qualifier 'it could be the case,' one gets the impression from these books that this principle is a basic assumption in the LJTT [Lakoff-Johnson-Turner Thesis]: human thought processes, and consequently all complex word meanings, are essentially metaphorical" (102–103). White charges: "Lakoff has idiosyncratically decided to use the word 'metaphor' to refer not primarily to a linguistic text but to the 'metaphoric conception', or comparison on which such text is based." He concludes: "I find such a way of talking, if not positively misleading, at the very least entirely unhelpful" (300).

[73] Steen's empirical research concerns this precise topic. He conducted a series of experiments designed to study how people understand metaphors found in literary texts by exploring "the effect on metaphor processing in literary texts of the two factors of reader knowledge and text structure" (52). By doing so, he aimed to restore "the equilibrium between metaphor as a kind of *expression* and metaphor as an *idea* in discourse" (6).

[74] See, for example the work of John Searle, who seeks to understand how a speaker can say metaphorically one thing ("S is P") and mean another ("S is R"), when P plainly does not mean R. He establishes a number of steps and principles involved as a hearer computes that the speaker means that "S is R" (John Searle, "Metaphor," in *Metaphor and Thought*, 2d edition, ed. Andrew Ortony [Cambridge: Cambridge University Press, 1993], 102). Researchers such as Raymond Gibbs approach the topic from the perspective of psychology, not philosophy; but they, too, seek to understand "how people make sense of tropes" and to identify the cognitive processes involved in comprehension of a metaphor (Raymond Gibbs Jr., "Process and Products in Making Sense of Tropes," in *Metaphor and Thought*, 2nd edition, ed. Andrew Ortony [Cambridge: Cambridge University Press, 1993], 253). For additional examples of this line of research, see Ortony's collection, *Metaphor and Thought*, and the recently published work in cognitive linguistics cited in chapter five.

2. *Linguistic Approaches to Metaphor*

In the 1996 work, *The Structure of Metaphor*, White prefaces his critique of the existing philosophical treatments of metaphor with a quotation from Simon Blackburn: "I think nobody would claim that the study of metaphor has been one of analytical philosophy's brighter achievements."[75] White charges that the debate among analytical philosophers "has, for so much of the time, appeared to be going nowhere, and has yielded so little insight,"[76] for two primary reasons. First, he cites "a poverty and . . . timidity in the choice of examples" and "a continual use of a few banal and hackneyed examples,"[77] such as "Man is a wolf"[78] or "Sam is a pig."[79] He argues that examples of such uncharacteristic linguistic simplicity do not reflect the diversity and complexity of metaphors encountered in speech and literature.

Second, he claims that "the participants in the debate have assumed at the outset a wrong account of the actual linguistic phenomenon itself."[80] He asserts: "Paradoxically, the main reason that analytic philosophy has failed in this area is that it has ignored the actual *language* of metaphor."[81] White endeavors to avoid this mistake by examining the way words combine to create a metaphoric statement. While he endorses Richard's claim that thought is metaphoric, he cautions that "it should not of course mislead one . . . into neglecting the actual nature of the *verbal* structure that lies at the heart of metaphoric communication."[82]

Likewise, other scholars before White have focused on the linguistic, instead of the conceptual, nature of metaphor. For example, Christine Brook-Rose produced an early alternative to the philosophic approach to metaphor in her 1958 study, *A Grammar of Metaphor*. Explaining the motivation behind her research, she writes:

> Most studies of metaphor, from Aristotle to present, have been concerned with the idea-content, rather than with form: what is the mental process involved in calling one thing another? Metaphor is expressed in words, and a metaphoric word reacts to other words to which it is syntactically

---

[75] Simon Blackburn, *Spreading the Word*; quoted in White, 1.
[76] White, 4.
[77] White, 1.
[78] Black, 73.
[79] Searle, 83.
[80] White, 4.
[81] White, 4.
[82] White, 105.

and grammatically related. The effect of this interaction varies considerably according to the nature of this grammatical relationship. Remarkably little work has been done on these lines. Limited though a purely grammatical approach to metaphor may be, it seems necessary if only to restore the balance.[83]

Conceiving of metaphor as the identification of one thing with another and the subsequent replacement of a more usual word or phrase with another,[84] Brooke-Rose argues: "Whatever the mental process involved in calling one thing by another name, the poet must use nouns, verbs, adverbs, adjectives, and prepositions."[85]

Janet Soskice also counters the prevailing trend in metaphor research when she insists that metaphors are not mental events, but a form of language use. In her 1985 book, *Metaphor and Religious Language*, she asserts:

> While it may be that the successful employment of metaphor involves non-linguistic observations, perceptions, and responses, it should not be thought that metaphor is primarily a process or a mental act, and only secondarily its manifestation in language.[86]

Instead, she maintains that metaphor should be considered a linguistic phenomenon, a figure of speech "whereby we speak about one thing in terms which are seen to be suggestive of another."[87]

As indicated by the title of the 1987 work, *Metaphor: Its Cognitive Force and Linguistic Structure*, Eva Kittay is concerned with both facets of metaphor. While she endorses the position that metaphors are conceptual and play a distinctively cognitive role, at the same time, she insists that "the conceptual requires an expressive medium."[88] She sees these two aspects of metaphor as intertwined, as she illustrates when she remarks: "Metaphor provides the linguistic realization for the cognitive activity by which a language speaker makes use of one

---

[83] Christine Brooke-Rose, *A Grammar of Metaphor* (London: Secker & Warburg, 1958), 1.

[84] Brooke-Rose, 17.

[85] Brooke-Rose, 15–16. Although her book proves useful for thinking about how to differentiate and label various types of metaphors, well beyond basic "A is B" type, the word-based, replacement theory of metaphor upon which the work is based diminishes the value and applicability of Brooke-Rose's research.

[86] Janet Martin Soskice, *Metaphor and Religious Language* (Oxford: Clarendon Press, 1985), 16.

[87] Soskice, 15.

[88] Kittay, 15.

linguistically articulated domain in order to gain an understanding of another experiential or conceptual domain."[89] In order to examine the linguistic aspects of metaphor, Kittay turns to the field of linguistics, applying componential semantics and other linguistic theories to enhance the study of metaphor.

IV. A REVIEW OF THE RESEARCH ON METAPHOR IN THE BIBLE

A. *"Avoidance of the Metaphorical"*

In contrast to the proliferation of research on metaphor in a wide range of academic disciplines, biblical scholars have produced a fairly modest amount of work on this topic. The previously mentioned bibliography on metaphor by van Noppen and Hols reflects this fact, for its lengthy, detailed index contains no entry for biblical studies. In an article on the role of metaphor in biblical poetry, Adele Berlin comments that "scant attention has been paid to [metaphor] in a systematic way" by modern biblicists.[90] Similarly, David Aaron observes that in the field of Bible, "very few scholars feel compelled to deal with the mechanics of metaphor."[91] In biblical translation, as well, one finds what Robert Alter characterizes as the "avoidance of the metaphorical."[92]

A number of factors may have contributed to the relative paucity of attention to metaphor in biblical scholarship. The avoidance of metaphor suggests that many biblical scholars have inherited the negative attitude toward metaphor that remained prominent from antiquity to the mid-twentieth century, an approach that tends to dismiss figurative language as ornamental, deviant, or deceptive. Marc Brettler agrees that "biblicists have shared philosophers' distrust of metaphor."[93] Aaron speculates that many biblical scholars have ignored metaphor "perhaps because figurative idioms are so commonly a part of our everyday speech acts."[94] John Lyons provides further insight into this

---

[89] Kittay, 14.
[90] Adele Berlin, "On Reading Biblical Poetry: The Role of Metaphor," *Congress Volume*, Cambridge 1995, ed. J. A. Emerton (Leiden: Brill, 1997), 26.
[91] Aaron, 9.
[92] Robert Alter, *Genesis* (New York: W. W. Norton & Company, 1996), xiii.
[93] Marc Zvi Brettler, *God Is King: Understanding an Israelite Metaphor* (Sheffield: Sheffield Academic Press, 1989), 26.
[94] Aaron, 9.

issue as he reflects upon the general neglect of semantics in modern linguistics. He proposes that this is due, in part, "to doubt about whether meaning can be studied as objectively and rigorously as grammar and phonology."[95] Likewise, in the field of Bible, metaphor falls within the domain of semantics and lacks the more orderly, tidy formal features of other aspects of biblical studies that have been extensively researched, such as grammar, syntax, or morphology. Ina Loewenberg's observation that "the unpopularity of the study of metaphor in linguistics undoubtedly has something to do with their syntactic unwieldiness as well as with their ubiquitousness"[96] may suggest another reason for the fairly limited bibliography on metaphor in the Bible.

B. *The Treatment of Metaphor in Studies of Biblical Poetry and Biblical Narrative*

Several authors address the topic of metaphor in the context of more comprehensive studies of biblical poetry or poetics. For example, in *A Manual of Hebrew Poetics*, Luis Alonso Schökel deals with metaphor in his chapter on biblical imagery. Central to his understanding of imagery is the idea of correlation, in which the poet, "who is the match-maker," places two panels of the image alongside each other.[97] In *The Language and Imagery of the Bible* by G. B. Caird and *Classical Hebrew Poetry* by Wilfred Watson, both authors provide rather traditional, word-based conceptions of metaphor involving the substitution of one term for another. They introduce Richard's terms "vehicle" and "tenor," but they do not expound upon the extant research on metaphor.[98] These three writers concentrate on categorization instead

---

[95] John Lyons, *Introduction to Theoretical Linguistics* (Cambridge: Cambridge University Press, 1968), 400. He also attributes this neglect to the fact that the "problem of meaning" might seem of equal, if not greater, concern to philosophy, logic, psychology, and other disciplines, such as anthropology or sociology (400).

[96] Ina Loewenberg, "Identifying Metaphors," *Foundations of Language* 12 (1974–75) 316.

[97] Luis Alonso Schökel, *A Manual of Hebrew Poetics* (Rome: Pontificio Istituto Biblico, 1988), 99.

[98] G. B. Caird, *The Language and Imagery of the Bible*, 2nd ed (Grand Rapids: William B. Eerdmans Publishing Company, 1997), 152; Wilfred Watson, *Classical Hebrew Poetry* (Sheffield: Sheffield Academic Press, 1995); 263. Justifying his lack of attention to metaphor research, Watson writes: "It can also be pointed out that the theory of metaphor is still being debated in the field of modern linguistics, so that it would be premature to offer a summary of the findings so far" (263). Likewise,

of theory, as seen in Caird's list of four classes of comparison and
Watson's catalogue of different kinds of metaphor and the main
functions of metaphor.[99] Such treatments of metaphor simplify a complicated topic without providing much exegetical assistance in unpacking biblical metaphors.

Most studies of biblical narrative, such as Alter's *Art of Biblical
Narrative* or Meir Sternberg's *The Poetics of Biblical Narrative*, make little
or no mention of metaphor.[100] Shimon Bar-Efrat's work on *Narrative
Art in the Bible* stands out as an exception to this trend, for he directly
addresses this subject. He points out that while metaphors are used
often in poetry, "they also feature in prose . . . particularly in the
speech of individual characters."[101] He insists that metaphors and
other linguistic features contain "expressive force" and should be val-
ued as "stylistically important," not "regarded merely as embellishments."[102] In his chapter on "Style," he defines metaphor as a word
"used in a non-literal sense" in which there is "similarity but no
direct continuity between its literal and non-literal meanings"; he
adds that "the things which the word indicates in its literal and non-
literal meanings belong to completely different and separate spheres."[103]
As in the books on biblical poetry examined above, Bar-Efrat avoids
introducing any of the research on metaphor found outside of the

---

Alonso Schökel does not discuss any of the theoretical literature on metaphor;
instead, he simply lists P. Ricoeur's work, *La metaphore vive*, as a reference (108).
Also see J. C. L. Gibson, *Language and Imagery in the Old Testament* (Peabody, MA:
Hendrickson Publishers, 1998).

[99] Caird, 145–49. Watson, 269–271. Similarly, Alonso Schökel categorizes the
ways nature, man, and God are transformed into images, such as through anima-
tion and personification (122–139).

[100] Robert Alter, *The Art of Biblical Narrative* (New York: Basic Books, Inc., 1981)
and Meir Sternberg, *The Poetics of Biblical Narrative* (Bloomington: Indiana University
Press, 1987), 12, 15, 194 (references not listed in the index). Other works surveyed
include Adele Berlin, *Poetics and Interpretation of Biblical Narrative* (Winona Lake:
Eisenbrauns, 1994); J. P. Fokkelman, *Reading Biblical Narrative* (Louisville: Westminster
John Knox Press, 1990); David M. Gunn and Danna Nolan Fewell, *Narrative in the
Hebrew Bible* (Oxford: Oxford University Press, 1993). The chapter of Gunn and
Fewell's book on "The Lure of Language" contains a section entitled "Multivalence,
ambiguity, and metaphor." They use the term "metaphor" broadly to refer to the
realm entered "once we move beyond the surface meanings of words to symbolic
or theological ones" (156); they do not address metaphor as a specific literary device.

[101] Shimon Bar-Efrat, *Narrative Art in the Bible* (Sheffield: Sheffield Academic Press,
1989), 209.

[102] Bar-Efrat, 198.

[103] Bar-Efrat, 209; he illustrates his definition with a list of examples of metaphors
found in biblical narrative.

field of biblical studies. Instead, he concentrates on the role metaphors play in biblical narrative. He asserts:

> The value of metaphors is that they are able to carry and transfer considerable emotional charge or illuminate in a something new (and sometimes surprising) way, often achieving a concrete representation or a vivid image.[104]

C. Patterns in Research on Metaphor in the Bible

The handful of biblical scholars who have written book-length studies of metaphor make more of an effort to acquaint their readers with some of the theoretical work on metaphor. The majority of books on metaphor fall into two categories: studies of specific metaphors in individual prophetic books[105] and works tracing one type of metaphor throughout the Bible.[106] Articles on metaphor follow a similar pattern: most of the research has concentrated on particular metaphors in the Prophets, with some attention given to other poetic material, such as Proverbs, Job, and Psalms.[107] For the most part, authors who have written books on metaphor in the Bible briefly discuss the broader metaphor research in an introductory chapter. They tend to summarize several of the most prominent theories and identify the ones which have influenced their own conceptions of metaphor. The majority of biblical scholars rely on the work of Richards and Black, particularly Richards' terminology of tenor and vehicle and Black's notion of associated commonplaces; some incorporate insights from Soskice, Paul Ricoeur, and Lakoff and Johnson, among others.

---

[104] Bar-Efrat, 209; also see his comments on the "emotional stance" expressed or aroused by metaphor, 56–57.

[105] See, for example, Kirsten Nielsen, *There is Hope for a Tree: The Tree as Metaphor in Isaiah* (Sheffield: JSOT Press, 1989); Katheryn Pfisterer Darr, *Isaiah's Vision and the Family of God* (Louisvile, KY: Westminster/John Knox Press, 1994); Julie Galambush, *Jerusalem in the Book of Ezekiel: The City as Yahweh's Wife* (Atlanta: Scholars Press, 1992); Bernhard Oestreich, *Metaphors and Similes for Yahweh in Hosea 14:2–9 (1–8)* (Frankfurt am Main: Peter Lang, 1998).

[106] For example, Marc Brettler, *God Is King: Understanding an Israelite Metaphor*; Elaine Adler, *Background for the Metaphor of Covenant as Marriage in the Hebrew Bible* (Ph.D. diss., University of California at Berkeley, 1990); Marjo Korpel, *A Rift in the Clouds: Ugaritic and Hebrew Descriptions of the Divine* (Munster: Ugarit-Verlag, 1990).

[107] See articles such as J. Cheryl Exum, "Of Broken Pots, Fluttering Birds and Visions in the Night: Extended Simile and Poetic Technique in Isaiah," *CBQ* 43 (1981) 331–52; Terence Kleven, "The Cows of Bashan: A Single Metaphor at Amos 4:1–3," *CBQ* 58 (1996) 215–227; William H. Irwin, "The Metaphor in Prov. 11:30," *Biblica* 65 (1984) 97–100.

When one turns from the introductory discussion to the biblical material under investigation, however, questions arise as to the extent to
which the various theories of metaphor affect the actual analysis of
the biblical text. Kirsten Nielsen broaches this issue when she asks
about her proposed definition of metaphor: "What is its use? Has it
any significance at all to the way in which we analyze specific Old
Testament texts, to whether we consider one theory of metaphor
more correct than the other?"[108] A comparison of a few works will
help answer this question.

In the first chapter of *Isaiah's Vision and the Family of God*, in a section entitled "Figurative Language and Contemporary Theory,"
Katheryn Pfisterer Darr articulates her intent to identify "a theory
of metaphor that will, with some adaptation, ground our interpretation."[109] She summarizes the work of Black and Richards, as well
as Soskice's critique of their theories. Convinced of the potential pit-
falls of Richards' work, Darr opts to rely on the work of J. David
Sapir. She explains:

> I abandon Richards's elegant "tenor" and "vehicle" terminology for
> the admittedly more cumbersome language employed by J. David Sapir
> in "The Anatomy of Metaphor" (1977:5). Sapir speaks of a metaphor's
> "topic" (i.e., "what we are talking about or referring to when we use
> the metaphor"), its "continuous term(s)" (those implying the topic . . .)
> and its "discontinuous term(s)."[110]

While Darr claims that "distinguishing among these three features
permits our analysis a greater degree of precision,"[111] she rarely uses
these terms in her analysis of the biblical text.[112] For example, when
she discusses the parent-child metaphor in Isa 1:2–3, she does so in
a more general manner, without specifying which elements in the
passage constitute the topic or the continuous and discontinuous
terms. Throughout her informative examination of a range of passages
from the book of Isaiah, she tends to speak about imagery more
broadly, without integrating the above-mentioned metaphor theory

---

[108] Nielsen, 66.
[109] Darr, 36.
[110] Darr, 39.
[111] Darr, 39.
[112] One of the rare instances in which Darr uses this terminology can be found
in the conclusion of chapter three, when she refers to "metaphors containing discontinuous terms from the argot of female adultery and prostitution" (122).

or delving into the inner-workings of a given metaphor. Similarly, in the introductory chapter, Darr distinguishes between metaphor and other tropes, such as synecdoche, metonymy, catachresis, and neologism.[113] Yet, in her analysis of Isaiah she does not use this terminology to label the various tropes found in the texts she examines or to differentiate them from metaphor.

The subsequent chapters of Darr's book demonstrate that she grounds her interpretation of the child and female imagery in Isaiah less on Sapir's work and more on aspects of metaphor introduced by two other scholars: Black's notion of "associated commonplaces"[114] and Nielsen's conception of the "informative and performative functions" of figurative language.[115] These facets of metaphor play a prominent part in Darr's research as she attempts to establish what stereotyped associations biblical imagery triggered in Isaiah's ancient audience and how they responded to this imagery. Because she argues that "knowledge of culturally-defined associated commonplaces is essential for construing figurative language," Darr relies on biblical and extra-biblical texts to help her "recover the complex associations surrounding a trope's terms in the world of ancient Israel."[116] When Isaiah speaks figuratively about a child, a prostitute, or a pregnant woman, she asks: What attitudes and associations did these images evoke for the ancient Israelites? To understand the child imagery in Isaiah, for instance, Darr begins by investigating the Israelite associations with children.[117] Similarly, she dedicates a chapter to "associations with females"[118] before examining the female imagery in the book.

Darr also adopts Nielsen's notion that figurative language contains an "informative function," referring to "imagery's ability to communicate ideas, data, perspectives, etc., to its audience," as well as a "performative function," meaning the "aspect of imagery intended to elicit participation on the part of readers or hearers."[119] Because

---

[113] Darr, 40.
[114] Darr, 37–38.
[115] Darr, 43.
[116] Darr, 41.
[117] Darr, 47–55. She identifies a range of associations: "limited knowledge, competence, and self-discipline; weakness and vulnerability; lovability; hope for familial longevity; disrespectful behavior; and rebelliousness" (47).
[118] Darr, 85–123.
[119] Darr, 43.

Darr views figurative language as "strategic speech,"[120] she repeatedly asks "how our familial model and selected metaphors enabled attempts (by authors and redactors) to persuade readers to particular perceptions of reality."[121] She argues that many texts in Isaiah employ images of mothers, wives, and daughters for persuasive purposes: not only "to convey" a particular message, but "to awaken sympathy" and to "structure the reader's understanding of what has gone wrong in the divine/human relation."[122] The strength of Darr's work lies in these two areas, her exploration of the rhetorical effects and mental associations of child and female imagery in Isaiah, not in her application of metaphor theory to analyze the mechanics of metaphor.

Whereas Darr claims to base her understanding of metaphor primarily on the work of Sapir, Black, Soskice, and Nielsen, Bernhard Oestreich attempts to follow the metaphor theories of H. Weinrich and Kittay.[123] He strives to interpret the metaphors and similes in Hosea 14:2–9 "according to the results of modern linguistics . . . as phenomena of language,"[124] meaning that he will use the vaguely defined concept of "semantic fields" to identify metaphors. While Oestreich identifies Weinrich and Kittay as the primary influences upon his notion of metaphor, he does not provide his readers with any background information about these two theories. For those unfamiliar with linguistics and the work of these two scholars, Oestreich's facile presentation masks, and thus distorts, the complex concepts he introduces. In the case of Kittay, he not only simplifies her discussion of semantic fields, but he ignores a central component of her research: the use of componential semantics to help understand metaphor.

In the textual analysis that follows his introductory chapter, Oestreich repeatedly refers to the concept of semantic fields as he explores how to interpret the metaphors in Hosea 14 and the book of Hosea as a whole. He recognizes the importance of identifying metaphorical language, which he establishes as the initial stage in his method of study: "The first step will clarify that an expression in the text is

---

[120] Darr, 42.
[121] Darr, 226.
[122] Darr, 122.
[123] Oestreich, 33.
[124] Oestreich, 227.

used metaphorically; that means that it recalls a semantic field different from the semantic field of the context."[125] Thus, when he analyzes Hos 14:5, which he translates as "I will heal their apostasy," he begins by raising the question of what makes this statement a metaphor. He concludes that the defining feature of this metaphor involves the juxtaposition of two distinct semantic fields.[126] According to Kittay, however, it is componential semantics that helps to illustrate the semantic anomaly that tags such an utterance as a metaphor. In other words, Oestreich draws upon only one facet of Kittay's multi-faceted theory of metaphor.

Oestreich's application of Kittay's research proves more limited than he suggests initially in another way as well. Early on he states his intent to adopt Kittay's terminology, labeling the two components that constitute a metaphor the "vehicle" and "topic," with the context of the metaphor called the "frame."[127] Outside of his introductory chapter, however, Oestreich does not apply the terms "vehicle," "topic," or "frame" to his analysis of specific passages. Like Darr, he selects the terminology of a particular researcher that supposedly will guide his subsequent study of biblical metaphor; however, neither Darr nor Oestreich thoroughly integrates this language into their textual analysis.[128]

A comparison of the methodologies practiced by Oestreich and Darr reveals a number of additional similarities between these two studies. After identifying the metaphoric language in a passage, the second step of Oestreich's method involves the "clarification of the concept used as the vehicle," meaning that he looks at the "general commonplaces," or "what people in general think of" the image.[129] For example, when Oestreich studies the divine image in Hos 14:6 ("I will be like the dew for Israel"), he first compiles factual data in

---

[125] Oestreich, 42.
[126] Oestreich, 58.
[127] Oestreich, 34.
[128] In contrast, Julie Galambush incorporates vocabulary coined by scholars of metaphor throughout her study of the marriage metaphor in Ezekiel, which lends her work greater precision and clarity. Galambush anchors her conception of metaphor in the work of Richards and Black (6). An example of her use of their terminology can be seen in her statement that in her study of Ezekiel 16 and 23, "both historical reconstruction (of the tenor) and literary analysis (of the vehicle) will be explored" (89).
[129] Oestreich, 42.

a section entitled, "Dew in Palestine;"[130] then, he explores the connotations of dew for ancient Israelites, information culled from a survey of dew images found throughout the Bible.[131] Similarly, as part
of her study of the female imagery in Isaiah, Darr explores two
aspects of the topic of prostitution: knowledge of "how and why
women were forced into prostitution," along with "stereotypical associations with the profession and its practitioners."[132]

Another stage in Oestreich's method of study involves examining
parallels of the imagery in Hosea in order to "decide if we are dealing with a conventional or a new metaphor."[133] In the case of the
dew image in Hos 14:6, for instance, Oestreich concludes that
"although Hosea uses the dew image in the traditional sense of blessing, he does not use it as a cliche," for "in several aspects he devi-
ates from the language traditions."[134] Darr also is sensitive to "the
biblical authors' penchant for traditional imagery."[135] Therefore, after
she traces the simile of a travailing woman in Mesopotamian texts,
Jeremiah, Psalms, and Isaiah, she concludes that the author of Isa
42:14 creates "a twist on an old cliche."[136] Like Darr, Oestreich
examines a range of biblical texts, beyond the immediate passage
and book under consideration, in addition to ancient Near Eastern
material, in order to provide perspective on and insight about the
particular metaphors under consideration.[137]

This comparison highlights a pattern found in other works on
metaphor in the Bible. In spite of differences in the approach to
metaphor articulated at the outset, in actual practice, studies of
metaphor in the Bible remain rather similar, exemplifying the standard
methodology of biblical scholarship: they closely examine the wording

---

[130] Oestreich, 157–160.
[131] Oestreich, 169–182.
[132] Darr, 115.
[133] Oestreich, 42.
[134] Oestreich, 185.
[135] Darr, 41.
[136] Darr, 105. She asserts: "One searches in vain for a better example of how
enlivening previously-suppressed associations with an established trope revives its
power to transform the reader's perception of reality" (105).
[137] Oestreich, 42. When he outlines the fourth stage of his method of study, "Old
Testament and Ancient Orient Background of the Metaphor," Oestreich insists on
looking for the immediate cultural context and placing a priority on biblical parallels (42). The fifth step of his method of study concerns the new aspects and particular meanings of the text in Hosea 14 (43).

of the passage at hand and glean information from relevant verses in other parts of the Bible and from extrabiblical sources. In response to Nielsen's previously quoted question, a survey of the literature on specific metaphors in the Bible suggests that, as the topic has been treated so far, there is little "significance at all to the way in which we analyze specific Old Testament texts . . . whether we consider one theory of metaphor more correct than the other."[138] Just as Nielsen posits that her description of metaphor results in a number of exegetical consequences,[139] this study will attempt to demonstrate that the theory of metaphor selected can affect, and indeed enhance, the interpretation of biblical texts.

D. *Works with a Theoretical Bent*

Several works fall outside of the two main categories of research, those that focus on particular metaphors in the prophetic books and scholarship tracing one metaphor throughout the Bible. Peter Macky's 1990 book, *The Centrality of Metaphors to Biblical Thought, A Method for Interpreting the Bible* aims to provide the "first monograph-length study of biblical metaphor yet published."[140] Macky evaluates a range of theories of metaphor and proposes his own working definition.[141] He outlines several systems for categorizing various metaphorical subtypes,[142] and he proposes a four-step method for exploring a metaphor.[143] In addition, he addresses some of the principal issues in the literature on metaphor, such as the question of what constitutes

---

[138] Nielsen, 66.

[139] Nielsen, 66–67.

[140] Peter W. Macky, *Centrality of Metaphors to Biblical Thought: A Method for Interpreting the Bible* (Lewston, NY: The Edwin Mellen Press, Ltd., 1990), 1. Markus Philipp Zehnder's book, *Wegmetaphorik im Alten Testament: Eine semantische Untersuchung der alttestamentlichen und altorientalischen Weg-Lexeme mit besonderer Berucksichtigung ihrer metaphorischen Verwendung* (Berlin: Walter de Gruyter, 1999) was discovered too late to be added to this section.

[141] Macky defines metaphor as "that figurative way of speaking (and meaning) in which one reality, the Subject, is depicted in terms that are more commonly associated with a different reality, the Symbol, which is related to it by Analogy" (49). He concludes that the definitions of metaphor proposed by Alston, Ricoeur, and Soskice "hit the target," proving the most useful for biblical interpretation.

[142] For example, he differentiates between prototypical and subsidiary metaphors, ornamental and comparative subsidiary metaphors, "twice-true metaphors" and metaphorical similes (57–71) and between novel, familiar, standard, hidden, and retired metaphors (72–80).

[143] Macky, 278–295.

literal versus figurative language[144] and the role of speech act theory in understanding metaphor.[145] When he turns from conceptual
issues to the biblical text itself, Macky generally quotes passages from
the Hebrew Bible and the New Testament, with little discussion of
the examples cited. Whereas the works discussed above concentrate
primarily on the analysis of specific biblical metaphors, with limited
attention given to the review and implementation of metaphor theory,
Macky focuses predominantly on general principles and methodology. In the end, his treatment of this topic raises the question: what
is the use of theory if it does not provide practical, exegetical benefits?
His work exemplifies the type of gap between theory and practice
observed in other studies on biblical metaphor.

David Aaron's recent book, *Biblical Ambiguities: Metaphor, Semantics
and Divine Imagery*, also concentrates heavily on the theory of metaphor.
Whereas other biblical scholars briefly summarize some of the more
familiar research on metaphor, Aaron presents a novel approach.
Bringing to the subject a sophisticated knowledge of semantics, he
builds an innovative interpretive strategy designed to "allow for more
accurate assessments of ancient utterances."[146] Aaron criticizes other
biblical scholars for making judgments about whether a statement
constitutes figurative or literal language, without articulating their
reasoning behind a particular interpretation.[147] He sets out to expose
the inadequacies of the existing research and to alter and advance
the treatment of this topic, as he explains:

> My goal is as much to cast doubt on the well-entrenched but unscrutinized
> methodologies that currently dominate biblical scholarship (regarding
> metaphor), as it is to offer a viable alternative to the standard approaches.[148]

The alternative approach he advocates is derived largely from Ray
Jackendoff's research on semantics and cognitive structure.[149]

---

[144] Macky, 32–38. Macky defines literal language as the "communicable, indepen-
dent use of words" and figurative language as the "dependent use of words" (25–26).

[145] Macky intends "to show that whenever we seek to understand and interpret
a biblical metaphor we must discover what the author's purpose was in the speech
act included in the metaphor" (243). He distinguishes metaphors based on the type
of speech act involved: expressive, evaluative, performative, exploratory, pedagogi-
cal, affective, transforming, and relational metaphors (243–261).

[146] Aaron, 69.

[147] Aaron, 50.

[148] Aaron, 9.

[149] Aaron, 69, with reference to Ray Jackendoff, *Semantics and Cognition* (Cambridge:
MIT Press, 1983) and *Consciousness and the Computational Mind* (Cambridge: MIT Press,
1987).

As a starting point, Aaron insists that scholarship on metaphor must "move away from [a] limiting, binary, either/or conception of figurative speech."[150] He proposes a "gradient model of meaning" that seeks to situate metaphor on a non-binary continuum of meaning. Instead of asking, "Is that statement metaphorical or not?" he urges readers to consider "the *degree* to which a statement is metaphorical and what causes the metaphoricalness."[151] In order to account for statements that fall in between the poles of "literal" and "metaphorical," Aaron introduces a third category called "conceptual ascription."[152] Because cases of conceptual ascription do not entail incongruity or anomaly, he does not consider them metaphors. Applying this concept to a biblical example, he asserts:

> Father-son language in the Hebrew Bible is fundamentally *ascriptival*, in both functional and structural ways, and for most of these expressions, metaphor is not involved. In this case, the functional ascription regards how one comes into the world (God as creator) and the structural ascription regards the attribution of authority to whomever it is that occupies the hierarchical station of "father" within a clan. Both are meant quite literally in the manner that ascription is closer to literal than it is to any figurative mode of expression. When we fail to recognize this, we guarantee a distortion of the biblical concept.[153]

In opposition to those who consider predicational statements about God like "God is king" as metaphors, Aaron insists that at certain times the ancient Israelites understood them literally.[154]

Aaron also distinguishes himself by exploring "the mechanics of metaphor." Describing what he means by this phrase, he writes:

> My goal here is to expose the underlying cognitive structure that functions when we make decisions regarding literal and non-literal meanings. By making our thinking patterns explicit, I hope to clarify

---

[150] Aaron, 4.

[151] Aaron, 29.

[152] The category of "conceptual ascription" accounts for the appositional or predicational statement, *A is B*, where B is not ontologically identical to A, but "A fulfills the proper function of B" or "A is perceived to have the same structure as B." The former example Aaron labels "functional ascription" and the latter, "structural ascription"(60).

[153] Aaron, 63.

[154] Aaron argues that "any notion of God as king of all celestial beings was understood as a literal charge of leadership" (41). In the same light, "the warrior deity, Yahweh, was understood quite literally to be an army . . . and to be a shield—again, literally, in the sense that he shielded Israel from its enemies" (59). Aaron also concludes that "ark-dwelling would have been literal for some sources" (178) and that certain psalm imagery "can be read quite literally" (52).

two stages of our interpretive process. The first is the way we decide *whether or not we can make a decision* as to what kind of language we are dealing with; the second stage is the actual computational process that decides where on the continuum a given statement falls.[155]

Aaron's work stands out from other studies of metaphor in the Bible both in its concern with providing a mechanism for identifying metaphor[156] and in its application of semantic theory to the study of figurative language.

V. THE CONTOURS OF THE PRESENT STUDY

In a number of respects, the aims of the present project parallel Aaron's goals. This volume also endeavors to explore the mechanics of metaphor and to provide a means of identifying metaphor and distinguishing it from other forms of figurative language. In addition, this study applies current linguistic research on metaphor to the biblical text in an attempt to advance our understanding of the ways metaphor functions in the Tanakh. Whereas Aaron relies primarily on Jackendoff's research on semantics and cognitive structure, this study utilizes the insights of linguists Eva Kittay and Asif Agha and philosopher Roger White to identify and interpret figurative language in the book of Samuel.

Reflecting on the contribution of his book, Aaron writes: "I do not consider the particulars of my textual interpretations as important as my attempt to establish solid footings for gradient interpretive strategies."[157] In contrast, textual interpretation plays a central role in this work. Like Macky, Aaron concentrates more on theory than on its actual application to the biblical text. For example, when illustrating his ideas, Aaron frequently looks outside the Bible, turning to quotations from Robert Frost, Shakespeare, and Lakoff and Turner;[158] and when utilizing biblical examples, he concentrates on simple appositional statements, such as "God is king."[159] This study

---

[155] Aaron, 101.

[156] Aaron proposes a diagnostic tool for identifying metaphor that will be discussed in chapter two.

[157] Aaron, 196.

[158] Aaron, 115, 121, 116, respectively.

[159] See, for instance, 38–41 or 57–59. Aaron tends to speak of phrases such as *God is sun, God is army, God is shield* out of context, without citing specific verses in which they are found.

will study the range of metaphors found in selected prose narratives in Samuel, not only in order to shed light on the mechanics of metaphor, but also to enhance the interpretation of the biblical text.

As the literature review above demonstrates, scholars have restricted their studies of metaphor primarily to the poetic sections of the Bible. No one has yet conducted an in-depth investigation of metaphor in biblical prose narrative. Just as parallelism, considered a defining characteristic of biblical poetry, also appears in prose passages,[160] so metaphor is utilized by writers of prose as well as poetry. While metaphor, like parallelism, does not dominate prose narrative the way it does poetic passages, nonetheless it functions as an important and effective literary device. Like other literary devices, metaphor provides a means by which "the text intimates its meanings"; it stands out as one of "the distinctive, artfully deployed features of ancient Hebrew prose and poetry that are the instruments for the articulation of all meaning, message, insight, and vision."[161] In addition, metaphors found in prose texts are not complicated to the same extent as those in poetic passages by the other intertwining features that define biblical poetry, such as terseness, parallelism, repetition and patterning.[162] These factors make biblical narrative a promising setting in which to examine metaphor and other forms of figurative language.

Whereas other studies of metaphor tend to isolate distinct metaphors, such as the metaphor of the tree or the metaphor of God and Israel as husband and wife, this volume will investigate the various metaphors found in a particular passage and situate them in their surrounding narrative context. Agha argues that "the real task of analysis is not merely to catalogue the cases of metaphor but to understand the dramatic and rhetorical effects of the implicit meanings conveyed by tropes."[163] Bar-Efrat emphasizes the value of this type of contextual strategy when he writes:

---

[160] Berlin, *Dynamics of Biblical Parallelism* (Bloomington: Indiana University Press, 1966), 4.

[161] Alter, *Genesis*, xii.

[162] See Adele Berlin, "Introduction to Hebrew Poetry," *The New Interpreter's Bible*, vol. IV (Nashville: Abingdon Press, 1996), 301–315. As noted above, such literary features appear in prose as well, but not in the same dominant, defining fashion.

[163] Agha, personal correspondence.

> The best approach to a discussion of style is by undertaking a stylistic
> analysis of an entire narrative unit. Only in this way can the stylistic
> phenomena be seen within their contexts . . . , the interaction between
> them observed and their special significances discerned.[164]

This study begins with an analysis of 1 Samuel 25 and a discussion
of how to identify and interpret the metaphors found in this chapter. Attention will be given to three main facets of metaphor: its
anomalous nature, its underlying analogy, and the interactional effects
it produces. Next, the metaphors in 2 Samuel 16:16–17:14 will be
compared with other tropes in this narrative unit, primarily metonymy
and simile. Finally, the notion of "dead" metaphors will be explored
and challenged in the course of an examination of the figurative language in 1 Samuel 24.

---

[164] Bar-Efrat, 200.

CHAPTER TWO

IDENTIFICATION OF BIBLICAL METAPHORS:
THE ANOMALOUS ASPECT OF METAPHOR

I. Introduction to 1 Samuel 25

First Samuel 25 tells the story of David, a fugitive future king who is slighted by a wealthy, churlish herdsman, aptly named Nabal.[1] David is determined to wreak his revenge upon Nabal and his household, but, in the nick of time, Nabal's clever wife Abigail convinces David to lay down his arms. The element of persuasion permeates this episode. First, David attempts to persuade Nabal to relinquish a portion of his bounty in compensation for the earlier protection provided by David's men (25:6–8). Next, Nabal's servant persuades Abigail to find a way to avert the calamitous consequences of Nabal's dismissive response to David (25:14–17). Finally, Abigail persuades David not to vanquish Nabal and his men (25:24–31). Of these three speeches, the latter two prove successful, in that the speaker induces the addressee to act in the desired manner. In both cases, the speakers, Nabal's servant and Abigail, pepper their words with metaphors.

Since the early twentieth century, commentators have drawn attention to the "elegance of Hebrew style"[2] found in 1 Samuel 25, which "stands out from among other chapters of this section by its distinctive style and diction."[3] Among more recent scholars, J. P. Fokkelman lauds "the long and excellent story of Nabal, Abigail, and David,"[4] a "highly praised story" that he calls "a masterpiece"[5] in part because of the "spectacular" and "bold" metaphors that make this a "rhetorical pearl."[6] David Gunn touts David's speech to his

---

[1] נבל means "fool" in Hebrew.

[2] S. R. Driver, *Notes on the Hebrew Text of the Books of Samuel* (Oxford: Clarendon Press, 1913), 201.

[3] M. H. Segal, *Studies in the Books of Samuel*, Part II (Philadelphia: Dropsie College for Hebrew and Cognate Learning, 1917); reprinted from *JQR* 8 (1917–18), 82.

[4] J. P. Fokkelman, *Narrative Art and Poetry in the Books of Samuel*, vol. II (Assen/Maastricht, The Netherlands: Van Gorcum, 1986), 474.

[5] Fokkelman, 477.

[6] Fokkelman, 506, 508.

servants (25:5–8) as a "model of rhetorical art" and Abigail's speech (25:24–31) as a "model of tact . . . designed to persuade."[7] Bar-Efrat emphasizes that the style of this chapter "is rich with literary and rhetorical means" such as metaphor, patterned word repetition, and rhetorical questions.[8]

Bar-Efrat distinguishes himself from other commentators in that he specifies which components of the chapter he classifies as a metaphor. In his introductory comments on chapter 25, he lists as metaphors the statements "they were a wall around us" (v. 16) and "my lord's life will be bound up in the bundle of the living . . . and the lives of your enemies He will sling from the hollow of the sling" (v. 29).[9] In the commentary that follows, Bar-Efrat explicates the meaning of several of these metaphoric utterances, especially those in v. 29.[10] In addition to the items on Bar-Efrat's list, questions arise about the metaphoric status of other elements in the chapter, such as the servant's remark that Nabal "swooped down" on David (v. 14)[11] and the narrator's comment that Nabal "was hard" (v. 3). Are there other expressions that qualify as metaphors? Before analyzing how a metaphor operates or interpreting how it functions in a given narrative, one must address the issue of identification and attempt to establish the defining features of a metaphor.

---

[7] David Gunn, *The Fate of King Saul* (Sheffield: Almond Press, 1980), 96, 99.

[8] Simon Bar-Efrat, *I Samuel* (Tel Aviv: Am Oved Publishers, Ltd., 1996), 313. Not all commentators share such a positive assessment of 1 Samuel 25. Kyle McCarter comments on the "flowery rhetoric" of Abigail's speech (*I Samuel* [New York: Doubleday, 1980], 401), and Peter Miscall notes that this and the surrounding chapters are marked by "lengthy" and "verbose" speeches (*I Samuel: A Literary Reading* [Bloomington: Indiana University Press, 1986], 144, 150). Robert Polzin writes in a footnote: "I am surprised that the contrived and artificial plot and characterization of chapters 24 and 26 are not more widely emphasized"; he adds, "Fokkelman, for example, is ecstatic over the art of these chapters, but in my opinion he neglects their artifice" (*Samuel and the Deuteronomist*, pt. 2 [Bloomington: Indiana University Press, 1993], 268).

[9] Bar-Efrat, *I Samuel*, 313. He identifies as similes the phrases "like the feast of a king" (v. 36) and "he became a stone" (v. 37).

[10] Bar-Efrat, *I Samuel*, 321–322.

[11] Bar-Efrat explains that the expression means that Nabal "attacked with words, like a bird of prey attacks prey" (*I Samuel*, 316), but neither in his comment on v. 14 nor in his introduction to this story does he label this as a metaphor.

II. The Identification of Metaphors

A. *The "Intractable Problem" of Identifying Metaphors*

Johnson provides a historical perspective on this issue. He observes that a number of contemporary scholars of metaphor insisted that an adequate theory of metaphor should be able to explain how we recognize metaphors and distinguish them from other tropes.[12] Albeit worthwhile, the task has remained a challenge. Johnson explains:

> This has seemed a reasonable starting point to almost everybody, since an answer to this question would both carve out a domain of discourse and identify the essential components of metaphoric comprehension. But although native speakers can easily identify figurative utterances and understand them, explaining *how* this is possible has proved to be one of the more intractable problems of metaphor.[13]

In the 1958 book *Aesthetics*, Monroe Beardsley proposes that "a metaphor is a significant attribution that is either indirectly self-contradictory or obviously false in its context."[14] In the 1981 revised edition of this work, Beardsley acknowledges that logical incompatibility or absurd falsity fails to account for all metaphors. For instance, a statement that denies a metaphor like "Marriage is not bed of roses" is literally true, but a metaphor nonetheless.[15] He remarks that "one of the persistent problems about metaphor is to identify the features that throw a word or phrase into a metaphorical stance and thus give rise to a metaphorical sense."[16] In spite of the challenges, Loewenberg insists on the importance of finding a solution to this problem. Although "our unreconstructed intuition as speakers of English permits us to recognize clear cases of metaphor,"[17] she asserts that "any satisfactory formulation of the principle of metaphor requires the identifiability of metaphors since they cannot be understood or produced unless recognized as such."[18]

---

[12] Johnson, 20.

[13] Johnson, 20–21.

[14] Monroe Beardsley, *Aesthetics* (Indianapolis: Hackett Publishing Company, Inc., 1981), 142.

[15] Beardsley, xxxv.

[16] Beardsley, xxxiv.

[17] Loewenberg, 315.

[18] Loewenberg, 316. While Johnson cites a number of worthwhile aspects of Loewenberg's work, he asserts: "Her attempt to remedy previous deficiencies falls short, because it still assumes that metaphors are identifiable, at least in part, by their literal falsity" (22).

In an article published in the mid-1950's, Black comments that "it would be satisfactory to have convincing answers" to a list of questions, including: "How do we recognize a case of metaphor?" and "Are there any criteria for the detection of metaphors?"[19] While he does not answer these questions in that essay, he returns to the topic twenty-five years later, when he denounces Beardsley's and Lowenberg's attempts to discover what he labels a "diagnostic criterion." Criticizing the ambitious search for "an observable and *necessary condition* for a statement to be metaphorical," he writes: "I use 'diagnostic criterion' here to suggest a bodily symptom, such as a rash, that serves as a reliable sign of some abnormal state though not necessarily qualifying as a defining condition."[20] He presents two objections to Beardsley's theory. First, the defining feature of logical incompatibility or absurd falsity applies to other tropes besides metaphor, such as hyperbole or oxymoron. Secondly, as Beardsley himself later realized, certain metaphors do not manifest logical contradiction or absurdity.[21] Black maintains that a range of reasons may prompt a metaphorical reading:

> The decisive reason for the choice of interpretation may be, as it often is, the patent falsity or incoherence of the literal reading—but it might equally be the banality of that reading's truth, its pointlessness, or its lack of congruence with the surrounding text and nonverbal setting.[22]

---

[19] Black, "Metaphor," 63–64.

[20] Black, "More about Metaphor," in *Metaphor and Thought*, ed. Andrew Ortony, 2d ed. (Cambridge: Cambridge University Press, 1993), 33. Black criticizes the general aim, not the details, of Loewenberg's "valuable essay" (34).

[21] Black, 34.

[22] Black, 34. Besides the truth or falsity test, scholars point to a range of other facets that mark a metaphor. For example, Earl MacCormac believes that the symptom of a metaphor is "emotional tension" (*A Cognitive Theory of Metaphor* [Cambridge: The MIT Press, 1985], 5). Similarly, Soskice states that with a metaphor, "one recognizes a dissonance or tension in a living metaphor whereby the terms of the utterance seem not strictly appropriate to the topic at hand" (71). Jackendoff and Aaron have designed a diagnostic tool that attempts to detect the kind of logical incongruity that they perceive in metaphor, one that "checks for both the presence of an incongruous mapping between domains and the applicability of this mapping to the sentence in question" (Jackendoff and Aaron, 326). The diagnostic involves translating a metaphor, such as "Our relationship is at a dead end," into the type of more general conceptual equations used by Lakoff and Turner, such as A RELATIONSHIP IS A JOURNEY. Then, the interpreter refashions the simple predicational statement into a sentence that acknowledges the incongruity involved when, using the terminology of Lakoff and Turner, the "source domain" is mapped onto the "target domain": "Of course, relationships are not really journeys—but if they were, you might say ours is at a dead end." Aaron explains: "The logic is overtly

In the end, he concludes that "there is no infallible test . . . to be expected in discriminating the metaphorical from the literal," for "every criterion for a metaphor's presence, however plausible, is defeasible in special circumstances."[23]

Given the complexity of metaphors and the tremendous diversity of definitions and approaches, it is not surprising that developing a foolproof means of identifying a metaphor has proven to be an elusive endeavor. When broaching this topic, researchers often acknowledge that the absence of a "diagnostic criterion" generally does not hamper the ability to process figurative language. For example, echoing the comments by Johnson and Loewenberg quoted above, Michael Toolan remarks:

> It is widely noted that informants readily understand utterances of all sorts without giving any indication, at the time or in subsequent tests, that they are at all concerned with categorizing those utterances as literal, or metaphoric, or metonymic, etc.[24]

Similarly, Kittay observes: "How do we recognize that an utterance is metaphorical rather than literal or inept and mistaken? Generally, we have little difficulty making such distinctions."[25] In spite of such confidence in the basic ability to identify metaphors, when closely examining a literary text, a section of discourse, or even the examples cited in the scholarly literature on metaphor, questionable cases frequently arise. If one convened a group of experts on metaphor and asked them to read 1 Samuel 25, would they agree as to what

---

expressed as follows: Since relationships *are not* journeys, when 'journey ideas' are used regarding relationships, one must be speaking about change in terms of movement in relationships. Ergo: statement is metaphorical" (Aaron, 116; Jackendoff and Aaron, 326). Jackendoff and Aaron contrast this example with the statement "My dog ran down the street," which evokes the equation ANIMALS ARE PEOPLE and translates into the diagnostic sentence, "Of course, animals aren't people—but if they were, you might say my dog ran down the street." They assert that such a sentence "has the curious flavor of a non sequitur or perhaps a bad pun." They continue: "The incongruity of treating dogs as human is acknowledged, but the relevance of this mapping to the expression *my dog ran down the street* is totally unclear." Having made such a subjective judgment, they conclude that the statement does not constitute a metaphor (Jackendoff and Aaron, 326–327; Aaron, 117). While this diagnostic tool may aim to make overt the cognitive procedure used to evaluate a metaphor, it does not provide a useful means of evaluating the complex, varied metaphors encountered in speech or literary texts.

[23] Black, 34–35.

[24] Michael Toolan, *Total Speech: An Integrational Linguistic Approach to Language* (Durham: Duke University Press, 1996), 77.

[25] Kittay, 40.

constitutes a metaphor in this chapter? While an "infallible test" for recognizing metaphor may be beyond our grasp, can we find a viable, helpful mechanism for identifying metaphors, particularly the uncertain or borderline cases? Can we find a diagnostic that may not be perfect but can be considered productive?

B. *Componential Semantics: A Model for Identifying Metaphor*

According to Kittay, the issue of the identification of an utterance as metaphorical "has received little attention" and "has never been adequately treated."[26] She attempts to rectify this situation, using componential semantics as the basis of her work. At the start of her chapter on "The Identification of Metaphor," she asks: "How do we recognize that an utterance is metaphorical . . . [W]hat are the criteria we use in so identifying utterances which ought to be metaphorically interpreted?"[27] Establishing the confines of her investigation, she writes:

> I am not asking for the psychological processes we undergo when we opt for a metaphorical interpretation. I am asking what conditions pertain when the appropriate interpretation of an utterance is metaphorical rather than literal, technical, fanciful, figurative but not metaphorical, or simply mistaken.[28]

Before examining Kittay's answers to these questions, a general introduction to componential semantics will provide the background needed to understand her work.

Componential semantics offers a way to analyze word meaning by breaking the sense of a lexeme into its component parts. Linguists commonly refer to the following examples to demonstrate how this approach extracts the basic constituents of a given word: "man" may be represented as comprising [human] [male] [adult], in contrast to "girl": [human] [female] [non-adult]. Similarly, "bull" is identified as [non-human] [male] [adult], whereas "calf" is represented as [non-human] [male/female] [non-adult].[29] This process involves the identification of "necessary and sufficient" features that distinguish the

---

[26] Kittay, 40.
[27] Kittay, 40.
[28] Kittay, 40.
[29] See, for example, John Lyons, *Linguistic Semantics* (Cambridge: Cambridge University Press, 1995), 108–110; Lyons, *Introduction to Theoretical Linguistics* (Cambridge: Cambridge University Press, 1968), 472; David Crystal, *The Cambridge Encyclopedia*

meaning of one word from others with common semantic components, those in the same semantic domain.[30] According to Lyons, the componential analysis of language "provides linguists, in principle, with a systematic and economic means of representing the sense-relations that hold among lexemes."[31]

Jerrold Katz and Jerry Fodor utilize componential semantics as they attempt to articulate a semantic theory that will provide a means of handling sentences that are grammatically well-formed but semantically ill-formed. For each lexeme, they first identify three elements: grammatical markers (unenclosed in the example below), semantic markers (in parentheses), and distinguishers (in square brackets). They explain: "The semantic markers and distinguishers are the means by which we can decompose the meaning of one sense of a lexical item into its atomic concepts," thereby allowing us not only to exhibit the semantic structure, but also to consider the semantic relations between lexemes.[32] For example, they distinguish three paths in the analysis of the lexeme *ball*:[33]

1. *Ball* → Noun concrete → (Social activity) → (Large) → (Assembly) → [For the purpose of social dancing]

2. *Ball* → Noun concrete → (Physical object) → [Having globular shape]

3. *Ball* → Noun concrete → (Physical object) → [Solid missile for projection by an engine of war]

Katz and Fodor introduce this type of lexical analysis in order to address the issue of concatenation, the means by which lexemes are combined into grammatically and semantically well-formed or ill-formed sentences. To delineate the semantically acceptable combinations

---

of Language, 2nd edition (Cambridge: Cambridge University Press, 1997), 107. Systems of notation vary: often contrasts are presented using + or −, such as + human or − human; some use brackets, where as others (such as Lyons) place the components in capital letters.

[30] Eugene A. Nida, *Componential Analysis of Meaning* (The Hague: Mouton, 1975), 32–33.

[31] Lyons, *Linguistic Semantics*, 114. Lyons acknowledges that componential semantics "has figured prominently in recent works on semantics and has guided a good deal of undoubtedly valuable research" (116). Nonetheless, he charges that "componential analysis is defective both theoretically and empirically" (116). See his critique, 114–116.

[32] Jerrold J. Katz and Jerry A. Fodor, "The Structure of Semantic Theory," *Language* 39 (1963) 185–186.

[33] Katz and Fodor, 198.

for a particular sense of a lexeme, they add a fourth element at the
end of each path (here in angled brackets). For instance, the relevant path for *spinster* contains: *spinster* → Adjective → (Human) →
(Adult) → (Female) → [Who has never married] <Human>, meaning that this adjective should modify a noun with the semantic marker
(Human). They explain:

> The expression *spinster insecticide* would be regarded as anomalous by
> speakers of English . . . because the path for *insecticide* does not contain
> the semantic marker (Human) which is necessary to satisfy the selec-
> tion restriction associated with *spinster*.[34]

As this example demonstrates, selection-restrictions indicate which
pairs of lexemes can be combined meaningfully in certain grammatical constructions.

A number of scholars have applied these linguistic theories to the
study of metaphor. Robert Matthews, for one, demonstrates how
componential semantics and selection restrictions relate to this topic.[35]
As he introduces his approach to metaphor, he states:

> An account of metaphor as a deviant but interpreted linguistic struc-
> ture involves the central notion of a RULE-VIOLATION which for-
> mally specifies just what is meant when we designate a structure as
> 'deviant.'[36]

To clarify, he analyzes the sentence, *the volcano burped*, in which the
selectional restriction violation involves the fact that a human attribute
(*burped*) is predicated of an inanimate noun (*volcano*).[37] Concerning
the familiar example, *the man is a wolf*, he writes:

---

[34] Katz and Fodor, 199.

[35] Robert J. Matthews, "Concerning a 'Linguistic Theory' of Metaphor," *Foundations
of Language* 7 (1971), 413–25. Other examples include L. Jonathan Cohen, "The
Semantics of Metaphor," in *Metaphor and Thought*, ed. Andrew Ortony, 2d ed.
(Cambridge: Cambridge University Press, 1993), 58–70; S. R. Levin, *The Semantics of
Metaphor* (Baltimore: Johns Hopkins University Press, 1977); U. Weinreich, "Explorations
in Semantic Theory," in T. A. Sebeok, ed., *Theoretical Foundations* (The Hague:
Mouton, 1966), 395–477. Jean-Marc Babut applies this approach to the Bible in
his book, *Idiomatic Expressions of the Hebrew Bible: Their Meaning and Translation through
Componential Analysis* (North Richland Hills, Texas: BIBAL Press, 1999). He engages in
a four-step process: (1) He defines the corpus in which the expression occurs, attempting to establish a linguistically homogeneous semantic domain. (2) He examines the
contexts in which the expressions appear in order to identify terms that have related
meanings. (3) He compares the items in the semantic domain, highlighting constant
features and distinctive components. (4) He determines the meaning of the idiomatic
expression and proposes a functionally equivalent translation (69–74).

[36] Matthews, 418.

[37] Matthews, 419–420.

We note that selections which *wolf* imposes upon the feature system of *man* have been violated: a member of the class having the feature [+ human] is being asserted to be a member of the class having the feature [+ canine (– human)].[38]

He also considers the more complex utterance, *Macbeth murders sleep.* The chart below illustrates the way that Matthews relies on semantic markers to locate the violation present in this metaphor.[39]

Macbeth. . . .	*murders. . . .*	*sleep*
[+human]	[+human agent]	[+physical state]
[+proper name]	[+human victim]	[+rest or quiescence]
	[+act of killing]	[+applies to animate object]
	[+malicious or premeditated]	
	[+unlawful]	

He explains:

> The selectional restrictions imposed by the verb upon the grammatical subject are satisfied: the agent is a human being. The selectional restriction imposed upon the grammatical object is, however not satisfied: only a human being can be said to be murdered. The feature [+ human victim] of *murders* is violated as *sleep* is [– human].[40]

Matthews concludes his article with a brief discussion of an utterance cited by Michael Reddy as a representative of a large class of sentences that do not involve any sort of selectional restriction violation but still may constitute a metaphor.[41] Reddy points out that the sentence *the rock is becoming brittle with age* reads differently in the context of a geological expedition as opposed to a description of an elderly professor emeritus. Matthews raises the question of whether or not this sentence should be termed a metaphor. He rejects the label of this statement as a metaphor and suggests: "Perhaps utterances of this type, although not metaphors themselves, are best viewed as having an underlying metaphor," such as *the old professor emeritus is a rock,* "which does involve restriction violation."[42] While Matthews does not dwell in depth on this example, he recognizes its significance,

---

[38] Matthews, 421–422.
[39] Matthews, 422.
[40] Matthews, 422–423.
[41] Michael J. Reddy, "A Semantic Approach to Metaphor," *Papers from the Fifth Regional Meeting, Chicago Linguistics Society* (Chicago: University of Chicago Department of Linguistics, 1969), 240–251.
[42] Matthews, 423.

admitting that "Reddy's contention that there is such a class of metaphors . . . questions the assertion that deviance is a necessary condition for a sentence to be metaphorical."[43] For others who utilize componential semantics to understand metaphor, and for their critics, this issue proves crucial to establishing a viable theory of metaphor.[44]

Kittay advances the linguistic study of metaphor by demonstrating how an utterance without an apparent selection restriction violation nevertheless qualifies as a metaphor. Her detailed, complex theory of metaphor incorporates certain tenets of the Katz-Fodor theory in conjunction with semantic field theory and the concept of first-order and second-order meaning.[45] Central to her theory of metaphor is the notion that "the unit of metaphor need not be coincident with the grammatical units of the single word or the sentence."[46] Instead of looking only at an isolated word or sentence, the evaluation of an utterance as metaphorical requires the interpreter to consider the larger textual unit created by the cohesion of separate but related sentences. Because the Katz-Fodor notion of selectional-restriction violation applies only to a sentence-length unit, their theory cannot capture the incongruity that results when an utterance like *the rock is becoming brittle with age* is placed within a larger context that equates the rock with an aging professor.

Kittay argues that in order to identify an utterance as metaphorical or literal, one must take into consideration the linguistic or situational context, for "the interpretation of an utterance-type is dependent upon the context."[47] To demonstrate, Kittay examines the

---

[43] Matthews, 423.

[44] For instance, reflecting on Matthews' work, Johnson writes: "The main problem with proposals of this sort is that they try to elevate a condition that frequently holds (namely, semantic deviance) into a necessary condition of metaphor. Semantic deviance (or violation of selectional restriction rules) cannot be a necessary condition of metaphor, because, as Loewenberg (1975) notes, '[a]ny sentence can be provided contexts . . . in which it can receive either literal or metaphorical interpretations'" (21). See Loewenberg, 321–322.

[45] The concepts of first-order and second-order meaning are derived from H. P. Grice's four-fold distinction between "timeless meaning," "applied timeless meaning," "occasion meaning," and "utterer's occasion meaning." See Kittay, 42–47 for her discussion of Grice's work. Note that what follows is a somewhat simplified presentation, eliminating many of the technical terms and notational symbols used by Kittay.

[46] Kittay, 50.

[47] Kittay, 55. Kittay provides examples of both types of contexts, linguistic and situational. The surrounding text constitutes the linguistic context, as in the following

non-deviant sentence, *Smith is a plumber*, which is complete as a grammatical utterance but incomplete as a metaphorical utterance.[48] She argues that its "completeness as metaphor requires a setting which renders [it] metaphorical," thereby allowing the interpreter to detect and analyze the incongruity revealed when the utterance is seen as part of a larger discourse. In the following sequence of sentences, the larger context signals to the hearer the presence of a metaphor: "Don't let Smith perform such a delicate surgical procedure. Smith is a plumber. His last two patients died."[49] In such a context, it becomes clear that Smith is actually a surgeon, and only metaphorically a plumber.

In order to locate the linguistic incongruity that marks a metaphor, Kittay modifies the Katz-Fodor projection rules so that they apply to units larger than a sentence. Katz-Fodor projection rules operate on the lowest-level constituents of a sentence by "bracketing together" the senses of the constituents and combining their senses according to appropriate syntactic rules. Kittay explains:

> We arrive at an interpretation of an utterance by choosing a given sense of a constituent of an utterance which can combine with the sense of another constituent in accordance with the sc-rules [semantic combination rules] of these senses.[50]

Because of the importance of taking the larger context into consideration, she expands the concept of projection rules to operate intra-sententially as well as inter-sententially so that they "characterize not only how a word combines within a sentence but also how a sentence coheres with its context."[51] She observes that a variety of cohesive elements bind together the separate sentences that form a semantic whole, such as demonstratives, pronouns, or elliptical phrases that require information in other sentences for their interpretation.[52] Within

---

sequence of sentences: "The rock is becoming brittle with age. He responds to his students' questions with none of his former subtlety." Illustrating a situational context, Kittay proposes that if the utterance *the rock is becoming brittle with age* "occurs as a sentence in an otherwise rambling conversation and is said as an aside, accompanied perhaps by a gesture, for example, a nod in the direction of the professor, we must take the relevant gesture as the situation context which can, at least in part, be rendered linguistically" (71).

[48] Kittay, 69.
[49] Kittay, 73.
[50] Kittay, 59.
[51] Kittay, 61.
[52] Kittay, 62. She lists a number of other examples of cohesive elements, including

a cohesive text, certain words stand in what Kittay calls a "substitutive relation" to one another if "terms may be substituted for one another in their respective sentences, preserving the sentences' syntactic well-formedness."[53] Given the substitutive relations in the plumber example cited above, cohesive projection rules allow the interpreter to form "conversion sentences"[54] that bring to the fore the metaphoric incongruity, as seen in the following example:

1. Original utterance: "Don't let <u>Smith</u> perform such a delicate surgical procedure. <u>Smith</u> is <u>a plumber</u>. <u>His</u> last two patients died."

2. Conversion sentence A: "Don't let <u>that plumber</u> perform such a delicate surgical procedure. <u>Smith's</u> last two patients died"

3. Conversion sentence B: "Don't let <u>Smith</u> perform such a delicate surgical procedure. <u>That plumber's</u> last two patients died."[55]

In such cases, the collocation of "plumber" with "surgical procedure" or "patients" creates a semantic incongruity. Kittay stresses that the original sentence did not violate selection-restriction rules; however, "the substitutions made possible by the cohesive coreferential relations yield structures which are contrary not just to empirical but also to linguistic fact."[56]

By expanding the unit of the metaphor and considering a broader context, Kittay affirms that componential semantics provides a viable model for locating the incongruity[57] or semantic rule-breaking[58] that marks a metaphor. Agha agrees that this type of grammatical analysis allows for the identification of the somewhat anomalous grammatical form found in a metaphor, the internal structural oddity that tags the text segment as a metaphor.[59] He stresses that the ability to identify and construe a metaphor requires a knowledge of the grammar of a language and an ability to distinguish what is syn-

---

the repetition of key words, the presence of conjuctives, and the use of lexically related words dispersed through the text (62).

[53] Kittay, 63.
[54] Kittay, 64.
[55] Kittay, 73 (underlining added).
[56] Kittay, 73.
[57] Kittay, 66.
[58] Kittay, 50.
[59] Agha, personal communication. Also see Asif Agha, "Tropic Aggression in the Clinton-Dole Presidential Debate," *Pragmatics* 7 (1996) 468.

tactically unmarked or unremarkable from what is syntactically remarkable, a position that presupposes a notion of convention.[60] Can this approach productively be applied to the Bible? First Samuel 25 provides a test case.

III. Application to 1 Samuel 25

A. *1 Samuel 25:16—*חומה היו עלינו *("They were a wall around us")*

One of the more obvious metaphors in this chapter appears in the speech of Nabal's servant, when he describes the prior benefaction provided by David's men: "They were a wall around us both night and day" (25:16). While this may be "a perfectly intelligible bit of metaphor,"[61] a question of identification remains: Precisely what

---

[60] Note that Kittay describes metaphor as involving a *semantic* incongruity, whereas Agha speaks about the *grammatical* anomaly that tags a metaphor. John Lyons addresses the relation between semantics and grammar in *Language and Linguistics* (Cambridge: Cambridge University Press, 1981). He states at the outset that "the meaning of a sentence is the product of both lexical and grammatical meaning: i.e., of the meaning of the constituent lexemes and of the grammatical constructions that relate one lexeme, syntagmatically, to another" (156). Further on, he acknowledges that "although there is a distinction between these two kinds of meaning in clear cases, the boundary between them is not always as easy to identify as we might like it to be" (163). To prove his point, he notes the fact that "what is lexicalized in one language may be grammaticalized in another language" (159). When Lyons addresses this issue in his later work, *Linguistic Semantics*, he uses two examples to demonstrate the inseparability of semantics and grammar: 'My friend existed a whole new village' and 'My friend frightened that it was raining.' Labeling these two sentences as "both grammatically and semantically ill-formed," he first explains the nature of the grammatical or syntactic anomaly: "Their ungrammaticality can be readily accounted for by saying that 'exist' is an intransitive verb (and therefore cannot take an object) and that 'frighten', unlike 'think', 'say', etc., cannot occur with a *that*-clause as its object" (218). Next, he describes the incongruous nature of these sentences as a matter of semantics: "The fact that they do not make sense—that they have no propositional content—can be explained by saying that it is inherent in the meaning of 'exist' that it cannot take an object, and that it is inherent in the meaning of 'frighten' that it cannot take as its object an expression referring to such abstract entities as facts and propositions" (218). As these examples demonstrate, although natural languages differ considerably in terms of what they grammaticalize or lexicalize, "there is, in all natural languages, some degree of congruence between semantic (or ontological) categories and certain grammatical categories, such a major parts of speech, gender, number, or tense" (218).

[61] McCarter, 397. Interestingly, although McCarter finds this metaphor "perfectly intelligible," he nonetheless suggests an emendation: "Still it is quite tempting to read *hamma* for *homma*, reckoning the *mater w* as late in any case, and translate: 'They were *a sun above us* at night as well as in the day. . . .'" (397). No textual or exegetical reason is given for this proposal. Berlin speculates that McCarter's reading

makes this utterance a metaphor? On an empirical level, the metaphor
implies that David's men were a wall, which is false. However, on
a linguistic level, componential semantics helps to highlight the nature
of the anomaly that qualifies this statement as a trope.

The word חומה generally refers to a city wall. The noun frequently
occurs in construct form followed by a city's name, as in "wall of
Tyre" (Amos 1:10) or "wall of Beth-shan" (1 Sam 31:10). Some passages describe walls being built or fortified; others tell of walls being
breached or torn down.[62] Out of the one hundred and thirty-three
times in which this lexeme appears in the Bible, rarely does a verse
detail the construction materials or methods.[63] Nevertheless, one reasonably can assume that the construction of a wall required solid,
weight-bearing building materials. Therefore, the following semantic
markers can be established for the word "wall": − animate, + made
of building material.

i. Original Utterance (1 Sam 25:16)

חומה	היו	עלינו
A wall	*they were*	*around us*
[f.s. noun, dir. obj.]$_N$	[ה.י.ה, *qal*, 3m.s., perf.]$_V$	[(prep.) + (1c.p. suf.)]$_{PP}$
− animate object	+/− animate subject	+ animate indir. obj.
+ made of building material		+ human indir. obj.

As this diagram shows, the utterance as it stands does not necessarily contain an anomaly. If the unstated subject of the verb "to
be" (היו) were a word like לבנים ("bricks") or עצים ("wood"), no incongruity would be involved.

ii. Conversion Sentence #1

חומה	היו (העצים)	עלינו
A wall	*(the wood) was*	*around us*
[f.s. noun, dir. obj.]$_N$	[ה.י.ה, *qal*, 3m.s., perf.]$_V$	[(prep.) + (1c.p. suf.)]$_{PP}$
	[(def. art.) + (m.p. subj.)]$_N$	
− animate object	**− animate subject**	+ animate indir. obj.
+ made of building material	**+ building material**	+ human indir. obj.

The anomaly becomes apparent when a conversion sentence is created
based on information provided by the surrounding literary context:

---

may have been influenced by the mention of "night and day" in the verse and/or
the prepositional phrase עלינו (personal correspondence).

[62] For examples, see 1 Kgs 3:1; Isa 22:10; 2 Kgs 14:13; Jer 50:15, respectively.

[63] See the following chapter for a more detailed discussion of this issue.

iii. Conversion Sentence #2

חוֹמָה	(הָאֲנָשִׁים) הָיוּ	עָלֵינוּ
A wall	*(the men) were*	*around us*
[f.s. noun, dir. obj.]ₙ	[ה.י.ה, *qal*, 3m.s., perf.]ᵥ	[(prep.) + (1c.p. suf.)]₍PP₎
	[(def. art.) + (m.p. subj.)]ₙ	
− **animate object**	+ **animate, + human subject**	+ animate indir. obj.
+ **made of building**	− **building material**	+ human indir. obj.
material		

In this case, the predicative statement equates animate beings (David's men), the implied subject of the verb, with an inanimate object (a wall).

The type of semantic anomaly at play in 1 Sam 25:16 can be found in a number of other biblical verses. Attempting to reassure Jeremiah, God declares: "And I will make you to this people a fortified wall of bronze. They will fight against you but will not prevail over you, for with you am I to deliver you and save you" (Jer 15:20).[64] In the Song of Songs, the brothers of the female protagonist announce their intentions to protect their sister: "If a wall she is, we will build upon it a silver battlement; if a door she is, we will panel it in cedar" (Song 8:9). In response, the sister proudly asserts: "I am a wall, and my breasts are like towers" (Song 8:10). In all of these examples, the selection restriction violation occurs when the lexeme "wall" is joined with nouns that refer to human beings.[65]

An interesting case appears in the book of Exodus, as part of the description of the Israelites' escape from the Egyptians after the splitting of the sea: "And the Israelites went into the sea on dry ground, and the waters were for them a wall" (Exod 14:22, 29). In most circumstances, a porous, non-weight-bearing substance like water (− animate; − building material) would not qualify as a standard material for constructing a wall (− animate; + made of building material), thereby creating a semantic anomaly.[66] However, given the miraculous

---

[64] A similar statement appears in Jer 1:18. In a hymn to the Pharaoh in an Amarna letter, the writer describes the Pharaoh as "the Sun who comes forth over me, and a brazen wall set up for him," thus enabling the speaker to feel at rest and confident (EA 147, 52–60; William Moran, *The Amarna Letters* [Baltimore: The John Hopkins University Press, 1992], 233).

[65] A slightly different type of violation appears in Isa 26:1: "[God] makes victory walls and a rampart." Here, the concatenation of an abstract concept (victory) and a more concrete noun (walls) produces the semantic anomaly.

[66] If the vocalization of Nah 3:8 is emended so that מִיָּם is changed to מִיָּם, a similar example exists when the prophet describes the city of No, "which sat by the Nile, water surrounding it, its rampart a sea, water its walls (מַיִם חוֹמָתָהּ)." Also

nature of the exodus episode, should the utterance be viewed as a semantic anomaly or a divine wonder? Does the verse imply that the waters amassed in a manner that resembled a wall, or that God actually formed a wall from water? When applying this method to the Bible, consideration should be given to the unique circumstances of a passages that explicitly involves God. How does the conception of metaphor change when an utterance involves a divine being who can only be spoken about figuratively? This issue deserves attention, but falls outside the confines of the present work.[67]

B. *1 Samuel 25:14*—ויעט בהם *("He swooped down on them")*

In the first verse of his speech, Nabal's servant uses a more complex metaphor when he depicts Nabal's reactions to David's messengers: "He swooped down on them (ויעט בהם)" (25:14). Translations of this verb vary. A number of translators focus on how Nabal responded verbally, emphasizing the tone of his voice: "He shrieked at them" (Fox); "He shouted insults at them" (*NRS*); "He flew at them screaming" (*NAB*).[68] Other translators depict how he responded physically, using figurative language drawn from the realm of animal behavior to characterize Nabal's treatment of the messengers: "He flew at them" (McCarter); "He flew at them screaming" (*NAB*); "He pounced on them" (Alter).[69] Still others comment on how Nabal responded emotionally, selecting verbs that suggest how Nabal felt and how he treated David's men: "He spurned them" (*JPS*); "He railed on them" (*KJV*); "He flared up at them" (*NJB, REB*).[70] How

---

see 4QPentParᵇ 6₅ (המים להם חמה, "the waters were to them a wall") and 4QpNah 3.3₁₀ (מים ה[ו]מ[ו]תיה, "water was its wall") (*DCH*, vol. 3, 172, s.v. חומה).

[67] Brettler and Aaron address the topic of figurative language used to depict God in the Bible.

[68] Everett Fox, *Give Us a King* (New York: Schocken Books, 1999), 123; *New Revised Standard Version* (*NRS*); *New American Bible* (*NAB*). The *NRS* adds a gloss that specifies not only how Nabal spoke ("he shouted") but what type of language he used ("insults"). The *NAB* translation fits in both of the first two categories since it combines a figurative verb ("he flew") with a modifying reference to Nabal's loud voice ("screaming"). Rashi's explanation resembles the *NAB* and *NRS*: "He flew at them with words."

[69] McCarter, 389–90; Robert Alter, *The David Story* (New York: W. W. Norton & Company, Inc., 1999), 155. The Septuagint reads, "and he fled from them," which McCarter speculates may represent ויש מהם (393).

[70] Jewish Publication Society *Tanakh* (*JPS*), *King James Version* (*KJV*), *New Jerusalem Bible* (*NJB*), *Revised English Bible* (*REB*). The use of the verb "flared up" introduces a metaphor not found in the Hebrew, the image of the enraged Nabal as flame. Similar to the *JPS*, Radak explains that Nabal "reproached them," adding that "he cut them down with evil words."

do these translators arrive at such different renditions of this verb?

Two other verbal attestations of this root appear in the Tanakh, both in 1 Samuel. First Samuel 14:32 tells how Saul's troops plundered the defeated Philistines: "And the troops swooped down on the booty (וַיַּעַשׂ] הָעָם אֶל [הַשָּׁלָל])."[71] In I Sam 15:19, Samuel accuses Saul of disobeying orders by pillaging the Amalekites: "And you swooped down on the booty (וַתַּעַט אֶל הַשָּׁלָל)." Biblical dictionaries differ in their treatment of the root, ע.י.ט. The *Brown-Driver-Briggs Hebrew and English Lexicon* provides one entry for the verb in 1 Sam 25:14 and another for the verbs in these other two passages. The first entry, עִיט, defines the lexeme, found only in 1 Sam 25:14, as "scream, shriek" and links it to the Arabic word for "scream, scold" and the Syriac for "anger, reviling"; the translation provided for this verse reads, "and he screamed at them." An entry for the noun עַיִט follows, "bird(s) of prey (from scream)," and then a listing for another verb עִיט, labeled a denominative verb and defined as "dart greedily (like a bird of prey)."[72] In contrast, the Koehler-Baumgartner Hebrew lexicon contains one entry for the verb עִיט, but cites two meanings, both of which share the common element of screaming: "shout at" in 1 Sam 25:14 and "fall upon screaming" in 1 Sam 15:19 and 14:32.[73] As seen in these two biblical dictionaries, some translate 1 Sam 25:14 based on the meanings of the proposed cognates and therefore depict Nabal as screaming at David's men (Fox, *NRS, NAB*). Others highlight the denominative nature of the verb by portraying Nabal as a bird of prey (McCarter, *NAB*).[74] A number of translators provide more of an interpretative gloss, using abstract terms like "spurn" or "rail on" to explain how Nabal reacted (*JPS, KJV*).

Which of these translations best captures the most coherent meaning of וַיַּעַשׂ in 1 Sam 25:14? One way to address the question is to examine the attestations of the noun עַיִט. In the six verses in which

---

[71] Both bracketed words represent the *qere* reading, which corresponds with the Septuagint; the *kethib* reads וַיַּעַשׂ הָעָם אֶל שָׁלָל. McCarter notes: "In 4QSamᵃ, though the verb is not extant, the succeeding preposition is *ʾl* (MT *l-*), which would be impossible with *wyʿś*" (246).

[72] F. Brown, S. R. Driver, Charles A. Briggs, *A Hebrew and English Lexicon of the Old Testament* (Oxford: Clarendon Press, 1951), 743 (hereafter *BDB*).

[73] L. Koehler and W. Baumgartner, *Hebräisches und aramäisches Lexikon zum Alten Testament*, vol. 3 (Leiden: E. J. Brill, 1983), 772. The entry cites two Arabic cognates, *ʿjṭ* (scream) and *ġjz* (anger), along with the Syriac *ʿajṭa*.

[74] Alter also preserves the figurative nature of the verb, but the translation "pounced on" could refer to any animal and does not imply a specific connection between Nabal and a bird of prey.

this lexeme occurs, the majority of cases connect the raptor with the act of consumption. In Gen 15:11, after Abram cuts apart several animals, birds of prey descend upon the carcasses. In an oracle against Ethiopia, Isaiah compares the enemy to shoots and branches that God will cut off and leave for the raptors and beasts of the earth to eat (Isa 18:5–6). Ezekiel announces that Gog and his battalions will be given as food to raptors and beasts of the field (Ezek 39:4). Jeremiah describes raptors circling around Israel and calls the beasts of the field to devour her (Jer 12:9). Of the remaining two verses, one focuses on the bird's flight, as Deutero-Isaiah metaphorically refers to Cyrus as a raptor summoned from the East (Isa 46:11); the other refers to the bird's vision when, in a comment about the remoteness and inaccessibility of mines of precious materials, Job states: "The path, no raptor knows it; the falcon's eye has not seen it" (Job 28:7).

The only potential connection between a raptor and screaming occurs in Jer 12:8–9:

> [8]She has become to me, my heritage
>   Like a <u>lion</u> in the forest
> She has given out her loud cry against me
>   For which reason I hate her
> [9]Is my heritage to me a speckled <u>bird of prey?</u>
>   Are the <u>birds of prey</u> circling round her?
> Go, gather <u>all the beasts of the field</u>
>   Bring them to consume[75]

In the first occurrence of עיט in v. 9, Jeremiah accuses Judah of acting like a bird of prey, but he does not specify what Judah has done wrong.[76] As a consequence of such behavior, in the second occurrence of עיט in this verse, Jeremiah predicts that Judah will become prey for birds and beasts. Does the chiastic connection between beasts and birds of prey in this pericope allow the reader to infer a con-

---

[75] Translation from Jack Lundbom, *Jeremiah 1–20* (New York: Doubleday, 1999), 650 (underlining added). For an explanation of the difficult phrase, העיט צבוע, see his commentary on this verse (654–655).

[76] Crediting Calvin with the correct interpretation of this passage, Lundbom writes: "God's heritage is simply a strange bird incapable of being tamed, a simple shift in metaphor from the roaring lion just mentioned (v 8). Calvin recognizes that the bird representing Judah is acting aggressively toward Yahweh, just as the lion is. It is not yet the victim, however soon it will be. The attacking birds function in the same capacity as the wild beasts next mentioned (v 9b)" (655).

nection between the actions of the raptor and those of the lion mentioned in the prior verse, who has sinned by raising a loud cry
against God? If so, this verse would stand out as the only passage
to hint, rather indirectly, at the vocal qualities of the bird of prey.

In a study of birds in the Bible, G. R. Driver observes: "Many
of the names of birds will be found to be in Hebrew as in other
languages onomatopoeic in origin; but no exact reproduction of a
bird's cry must be expected." As an example, he cites the *'ayiṭ*,
"screamers," which he links to the Arabic, *'ayyaṭa* ("screamed").[77]
Interestingly, in spite of the origin of the name, according to ornithol-
ogist Nigel Clark, "birds of prey are not very vocal except when on
their breeding territories or during courtship."[78] Confirmation of
Clark's observation can be found in Dick Forsman's handbook for
identifying raptors. He outlines a number of ways to distinguish raptors in the field, such as the bird's plumage or the size, shape, and
structure of the bird; yet absent from the list of identifying features
is any discussion of vocal characteristics.[79] Similarly, the index of
another reference work on birds of prey contains entries like beak,
ear, sense of smell, and vision, but no mention is made of the sounds
produced by a raptor.[80]

When Nabal's servant uses the verb עיט, does he intend to comment on Nabal's tone of voice and imply that Nabal screamed? Or,
instead, does he evoke the image of a raptor descending upon its
prey, the element that is central to 1 Sam 15:19 and 14:32 and the
majority of passages containing the noun עיט? Further insight into

---

[77] G. R. Driver, "Birds in the Old Testament," *Palestine Exploration Quarterly* (1955),
5. He explains that this term "denotes primarily all the *raptores* (*vulturidae, falconidae,*
and also *strigidae*) but can presumably denote individual members of the class when
suitably qualified" (5).

[78] Personal correspondence with Nigel Clark, Head of Projects at the British Trust
for Ornithology (July, 2002). Brian Millsap, President of the Raptor Research
Foundation, elaborates: "Many species of birds of prey do have what is best described
as a scream as part of their vocal repertoire. The 'scream' vocalizations are usually given either while defending a territory from an intruding individual of the
same or a competing species, or during courtship when soliciting or displaying to
a prospective or confirmed mates. Some owls and hawks also have a scream-type
call that is given by the young when begging for food from parents. This scream
probably serves to help the adult find the fledgling once it is out of the nest" (personal correspondence, August, 2002).

[79] Dick Forsman, *The Raptors of Europe and The Middle East* (London: T & AD
Poyser, 1999).

[80] Leslie Brown, *Birds of Prey: Their Biology and Ecology* (New York: A & W Publishers,
Inc, 1977).

the meaning of the verb in 1 Sam 25:14 is provided by the prior
narrative account of Nabal's interaction with the messengers. The
statement in v. 14, ויעט בהם, reflects how Nabal's servant interprets
Nabal's actions and how he chooses to characterize them when speaking to Abigail. But to what extent does the servant's version of
the events comport with the narrator's record of what Nabal said
and how he acted? After succinctly relaying the information that
"David's lads came and spoke to Nabal all these words in David's
name" (25:9), the narrator introduces Nabal's response with the
generic wording, "And Nabal answered David's servants and said
(ויען . . . ויאמר)" (25:10), without indicating that Nabal spoke in a
loud voice. Furthermore, nothing in Nabal's actual speech (25:10–11)
explicitly indicates that Nabal screamed at the messengers. To say that
Nabal "spurned," "railed on," or "flared up at" David's men may capture the spirit of what transpired during the confrontation; however,
Nabal's servant does not use an abstract term like הבעיס or חרף.[81]
Instead, he selects a verb that metaphorically depicts Nabal as a raptor swooping down upon his victims, chewing them out, to use a
slang expression, or, as Fokkelman puts it, biting their heads off.[82]
Thus, the literary context and patterns of usage within the Bible,
not the presumed etymology, determine the nuance of the verb in
this particular passage.

What tags the statement ויעט בהם as a metaphor? There is nothing distinctive about the verb "swooped down" in and of itself. It
becomes a metaphor when combined with the other words in this
sentence, mainly the implied subject, Nabal.

i. Original Utterance (1 Sam 25:14)

ויעט	בהם
It/he swooped down	*on it/them.*
[(conj.) + (ע.י.ט, qal, 3m.s., imperf.)]$_V$	[(prep.) + (3m.p. suf.)]$_{PP}$
– human verb	+/– animate indir. obj.
+/– human subj.	+/– human indir. obj.

In the original utterance, both the subject and object are unspecified.
If the sentence appeared in the midst of a conversation about vultures, one might imagine the following conversion sentence:

---

[81] *The Dictionary of Classical Hebrew* (hereafter *DCH*), ed. David Clines (Sheffield Academic Press, 1993–2001), defines הכעיס as "provoke (to anger), . . . offend, insult" and חרף I (*pi'el*) as "reproach, revile."
[82] Fokkelman, 491.

ii. Conversion Sentence #1

ו)עט (ועיט	ב)פגר)ים(
(The raptor) swooped down	*on (the corpses).*
[(conj.) + (.ט.י.ע, *qal*, 3m.s., imperf.)]$_V$	[(prep.) + (3m.p., indir. obj.)]$_{PP}$
[(def. art.) + (m.s. subj.)]$_N$	
– human, + ornithological verb	– animate indir. obj.
– human, + ornithological subj.	+/– human indir. obj.

In this case, no anomaly is involved, for a verb that demands an ornithological subject ("swooped down") is paired with a fitting noun ("raptor"). In the context of 1 Samuel 25, however, a conversion sentence reveals the incongruity that arises when a verb associated, in principle, with a non-human creature, a bird of prey, is used in conjunction with a human subject, thereby producing a selection restriction violation.

iii. Conversion Sentence #2

ויעט (נבל)	ב)אנשים(
(Nabal) swooped down	*on (the men).*
[(conj.) + (.ט.י.ע, *qal*, 3m.s., imperf.)]$_V$	[(prep.) + (3m.p., indir. obj.)]$_{PP}$
[personal name]$_N$	
– human, + ornithological verb	+ animate indir. obj.
+ human, – ornithological subj.	+ human indir. obj.

Admittedly, this explanation contains a number of complications. First of all, it elicits questions about the criteria used to establish a selection restriction violation. In Pelio Fronzaroli's critique of componential semantics, he highlights what he views as a fundamental limitation of this approach: the reliance upon intuitive criteria in identifying the features of a particular lexeme and judging when individual words belong to a given semantic field. While some scholars depend on lexicographic descriptions or context, many resort to their own intuition, which prompts Fronzaroli to call for a method to apply when making such judgments.[83] Upon what basis has it been determined that the non-anomalous usage of the verb עיט involves an ornithological subject? How does one decide that the verb עיט carries the selection restriction, "– human"? In the case at hand, conclusions about the collocational restrictions of עיט were based on the fact that it constitutes a denominative verb fundamentally used to describe the action of a raptor. However, neither context nor actual usage in the biblical text reinforces such an interpretation. After all, this verb only appears three times in the Bible (1 Sam 14:32; 15:19;

---

[83] Pelio Fronzaroli, "Componential Analysis," *ZAH* 6 (1993) 86–91.

25:14), all in narrative contexts in which the verb functions metaphorically to describe human beings swooping down on their purported
prey, booty in the first two citations and messengers in the third;
never is the verb used with a bird as the subject.

This pattern of usage draws attention to another issue that arises
when attempting to apply componential semantics to the Bible and
to identify metaphor through the presence of a semantic anomaly.
Agha points out that the ability to construe a metaphor requires a
knowledge of the grammar of a language and an ability to distinguish that which is syntactically unmarked or unremarkable, the normal way of speaking, from that which is syntactically remarkable.
He notes that the concept of a trope involving an anomaly introduces a question of the norm: What is the base-line relative to which
something counts as a deviation?[84] For biblical studies, this question
proves particularly difficult to answer. Because of both the relatively
small corpus of ancient Hebrew texts and the literary nature of biblical Hebrew, one cannot always draw a clear line between normalcy
and anomaly. Does the pattern of usage for עיט mean that it was
normative to employ the verb in conjunction with human beings,
and thus should not be considered anomalous? Or, instead, does it
simply reflect the fact that the available evidence is skewed? In other
words, should we attribute the absence of nonfigurative attestations
of this verb in the Bible and other relevant ancient Near Eastern
texts to the "luck of the spade," to the fact that, by chance, we have
not uncovered any extra-biblical, nonmetaphoric applications of this
verb? Alternatively, or in addition, we should factor in the literary
nature of the Bible, a corpus containing largely poetic material and
prose written in a formal literary language. While a thorough investigation of distributional patterns of usage, etymology, and comparative Semitic languages can yield important information, these questions
cannot be resolved definitively.

This example exposes some of the problems inherent in working
with a language preserved in a limited, closed corpus. The papers
written for the 1992 European Science Foundation Workshop on
the Semantics of Classical Hebrew focus on the challenges involved
in studying a "dead language"[85] with a rather restricted body of

---

[84] Agha, personal communication.
[85] Johannes Hendrik Hospers warns "that the qualification 'dead' might lead to
a misunderstanding as Classical Hebrew has never wholly become a 'dead' lan-

texts. Ida Zatelli points out that Classical Hebrew is limited in the applications of linguistic theories because of the absence of speakers.[86] For Fronzaroli, the limited corpus means that the degree of intuitive knowledge about semantic fields and semantic components "will probably remain limited."[87] James Barr cautions:

> The restriction of the corpus means that all sorts of statements, however profound and accurate, have to be qualified by the implication: 'this is true of the corpus, we cannot say whether it is true of the language.'[88]

Likewise, Bar-Efrat recognizes the limitations involved in the study of biblican Hebrew. He observes:

> Since we are unaware of the full extent and precise nature of the Hebrew language in biblical times (the Bible itself contains a very limited part of the language used at the time) it is impossible to assess accurately the rarity or deviance of any given word or linguistic phenomenon.

He concludes that "we have no choice but to be content with the little we can wrest from the Bible."[89]

Although the means used to identify the metaphoric nature of ויעט בהם in 1 Sam 25:14 remain imprecise, this does not invalidate the notion of a metaphor as marked by anomaly. In this instance, while the data about the verb עיט remain limited and thus conclusions tentative, one can look to the larger corpus of biblical narrative to appreciate the anomalous nature of this sentence. Alter characterizes the Hebrew of the Bible as "a conventionally delimited language" in which "only certain words were appropriate for the literary rendering of events."[90] He concludes:

> All this strongly suggests that the language of biblical narrative in its own time was stylized, decorous, dignified, and readily identified by

---

guage in the true sense of the word," like Akkadian or Phoenician. Instead, he stipulates: "Classical Hebrew can be characterized, however, as a language phase from the past with a limited corpus" ("Polysemy and Homonymy," *ZAH* 6 (1993) 120).

[86] Yet she affirms that "nevertheless the existing corpus seems to offer sufficient matter for adequate and profitable study." Ida Zatelli, "Pragmalinguistics and Speech-Act Theory as Applied to Classical Hebrew," *ZAH* 6 (1993) 71.

[87] Fronzaroli, 90.

[88] Barr, 5. Similarly, Hospers acknowledges: "Various questions posed to this material cannot easily be answered" (121).

[89] Bar-Efrat, *Narrative Art in the Bible*, 199–200.

[90] Alter, *Genesis*, xxiii. Also see the introduction to Alter, *The Five Books of Moses* (New York: W. W. Norton & Company, 2004).

its audiences as a language of literature, in certain ways distinct from
the language of quotidian reality. The tricky complication, however,
is that in most respects it also was not a lofty style, and was certainly
neither ornate nor euphemistic. If some of its vocabulary may have
reflected a specialized literary lexicon, the language of biblical narrative also made abundant use of ordinary Hebrew words that must have
been in everyone's mouth from day to day. . . . Biblical prose, then, is
a formal literary language but also, paradoxically, a plainspoken one,
and, moreover, a language that evinces a strong commitment to using
a limited set of terms again and again, making an aesthetic virtue out
of the repetition.[91]

In 1 Sam 25:14, the servant could have employed a more common
verb or a more direct way to describe Nabal's actions. When considered in light of the general tenor of biblical prose narrative, a
verb like עיט certainly appears to be unusual and remarkable, standing out from the straight-forward language used most often in these
texts.

C. *1 Samuel 25:29b[1]*—והיתה נפש אדני צרורה בצרור החיים את יי אלהיך
("May my lord's life be bound in the bundle of the living with/
by YHWH your God")

Spurred into action by the persuasive speech of Nabal's servant,
Abigail hurriedly amasses copious provisions—"two hundred loaves
of bread and two jugs of wine and five dressed sheep and five seahs
of parched grain and a hundred raisin cakes and two hundred fig
cakes" (25:18)—and rushes to intercept David before he fulfills his
lethal vow. Her lengthy, obsequious speech is laden with figurative
language, particularly in v. 29, when Abigail prays for deliverance
for David and destruction for his enemies: "And when a person rises
up to pursue you and to seek your life, may my lord's life be bound
in the bundle of the living[92] with YHWH your God, and the life of
your enemies, may He sling from the hollow of the sling" (25:29).
Fokkelman extols this verse as a "rhetorical pearl . . . mainly thanks
to the spectacular metaphors."[93] Alter also comments on the shrewdly

---

[91] Alter, *Genesis*, xxv.
[92] One can treat the phrase, צרור החיים, in two ways. The translation "bundle
of life" renders חיים as an abstract concept ("life") that refers to a condition of animate existence. In the translation, "bundle of the living," חיים functions as a collective noun representing animate beings. *JPS* and Fox translate the lexeme in the
former manner, Alter and *NRS* in the latter. The preference for the translation "the
living" will be explained in the following chapter.
[93] Fokkelman, 506.

chosen metaphors in this section of Abigail's "extraordinary speech," as does Bar-Efrat.[94] What, precisely, marks these statements as metaphors? To what extent can a linguistic analysis of their components lead to a better understanding of how they operate metaphorically?

An assessment of whether or not the statement "may my lord's life be bound in the bundle of the living with YHWH your God" contains a semantic incongruity requires a study of patterns of usage in order to establish the selection restrictions for its constituents. Given the complexity and ubiquitousness of the lexeme נפשׁ,[95] it will be more productive to concentrate on the verbal and nominal attestations of the root I צ.ר.ר. *BDB* divides the entry for I צרר into two sections, transitive and intransitive forms,[96] the former having a *qal* definition of "bind or tie up."[97] The transitive verb is used with a number of concrete objects. In Josh 9:4, the *puʿal* participle מצררים describes a wrapped up or mended <u>wineskin</u>. In Exod 12:34, the Israelites wrap their <u>kneading bowls</u> <u>in their cloaks</u> as they hastily prepare to leave Egypt. According to most, Prov 26:8 speaks of a <u>stone</u> bound <u>in a sling</u>.[98] Proverbs 30:4 asks the hyperbolic question:

---

[94] Alter, *The David Story*, 156, 158; Bar-Efrat, *1 Samuel*, 321.

[95] The noun occurs 754 times. Dictionaries identify anywhere from six to twelve categories of meaning and usage: *Theological Lexicon of the Old Testament* (hereafter *TLOT*) and *Theological Dictionary of the Old Testament* (hereafter *TDOT*) delineate six; *BDB* lists ten; *DCH* outlines twelve. For example, the *nepeš* entry in *TLOT* organizes the entry for "one of the most studied words in the OT" (744) as follows: (1) Concrete meanings: (a) breath, (b) throat/gullet; (2) Longing/desire/craving: (a) hunger, (b) vengeance, (c) desire/wish/choice; (3) Soul: (a) desirous, (b) hungry/sated, (c) melancholy/happy, (d) hoping, (e) loving/hating, (f) alive; (4) Life: (a) deliverance/protection/maintenance, (b) threat/detriment; (5) Living being/person; (6) Corpse (744). The lexeme attested three times in 1 Sam 25:25 falls into the fourth category, referring to an "individuated life" (*TDOT*, 512–513). See *Theological Lexicon of the Old Testament*, ed. E. Jenni and C. Westermann, trans. Mark Biddle (Peabody, MA: Hendrickson Publishers, 1997), s.v. נפשׁ; *Theological Dictionary of the Old Testament*, ed. G. J. Botterweck and H. Ringgren, trans. David Green (Grand Rapids: Eerdmans, 1990), s.v. נפשׁ.

[96] Koehler-Baumgartner does the same (s.v. שׁפנ).

[97] According to *BDB*, the intransitive means "to be scant, cramped" in the *qal* and "to make narrow for, press hard upon, cause distress to" in the *hipʿil*.

[98] Scholars disagree about the expression in Prov 26:8, כצרור אבן במרגמה. A number of scholars consider צרור a verbal form derived from I צרר (see *BDB*, Koehler-Baumgartner, *GKC*, *DCH* [s.v. I מרגמה]; *BHS* proposes reading the verb as a participle, צורר, instead of an infinitive). Others consider the lexeme a noun from the homonymous root, צורר, as found in 2 Sam 17:13 and Amos 9:9 (see *DCH* [s.v. II מרגמה] and Shalom Paul, *Amos* [Minneapolis: Fortress Press, 1991], 286); in Prov 26:8, this interpretation results in a redundant phrase, "like a pebble of a stone." Adding to the confusion is the uncertainty about the meaning of מרגמה. *DCH* suggests three possibilities: (1) I מרגמה, meaning "sling," used with the verb

"Who has wrapped the <u>waters</u> <u>in his garment</u>?" Similarly, Job 26:8 marvels at God, who "wrapped up the <u>waters</u> <u>in His clouds</u>."[99] Second Samuel 20:3 conveys a slightly different nuance, for it describes how David's ten <u>concubines</u> "were shut up (וַתִּהְיֶינָה צְרֻרוֹת)" <u>in a house</u> under watch.[100] In Isa 8:16, the prophet exclaims: "Tie up the <u>message</u>, seal the instruction with My disciples." Here, does Isaiah refer to a physical object, as in the previous quotations, or, instead, does he speak metaphorically about an intangible entity? Joseph Blenkinsopp argues for the first interpretation, as he concludes:

> In the final and somber act of the drama Isaiah has his utterances delivered during the crisis sealed, secured in a receptacle of some kind, and committed to his disciples. It is possible that the verbs are used metaphorically . . ., or at least in the sense that Isaiah's discourses are committed to memory by disciples. However, the parallel with 29:11–12, referring to the words of a sealed book (*dibre hasseper hehatum*), and with 30:8–11, which speaks of a tablet and a book serving as witness, both in the context of prophecy as problematic, suggests that we take them literally. In that case the message and instruction indicate a text written on papyrus, wrapped <u>in cloth</u>, and put for safekeeping in a jar or other container.[101]

In light of the pattern of usage established by the above citations, Hos 13:12 stands out. In this verse, the prophet pairs the transitive verb, I צרר, with an abstract noun, עָוֹן ("iniquity"), when he declares: "Ephraim's <u>iniquity</u> is bound up, his sin is stored away." In contrast to the ambiguity of Isa 8:16, this verse clearly exemplifies a figurative application this verb.

Of the nine verses containing the noun, צְרוֹר ("bundle" or "bag"), three citations place this lexeme in a construct phrase, teaming it

---

צרר; (2) II מַרְגֵּמָה, meaning "heap of stones," used with the noun צְרוֹר, "like a pebble in a heap of stones"; (3) emend the phrase to read, בְּמַרְגָּלִית, "in a jewel." Additional questions underlie these proposals: How does this phrase function in relation to the second half of the verse, as a metaphor for paying honor to a dullard? Which reading makes the most sense not only in light of what we know about the individual lexemes, but also in accordance with broader point of the proverb?

[99] In "one of the most obscure and difficult passages in Hosea" (F. Andersen and D. Freedman, *Hosea* [New York: Doubleday, 1980], 375), Hosea uses this verb in a verse that reads: "A wind has bound her up <u>in her wings</u> (צָרַר רוּחַ אוֹתָהּ בִּכְנָפֶיהָ)" (4:19). Translations of this statement and interpretations of the intended direct object ("her") vary considerably.

[100] Koehler-Baumgartner assign this verse a separate meaning ("lock up"), distinct from "wrap up" in most other passages (with the exception of Prov 26:8).

[101] Joseph Blenkinsopp, *Isaiah 1–39* (New York: Doubleday, 2000), 243 (underlining added).

with the concrete object found in the pouch: "bag of <u>money</u>" (Gen 42:35; Prov 7:20) and "bag of <u>myrrh</u>" (Song 1:13). Of the remaining verses, Hag 1:6 describes a person who futilely and foolishly places his <u>wages</u> in a bag with holes, leaving him with nothing to show for his labor: "The one who earns wages earns wages for a pierced bag." Job 14:17 differs from the above passages, for, like Hos 13:12, it depicts an abstract entity, פשע ("transgression"), hidden away in a pouch: "Sealed <u>in a bag</u> would be my <u>transgression</u>; and you would plaster over my iniquity."

Whereas the paucity of citations using the root ע.י.ט. made it more difficult to differentiate between standard and incongruous forms, in the case of the root I צ.ר.ר, clear patterns of usage emerge from the available evidence which allow us to establish general selection restrictions. In all attested cases, the verb צרר is used with a human or divine subject, as is the case in 1 Sam 25:29. In the majority of the non-figurative passages, the object accompanying the verb constitutes an inanimate, physical object: kneading bowls, water, a stone, and, if Blenkinsopp is correct, a message written on papyrus. A number of instances also include a prepositional phrase that specifies the material in which the object has been wrapped: in a garment, in clouds, in a sling, and, according to Blenkinsopp, in a piece of cloth. In terms of the nominal usage of צרור, all citations except for 1 Sam 25: 29 and Job 14:17 identify the contents of the bundle as a concrete, inanimate object: money or myrrh. The following diagram summarizes the selection restrictions for I צרר when it carries the sense of "to bind up":

I צרר	Standard Usage	1 Sam 25:29
Subject:	Human or Divine	Divine
Object:	− animate[102]	+ animate
Prepositional Phrase:	(prep.) + (− animate indir. obj.)	(prep.) + (− animate indir. obj.)
Construct Phrase:	(צרור) + (− animate entity)	(צרור) + (+ animate entity)[103]

---

[102] The empirical possibility exists that a person or animal literally could be bound up in some sort of sack, though no such examples appear in the Bible. Note that 2 Sam 20:3 involves an animate direct object, but David's concubines are locked in a house, not wrapped in some apparatus for transport or storage. Because of the distinct features and nuance of the verb צרר in 2 Sam 20:3, where it means "lock up" or "shut up" instead of "bound up," this passage has not been included in the following chart.

[103] This construal is based on the translation of חיים as "the living (beings)." The

As this chart indicates, a semantic analysis pinpoints the anomalous features that mark this utterance as a metaphor: (a) the collocation of the transitive verb, I צרר, with the animate direct object, נפש אדני ("life of my lord"), and (b) the co-occurrence of the nouns, צרור and חיים, "bundle" and "living."

A secondary way to appreciate the unusual nature of Abigail's statement is to examine the other verbs used to express a similar notion of salvation. In his נפש article in *Theological Lexicon of the Old Testament*, Claus Westermann compiles the verbs used with the object נפש to speak about the deliverance of life. Looking at only the instances in which God functions as the subject, his list of thirteen verbs includes predominately straightforward, nonfigurative verbs like נצל (*hipʿil*) "to deliver" or פדה (*qal*) "to redeem."[104] As noted in the discussion of 1 Sam 25:14, this type of observation about the unique nature of an expression in light of the general norm of biblical prose supplements the identification of the incongruity that results from a semantic analysis of the constituent lexemes.

D. *1 Samuel 25:29b²*—ואת נפש איביך יקלענה בתוך כף הקלע
("And the life of your enemies He will sling from the hollow of the sling")

In the remainder of v. 29, Abigail shifts her attention from "the life of my lord" to "the life of your enemies" as she contrasts the positive future envisioned for David with the negative fate foreseen for his foes: "And the life of your enemies He will sling from the hollow of the sling." Like the statement that precedes it, the anomalous element of this utterance stems from the collocation of its lexemes. The focal points of this sentence, a verb and noun from the root I ק.ל.ע,

---

alternate translation, "life," represents an abstract concept, which also fails to conform with the standard pattern.

[104] The complete list of verbs used with God as the subject and נפש as the object to express deliverance reads (definitions from Westermann): נצל *hi.* "to deliver" (Jer 20:13; Ps 22:21; 33:19; 56:14; 86:13; 116:8; 120:2; *ni.* Gen 32:31), מלט *pi.* "to deliver" (Ps 116:4; *ni.* Ps 124:7), חלץ *pi.* "to deliver" (Ps 6:5), פלט *pi.* "to deliver" (Ps 17:13), ישע *hi.* "to help" (Ps 72:13), פדה *qal* "to redeem" (2 Sam 4:9; 1 Kgs 1:29; Ps 34:23; 49:16; 55:19; 71:23; Job 33:28), גאל *qal* "to redeem" (Ps 69:19; 72:14), שוב *hi.* "to return" (Ps 35:17; Job 33:30), שלח *pi.* "to return" (Ezek 13:20), יצא *hi.* "to lead out" (Ps 142:8; 143:11), עלה *hi.* "to lead up" (Ps 30:4), רפא *qal* "to heal" (Ps 41:5) (*TLOT*, 752). Note that the majority of these citations appear in poetic passages.

are not attested as often as their counterparts from the root I צ.ר.ר.
in the prior part of the verse. Nonetheless, the citations provide
enough information to determine a pattern of usage and selection
restrictions.

It is hardly coincidental that Abigail's speech contains a root that
dominates another pivotal episode in the David story: David's victory over Goliath in 1 Samuel 17. In this earlier chapter, the narrative records in detail David's preparations for battle: He chooses
five smooth stones (חלקי אבנים) from the creek and places them in
his shepherd's satchel. Then, slingshot in hand (וקלעו בידו), he
approaches Goliath (17:40). After some verbal sparring, David takes
a stone (אבן) from his bag and slings it (ויקלע), striking Goliath in
the forehead (17:49). The narrator reports: "And David prevailed
over the Philistine with sling and stone (בקלע ובאבן), and he struck
down the Philistine and killed him, and no sword was in David's
hand" (17:50). Of the ten verses in the Bible that contain either the
verb קלע or the noun קלע, seven also mention stones. In addition
to the verses cited above, three passages contain a form of the
phrase, אבני קלע ("slingstones").[105] Second Kings 3:25, the only attestation of the noun קלע ("slinger"), also connects the act of slinging
with stones. The verse recounts how the Israelites attacked Moab,
"throwing stones (וישליכי איש אבנו) into every fertile plot, filling it up,
stopping up every spring . . . leaving only the stones (אבניה) of
Kirhareseth (intact), which the slingers surrounded (ויסבו הקלעים) and
attacked."[106]

Only two verses break this pattern, using a different object and
subject with the verb קלע. In the verse at hand, Abigail envisions
God slinging human beings from a slingshot. In Jer 10:18, the prophet
employs the same imagery, but without explicit mention of the slingshot: "For thus said YHWH: Look I am slinging out the dwellers
of the land at this time." The chart below summarizes the selection
restriction violations found in these two verses:

---

[105] Zech 9:15; Job 41:20; 2 Chr 26:14. Also see Judg 20:16, which describes how
the left-handed men mustered by the Benjaminites could sling a stone at a hair
and not miss (קלע באבן).

[106] Translation from M. Cogan and H. Tadmor, *II Kings* (New York: Doubleday,
1988), 42.

קלע *I*	*Standard usage*	*1 Sam 25:29*	*Jer 10:18*
Subject:	Men	God	God
	+ human	**– human**	**– human**
Object:	Stones	David's enemies	Dwellers of the land
	– animate	**+ animate**	**+ animate**

Reinforcing this conclusion about the semantically anomalous nature of the language in 1 Sam 25:29 is the rarity of such expressions in biblical narrative and the predominance of other, nonfigurative ways to articulate the demise of an individual. For example, Abigail could have used a common, straightforward verb like הרג ("to kill") or נכה *hi.* ("to strike").[107] The reasons why Abigail chose these two unusual expressions in v. 29 will be explored in subsequent chapters.

E. *1 Samuel 25:31*—ולא תהיה זאת לך לפוקה ולמכשול לב לאדני
("Let this not be for you a tottering or a stumbling block of the heart for my lord")

Abigail concludes her speech by reminding David of what he risks if he carries out his resolve to kill Nabal and his men. Since God has planned a bright future for David, which includes making him king, Abigail cautions David not to stain his reputation with "blood shed for no cause." "YHWH will do well with my lord," she assures him, so do not carry out your vengeance yourself (25:30–31). As Abigail delivers this message, she warns: "And let this not be for you a פוקה or a מכשול לב for my lord" (25:31). Translations of these two chiastically arranged expressions vary considerably. Some translate both phrases as abstract concepts: "my lord shall have no cause of grief, or pangs of conscience" (*NRS*).[108] Others render these nouns as concrete objects: "then do not let this be for you an obstacle or

---

[107] Westermann compiles a list of verbs used with נפש to indicate violent loss of life: נכה *hi.* "to smite" (Gen 37:21; Lev 24:17f.; Num 35:11, 15, 30a; Deut 19:6, 11; Josh 20:3, 9; Jer 40:14f.), לקח "to take away"(Ezek 33:6; Ps 31:14; Prov 1:19; 11:30), uniquely אבד *pi.* "to destroy" (Ezek 22:27), אכל "to devour" (Ezek 22:25), הרג "to kill" (Num 31:19; cf. Jer 4:31), כרת *hi.* "to exterminate" (Ezek 17:17), מות *hi.* "to kill" (Ezek 13:19), and רצח "to slay" (Deut 22:26). He adds a number of less formulaic expressions for dying that use נפש, such as מות "to die" (Judg 16:30; Job 36:14; Num 23:10) or נפח "to expire" (Jer 15:9; *hi.* Job 31:39; cf. Job 11:20) (*TLOT*, 754).

[108] Similar translations include: "you shall not have this as a qualm or burden on your conscience" (*NAB*); "you must have no anxiety, my lord, no remorse" (*NJB*); "That this shall be no grief unto thee, nor offence of heart unto my lord" (*KJV*).

a stumbling-block of the heart (to) my lord" (Fox).[109] What, precisely, do these expressions mean? Does either one constitute a metaphor? While a reader of the *NRS* translation would answer this question negatively, a translation like Fox's leads one to consider this possibility. The linguistic approach used in the prior examples will be applied to these expressions in order to evaluate the figurative status of this verse.

The diverse translations of v. 31 reflect a degree of uncertainty about both the meaning of the scarcely attested first term, פוקה, as well as its relationship to the subsequent expression, מכשול לב. Turning first to the more commonly used noun, מכשול, relevant citations fall into a distinct pattern of usage. In several passages, מכשול denotes a material object that can cause a person to stumble physically and fall down. In Isa 57:14, the prophet instructs the people to prepare a road by eliminating any obstructions found on the ground: "Build up, build up (a highway). Clear a road. Remove a stumbling block from the road of my people (הרימו מכשול מדרך עמי)."[110] Leviticus 19:14 also uses מכשול to refer to a concrete object on the ground that can cause physical injury, particularly to those unable to see it: "You shall not place a stumbling block before the blind (ולפני עור לא תתן מכשל)."

A number of passages depict God placing some sort of obstacle before an individual in order to make that person stumble. For instance, God warns that if a righteous person changes ways and begins to sin, "when I put a stumbling block before him, he shall die" (Ezek 3:20).[111] In a similar statement, God declares: "I am giving this people stumbling blocks and they shall stumble over them . . . and they shall perish" (Jer 6:21). In Isa 8:14, Isaiah delivers an ominous

---

[109] Also see McCarter's version: "this must not be an obstacle or stumbling block." The following translations fall in between these two ends of the spectrum: "do not let this be a cause of stumbling and of faltering courage to my lord" (*JPS*), "there will be no reason why you should stumble or your courage should falter" (*REB*), and "this will not be a stumbling and a trepidation of the heart to my lord" (Alter).

[110] Isaiah 62:10 expresses the same concept with slightly different vocabulary: "Clear a road for the people. Build up, build up a highway. Remove the rocks (סקלו מאבן)."

[111] Of the fourteen attestations of the noun מכשול, over half appear in the book of Ezekiel. Six of these eight citations contain some form of the phase unique to Ezekiel, מכשול עון. Moshe Greenberg explains: "In accord with Ezekiel's use of 'stumbling-block,' the phrase means 'cause of downfall (consisting) of iniquity'; or 'the iniquitous cause of their downfall'" (*Ezekiel 1–20* [New York: Doubleday, 1983], 153).

message, insisting that God will be "a stone of striking (וְלָאֶבֶן נֶגֶף)
and a rock of stumbling (וּלְצוּר מִכְשׁוֹל) for the two Houses of Israel,
a trap and a snare (לְפַח וּלְמוֹקֵשׁ) for those who dwell in Jerusalem."
The verse that follows emphasizes what will happen to those who
encounter the rock: "And many shall stumble over them (וְכָשְׁלוּ בָם
רַבִּים), and they shall fall and be broken"; those who chance upon
the trap "shall be snared and captured" (Isa 8:15). Psalm 119:165
presents the absence of a stumbling block as a sign of God's blessing, announcing that "there will be well being (שָׁלוֹם רָב) for those
who love God's teaching, and they will not encounter a stumbling
block (וְאֵין לָמוֹ מִכְשׁוֹל)." This verse, like 1 Sam 25:31, implies, but
does not state directly, that God situates the stumbling block in
response to human behavior. Unlike Isa 57:14 or Lev 19:14, which
refer to concrete objects set on the ground by human beings, this
second group of texts uses מִכְשׁוֹל figuratively. Such passages envision
the misfortunes of life—perhaps illness or crop failure or military
defeat—as the sort of divinely ordained punishments that disrupt a
person's life and possibly result in death. In such instances, a מִכְשׁוֹל
("stumbling block") refers to an unspecified occurrence in life, not a
physical object.

Verbs from the root כ.שׁ.ל. follow a similar pattern. Some citations speak about the literal, physical act of stumbling, like the description of the warriors who stumble against one another and fall down"
(Jer 46:12).[112] Lamentations 5:13 mentions young men who stumble
or stagger under the weight of a heavy load of wood.[113] Psalm 105:37
boasts that when God led the tribes out of Egypt, none of them
stumbled.[114] Likewise, Jeremiah predicts that the absence of physical
stumbling will serve as a sign of divine providence when the Israelites
return from exile: "I will lead them to streams of water, by a level
road where they shall not stumble" (Jer 31:9). In a larger percent-
age of the sixty-three attestations of the verb כשׁל however, this root
functions figuratively. Subjects consist of those deserving of punish-

---

[112] Other examples of warriors include Isa 5:27; Jer 46:6; Nah 3:3; also see Lev
26:37. Often the act of stumbling is connected with the act of falling, as either a
synonymous or sequential act. See, for example, Isa 8:15; Jer 46:6, 12; 50:32; Ps
27:2.
[113] Similarly, Isa 40:30 refers to faint and weary youths who stumble.
[114] Another reference to an absence of stumbling during the exodus occurs in
Isa 63:13.

ment, such as the wicked,[115] disobedient priests, or the arrogant.[116] Several times, accompanying clauses specify that people stumble "because of their sin."[117] A passage from Deutero-Isaiah fits into both categories, for in describing a blind man groping along a wall and stumbling, the image in turn depicts the people's sense of despondency and disorientation, the feeling that they "stumble at noon as if in the dark" (Isa 59:10). Rarely do such passages identify what, precisely, it means to stumble in a non-physical manner, though the negative connotations are clear.[118] For instance, Prov 24:16 instructs: "Seven times the righteous man falls and gets up, while the wicked stumble with one misfortune (ורשעים יכשלו ברעה)." Similarly, Hos 14:10 contrasts the fate of the righteous, who walk on the paths of YHWH, with the sinners, who "stumble on them."

The preceding analysis of the root כ.ש.ל shows that the noun "stumbling block" and the verb "to stumble" function both figuratively and nonfiguratively in the Tanakh. In 1 Samuel 25, two features signal a metaphoric use of מכשול in v. 31. First, when Abigail warns David, "let this not be . . . a stumbling block of the heart for my lord," she does not identify what "this" refers to until the end of the verse: "to shed blood for no cause and for my lord to have carried out his own deliverance" (25:31).[119] As in prior cases, the presence of a semantic incongruity depends on the referent of the demonstrative pronoun. If "this" refers to a brick, the branch of a tree, or something else lying on the ground over which a person might trip and fall, then the utterance contains no anomaly.

i. Modified Original Utterance (1 Sam 25:31)

ולא תהיה זאת	למכשול
Let this not be	*a stumbling block.*
[(conj. + neg. part.) + (.ה.י.ה, *qal*, 3f.s.) + (f.s. demonst. pron.)]$_{VP}$	(prep.) + (m.s. indir. obj.)]$_{PP}$
+ / − animate	− animate
	+ located on the ground

---

[115] Hos 14:10; Ps 27:2; Prov 4:19; 24:16; cf. Ezek 33:12.

[116] Hos 4:5 and Jer 50:32, respectively.

[117] See, for example, Hos 5:5; 14:2; Ps 31:11; Prov 24:16.

[118] In this regard, Jer 50:32 stands out, for when it states that "arrogance will stumble and fall, with none to raise her up," the passage specifies that this means that God "will set her cities on fire, and it shall consume everything around her."

[119] Alter's translation.

ii. Conversion Sentence #1

ולא תהיה (הלבנה)	למכשול
Let the brick not be	*a stumbling block.*
[(conj. + neg. part.) + (ה.י.ה, *qal*, 3f.s.) + (f.s. subj.)]$_{VP}$	[(prep.) + (m.s. indir. obj.)]$_{PP}$
– animate entity	**– animate entity**
+ located on the ground	**+ located on the ground**

However, in the present context, "this" refers to an action, not an object. The following chart illustrates the semantic disjunction produced by the equation of murder and an obstacle:

iii. Conversion Sentence #2

ולא תהיה [120](שפכת דם)	למכשול
Let the shedding of blood not be	*a stumbling block.*
[(conj. + neg. part.) + (ה.י.ה, *qal*, 3f.s.) + ((f.s. participle) + (m.s. noun))]$_{VP}$	[(prep.) + (m.s. indir. obj.)]$_{PP}$
action	**– animate entity**
– located on the ground	**+ located on the ground**

The second feature of this expression that marks it as a metaphor is the unique collocation of מכשול ("stumbling block") and לב ("heart"):

מכשול	לב
stumbling block	*of the heart*
– animate entity	**body part**
located on the ground	**belonging to + animate being**

The diagram helps to highlight the incongruous nature of a construct phrase that, in a sense, situates a concrete, physical object in the heart, not on the ground. Contrast this expression with the construct phrase, צור מכשול "rock of stumbling" (Isa 8:14), which fittingly pairs an inanimate object located on the ground with the word מכשול.[121] The word לב ("heart") serves as the *nomen rectum*, the "governed noun," in sixty-five genitival expressions in the Tanakh.[122] In the majority of cases, the substantival or adjectival *nomen regens*, the "governing noun," functions attributively as a descriptor of the person's intellect, emotional state, or character, as in the expressions "wise of heart" (חכם לב), "joy of heart" (שמחת לב), "stubbornness of heart" (שרדות לב).[123] A number of instances clearly deviate from this

---

[120] This phrase appears in Ezek 22:3.
[121] See above note regarding the construct phrase משכול עון in Ezekiel.
[122] Twenty-five construct expressions contain לבב as *nomen rectum*.
[123] Exod 31:6; 35:10; 36:1, 2, 8 (חכם לב); Song 3:11 and Eccl 5:19 (שמחת לבו);

pattern. When various passages speak of circumcising the "foreskin of the heart (ערלת לבב or ערל לב)," the message is that the Israelites need to remove the metaphoric covering over the heart that "renders it inaccessible to God's teaching."[124] Another figurative expression occurs when Jeremiah declares that the sins of Judah will be engraved on the "tablet of their heart (לוח לבם)" with an iron pen (Jer 17:1). Similarly, twice in Proverbs the speaker adjures his listeners to bind the teachings on a part of the body and write them on the "tablet of your heart (כתבם על לוח לבך)."[125] As in 1 Sam 25:31, the anomaly that marks this trope arises from the collocation of a concrete object, a לוח ("tablet"), and a body part, לב ("heart").

In her attempt to dissuade David from following through on his vengeful plan, Abigail also employs the less familiar word פּוּקָה. This nominal form only appears in the verse at hand, just as the related noun, פּק, occurs once; two verses contain verbs from the root I פ.ו.ק., one in the qal and the other in the hip'il. In Jer 10:1–5, the prophet paints a satirical picture of idols and those who make them as he describes how a craftsman decorates the idol and then secures it in place with hammers and nails "so it will not totter (ולא יפיק)" (Jer 10:4). In a number of passages that ridicule idolatry with a similar tone and message, Deutero-Isaiah expresses the identical concern that the idol not wobble and fall over. Twice he uses a different, more commonly attested verb, from the root מ.ו.ט., such as when he pokes fun at the skilled woodworker who attempts to make firm the idol and ensure that "it will not totter (להכין פסל לא ימוט)" (Isa 40:20).[126] The related passages in Deutero-Isaiah confirm the sense of יפיק in Jer 10:4, which therefore means "to totter." This root also appears in a diatribe against the religious leaders in Isa 28:7, when

---

Deut 29:18 and Jer 7:24; 9:13; 11:8; 13:10; 16:12; 18:12; 23:17 and Ps 81:13 (שרירות לב). The *TDOT* entry on לב arranges construct phrases with לב as the *nomen rectum* into four main categorizes: anthropological, emotional, noetic, and ethical (408).

[124] Jeffrey Tigay, *Deuteronomy* (Philadelphia: Jewish Publication Society, 1996), 107. Commenting of Deut 10:16, he explains that foreskin "is a metaphor for a mental block that has made Israel stubborn" (108). Other citations include Jer 4:4; 9:25; Ezek 44:7, 9; cf. Lev 26:41 and Deut 30:6.

[125] Proverbs 3:3 speaks of binding the commandments on the throat and 7:3 on the fingers.

[126] Deutero-Isaiah uses the same vocabulary in Isa 41:7 when he describes how the woodworker strengthens the idol with nails so that "it will not topple (לא ימוט)." He varies the wording somewhat in Isa 46:7: "When they put it down, it stands; from its place it cannot move (לא ימיש)."

Isaiah repeats the roots ש.נ.ה. three times and ת.ע.ה. twice as he depicts the physical effects of alcohol: "And also these from wine stagger (שׁגוּ) and from liquor reel (תעוּ). Priest and prophet stagger (שׁגוּ) from liquor. They are confused (נבלעוּ) from wine. They reel (תעוּ) from liquor." Isaiah concludes the verse with the following statement: שׁגוּ בראה פקוּ פליליה. Assuming that the third instance of the verb שׁגה mirrors the first two,[127] then this sentence describes the unsteady physical movements of the priest and prophet: They stagger about drunk while they see visions, and they totter intoxicated as they render judgments. Nahum uses a nominal form of this root when he illustrates four ways in which the body reacts to "desolation, devastation, and destruction": "the heart melts, and tottering of knees (ופק ברכים), and trembling in all loins, and everyone's faces turn ashen" (Nah 2:11).[128]

Thus, the root פ.ו.ק. describes a physical movement, the unsteady gait or swaying to and fro witnessed in drunks, the knees of individual in a state of panic or fear, and unsecured wooden idols. What does it mean, then, when Abigail cautions David: "Let this not be for you a tottering" (25:31)? Some interpret the statement as meaning: let this not cause you to totter or stumble. Whereas Alter leaves the expression vague, "this will not be a stumbling," *JPS* makes the causative nuance explicit, "do not let this be a cause of stumbling." Both translations distinguish פוקה from the expression that follows, מכשול לב ("stumbling block of the heart"), differentiating between the physical action of stumbling and the emotional state of fear, "trepidation of the heart," or "faltering of courage."[129] Fox and McCarter go one step further, rendering the noun פוקה not as an action, but

---

[127] Because שׁגה also can mean to err or go astray morally (see, for example, 1 Sam 26:21; Prov 5:23; Job 6:24; 19:4), Isaiah may have intended not simply to characterize the instability of the movement of the priests and prophets, but to criticize the inferiority and unreliability of their work as well. The translations of שׁגוּ בראה by *JPS* and Brevard Childs (*Isaiah* [Louisville: Westminster John Knox Press, 2001], 201) carry such a nuance: "They are muddled in their visions," as does Blenkinsopp's translation of פקוּ פליליה as "go astray in giving judgment" (386). *JPS* and Childs translate פקוּ as "stumble."

[128] *JPS* translation, with a note that this phrase (ופנו כלם קבצו פארור) is uncertain. *NRS* translates: "grow pale." A similar image appears in Isa 35:3, with the verb כשל to describe the shaking knees which, like slack hands, are exterior signs of fear.

[129] Alter and *JPS*, respectively. Because these two translations differentiate between these two terms, they both translate the conjunction as "and," whereas those who treat the expressions as synonyms render the conjunction as "or."

as the concrete object that prompts the action: "obstacle." According to this line of interpretation, פוקה refers elliptically to the actual cause of the unsteady motion and functions as a synonym of מכשול ("stumbling block"). Others take a different approach and consider פוקה a physical sign of fear, meaning, let this not be something that causes your body to tremble. For instance, Bar-Efrat explains that "it is a matter of trembling (from fear)," the point being that when David becomes king, he will fear that God will punish him for spilling Nabal's blood.[130] This type of understanding of the expression leads to the less precise, more exegetical translations of פוקה as "grief" or "anxiety."[131] Such translations tend to equate פוקה and מכשול לב, treating both terms as synonyms for an emotion, such as "anxiety" and "remorse" or "cause of grief" and "pangs of conscience."[132]

The judgment as to whether or not this utterance contains a semantic incongruity varies depending on the meaning assigned to פוקה. If, as Bar-Efrat and others argue, פוקה depicts the trembling body of a person in fear, then this utterance does not prove semantically anomalous. Abigail cautions David that following through on his resolve to kill Nabal and his men eventually may cause his body to shiver from fear as he worries about the divine punishment that may result from his rash deed. There is nothing incongruous about stating that one act (murder) may elicit an emotional response (fear) which will manifest itself by a physical movement (trembling). In this case, פוקה functions as a descriptive term, portraying the exterior, bodily expression that reflects a particular internal emotion, much like the tottering knees and ashen face mentioned in Nah 2:11. If the utterance "Let this not be for you a tottering" stood alone, this interpretation would prove more convincing. Its weakness lies in the failure to account for the second half of the parallelism and to address the incongruity that then arises between the vision of David trembling in fear and the image of him stumbling over an obstacle.

On the other hand, if, as several scholars suggest, פוקה signifies a concrete object that can cause a person to stumble, then the analysis resembles that provided for מכשול. According to this reading, the

---

[130] Bar-Efrat, *I Samuel*, 322. This argument would be more convincing if לב was attached to פוקה, as in the phrase, מכשול לב. This would clarify that the expression refers to the trembling of the heart in fear, not the tottering of the entire body.

[131] For instance, "my lord shall have no cause of grief" (*NRS*); "That this shall be no grief unto thee" (*KJV*) and "you must have no anxiety" (*NJB*), respectively.

[132] *NJB* and *NRS*, respectively; similarly, see *KJV* and *NAB*.

two nouns in these parallel phrases serve as near synonyms. In both
cases, locating the semantic incongruity requires expanding the unit
of the metaphor to include the entire verse and then creating a
conversion sentence: Let the shedding of blood for no cause and
the carrying out of your own deliverance not be for you an (object
that causes) tottering. In other words, Abigail cautions David not to
let the killing of Nabal and his men be an obstacle to his future
success. Such a notion metaphorically equates the act of murder
with a concrete object on the ground over which a person might
trip and stumble.

A third, and preferred, approach understands פוקה as a physical
action, "tottering." Abigail reminds David that following through on
his vow to kill "every pisser against the wall" (25:22) may have negative consequences on his future as a ruler of Israel. She suggests
not that he literally will stagger when he walks, but that he risks
some sort of personal or political downfall. Instead of viewing פוקה
in a paradigmatic relationship with מכשול, this line of reasoning conceives of the two terms as functioning more in a syntagmatic relationship: the first term describes the effect of the second. Admittedly,
this argument would be stronger if the nouns appeared in the reverse
order: cause ("stumbling block") and then the result ("trembling").[133]
While the general message of the two expressions is similar, both
parts of the utterance do not necessarily operate the same figuratively.
Instead of equating an action (murder) with a physical object (an
obstacle), the utterance implies that one act (murder) may result in
another (tottering). What is the appropriate label for such a trope?
This questions will be addressed in chapter five.

F. *1 Samuel 25:37b¹—וימת לבו בקרבו*
("And his heart died within him")

Abigail's speech proves successful, as she dissuades David from carrying out his vengeful plans. David accepts her gifts and praises God
for sending a woman of such good sense to prevent him from "coming into blood guilt" (25:33). She waits until the light of the following morning, when Nabal has awakened from the festivities of
the prior night, to inform her husband of her encounter with David.
The narrator describes Nabal's response to Abigail's news: his heart,

---

[133] Cf. עצבונך והרנך (lit. "your pain and your pregnancy") in Gen 3:16.

which "was of good cheer" the night before (25:36), "died within him, and he became a stone" (25:37). What do each of these phrases mean independently? What is the semantic relationship between the two? Do they both qualify as metaphors?

The surrounding narrative context makes it clear that neither expression denotes Nabal's actual death, for the subsequent verse states that Nabal did not die until ten days later. Interpretations of v. 37 vary, from those who read the two statements as indicating that Nabal experienced some sort of physiological reaction, such as a heart attack or stroke,[134] to those who understand the utterances as suggesting an emotional response, namely a loss of courage.[135] Several medieval commentators compound the negative portrayal of Nabal by explaining that Nabal experienced a sense of worry or regret about the amount of goods given away to David, not concern about the fact that he and his men narrowly escaped death.[136]

The dissonance between the comment in v. 37 that "his heart died within him" and the statement in v. 38 that "it was about ten days later that YHWH smote Nabal and he died" signals a figurative application of the root מ.ו.ת. ("to die") in the former verse. In addition, a survey of patterns of usage for the verb in this expression indicates an anomalous collocation of words. Of the eight hundred and forty two attestations of the verb מות in the Bible, only in this instance is it paired with the subject לב ("heart"). In the majority of cases, the verb is used with a personal name or a noun referring to specific individuals or a collective body of human beings, such as אב ("father") or עם ("people"). Animals appear as the subject less frequently. Only in a handful of instances is the verb used with inanimate subjects, such as land (Gen 47:19) or wisdom (Job 12:2).[137] Having established that the sentence "And his heart died within him" constitutes a figurative pairing of subject and verb, the question arises as to whether this statement qualifies as a metaphor or some other trope. This decision depends upon the understanding of the meaning of the word לב in this verse and on the perception of an analogy, issues which will be addressed in the following chapter.

---

[134] See, for instance, Alter, *The David Story*, 160 or Bar-Efrat, *I Samuel*, 324.

[135] See, for instance, *JPS* or *NAB*.

[136] Rashi, Radak, Ralbag.

[137] For additional citations, see *DCH*, s.v. מות. נפש appears as the subject in about fourteen verses, where this noun functions as pronoun (e.g., Num 23:10 or Judg 16:16).

G. *1 Samuel 25:37b²*—וְהוּא הָיָה לְאָבֶן *("And he became a stone")*

Most translators treat the subsequent statement in v. 37 as a simile: "and he became *like* a stone."[138] Does such a translation accurately render the nuance of this grammatical construction? The *Dictionary of Classical Hebrew* article on the preposition לְ discusses the verb form, הָיָה לְ, "be as, i.e. become, turn into." Of the nine examples cited, such as "may my lord the king's word become . . . a comfort" (2 Sam 14:17), none contains "like" or "as" in the translations provided in *DCH*.[139] In the same manner, a survey of how some of the translators mentioned above render other examples of this grammatical form in Samuel shows that nowhere else do they add the word "like."[140] So what motivates the insertion of "like" in v. 37? Is it intended to clarify to the reader that the narrator uses an analogy? Or does it reflect a certain discomfort with and desire to soften the figurative statement? From a linguistic perspective, what makes this utterance a metaphor?

As in prior examples, the analysis of the statement "and he became a stone" depends on the determination of the referent of the unspecified subject. In Hebrew, the masculine pronoun הוּא can refer to either a person ("he") or an object ("it"). If the broader context concerned a builder who ran out of stone and substituted wood instead, the sentence might read, וְהוּא הָיָה לְאָבֶן, meaning, "And it (the wood) served as stone." In that case, the utterance would not contain a semantic incongruity, for one concrete object substitutes for a related building material. A similar statement occurs in the account of the Tower of Babel, when the narrator remarks that "brick served them as stone (וַתְּהִי לָהֶם הַלְּבֵנָה לְאָבֶן)" (Gen 11:3). In 1 Sam 25:37, however, the subject consists of either a human being, הוּא ("him") denoting Nabal, or a body part, הוּא ("it") referring to the heart mentioned in the preceding sentence. According to Bar-Efrat, the subject of הוּא must be read as "(the body of) Nabal," for he claims the sentence would read וַיְהִי לְאָבֶן if the "heart" constituted the subject.[141]

---

[138] See, for example, *JPS*, *NRS*, Alter; Fox puts the insertion "like a" in parentheses. McCarter translates: "he became a stone."

[139] *DCH*, s.v. לְ, 3c (481a).

[140] In translations of similar expressions with הָיָה לְ and a substantive in the book of Samuel, *JPS*, *NRS*, and Alter do not render these expressions with "like" or "as"; see 1 Sam 4:9; 10:12; 18:21 (*JPS* is an exception here); 2 Sam 7:14; 15:33.

[141] Bar-Efrat, *1 Samuel*, 324.

An examination of other passages containing the phrase ל היה with a substantive following the preposition ל reveals two categories. In a number of examples like Gen 11:3, the phrase indicates that one thing functions as something else or someone serves a particular role. For instance, God reminds the Israelites: "I also gave them my sabbaths to serve as a sign between me and them (להיות לאות)" (Ezek 20:12).[142] Elsewhere, the people recall to David God's earlier decision: "And it is you who will be (or function as) prince (ואתה תהיה לנגיד) over Israel" (2 Sam 5:2).[143] In other verses, this grammatical construction is used in a somewhat different manner, to indicate a transformation, as defined in *DCH* as, "be as, i.e. become, turn into." In Exod 4:9, God instructs Moses to pour water from the Nile on the floor, "and it will turn to blood on the dry ground (והיו לדם ביבשת)." When Ahab attempts to commandeer Naboth's garden, he orders: "Give me your vineyard, so that it may become a vegetable garden for me (ויהי לי לגן ירק)" (1 Kgs 21:2). In Ps 118:22, the psalmist marvels: "The stone that the builders rejected has become the chief cornerstone (אבן מאסו הבונים היתה לראש פנה)." In all of these examples, one entity becomes a different, but related entity; both objects stay within the same basic semantic field, that of a stone, an agricultural plot, or a liquid substance.[144] In contrast, in other cases the transformation involves separate semantic fields. For example, God complains that "the house of Israel have become dross (היות כלכם לסגים)" (Ezek 22:19).[145] Elsewhere, a scheming Saul agrees to give Michal to David so "she will be a snare for him (ותהי לו למוקש)" (1 Sam 18:21).[146] Similarly, David advises Hushai: "If you cross over with me, you will be a burden to me (והית עלי

---

[142] For similar examples, see Gen 17:11; Exod 13:16; Num 17:3; Deut 6:8; 11:18.

[143] For similar examples, see Judg 11:6, 8, 9; 18:19; 1 Sam 23:17; 2 Sam 5:2.

[144] Also see Deut 28:26; 1 Sam 10:12 (cf. Ps 69:12); Isa 1:22; Ezek 34:8. In cases where ל היה carries the nuance of "function or serve as," many instances function literally; the subject and object are both from the same semantic field, such as animate beings (2 Sam 5:2) or inanimate objects (Gen 11:3). On the other hand, other examples involve a crossing over of semantic fields, as when God explains that Aaron with serve as Moses' mouth (יהיה לך לפה) (Exod 4:16) or when Moses tells his father-in-law: "You can be our eyes (והיית לנו לעינים)" (Num 10:31). Many statements about God fit in this category, like Ps 71:3: "Be a sheltering rock for me (היה לי לצור מעון)."

[145] The same expression also appears in Ezek 22:18; see Greenberg's comments, *Ezekiel 21–37* (New York: Doubleday, 1997), 458.

[146] Also see Exod 34:12; cf. Ps 69:23.

(למשׂא)" (2 Sam 15:33).[147] In such cases, as in 1 Sam 25:37, an animate being is described as becoming something inanimate.[148] In the Samuel passage at hand, the semantic incongruity results from the association of lexemes from distinct semantic fields. Not only is it empirically impossible for a human being to become a stone, but it is linguistically anomalous to identify an animate being with an inanimate object.

H. *1 Samuel 25:3—*קשׂה וְהָאִישׁ *("And the man was hard")*

The final case under consideration comes from the introductory section of the chapter. In 1 Sam 25:2–3, the narrator sets up a contrast between Abigail, who is described first as having "a good mind and lovely looks," and Nabal, about whom it is written: "and the man was hard and evil in deeds" (25:3). Translations of the statement וְהָאִישׁ קשׂה differ, from those who translate קשׂה as "hard" (Alter, *JPS*) to those who render the phrase more exegetically as "churlish" (*KJV*), "surly" (*NRS*), or "miserly" (*NJB*).[149] What, precisely, does it mean for a person to be "a hard man"? Most exegetes, from Rashi and Radak to McCarter and Alter, make no comment on the expression.[150] Can this ambiguous utterance be viewed as anomalous and therefore possibly metaphoric? An assessment of the figurative nature of the statement first requires a survey of patterns of usage for the root ק.שׂ.ה. and then, in the following chapter, a determination as to whether or not the sentence contains an underlying analogy.

The adjective קשׂה modifies a variety of nouns and carries a range of nuances. The Torah characterizes the exceedingly <u>taxing labor</u> performed by the Israelites in Egypt as קשׂה.[151] A number of pas-

---

[147] Also see Job 7:20.

[148] The opposite sort of transformation occurs when Isaiah laments that the faithful city, Jerusalem, has become a harlot (הָיְתָה לְזוֹנָה קִרְיָה נֶאֱמָנָה) (Isa 1:21). Another example includes the statement in the Psalms that one inanimate object will become a different inanimate object: "May their table be a trap for them, a snare for their allies (יְהִי שֻׁלְחָנָם לִפְנֵיהֶם לְפָח וְלִשְׁלוֹמִים לְמוֹקֵשׁ)" (Ps 69:23).

[149] Other translations include "rough" (Fox) and "harsh" (*NAB*).

[150] Fokkelman is an exception; he remarks: "Nabal is given only three words and is finished off as 'hard', which has no counterweight but is simply continued and explained with 'evil-doer'" (482).

[151] Exod 1:14; 6:9; Deut 26:6; 1 Kgs 12:4 and 2 Chr 10:4 concern the harsh work and heavy yoke imposed by Solomon. Also see Isa 14:3. Verbally, this root characterizes Rachel's severe labor, which resulted in the birth of Benjamin and the death of Rachel (Gen 35:16).

sages describe a person's <u>manner of speaking</u> as קָשֶׁה, such as when Joseph speaks "<u>harshly</u>" to his brothers (Gen 42:7, 30) or when David questions how Saul might respond to Jonathan (1 Sam 20:10).[152] In Exod 18:26, קָשֶׁה appears in opposition to the adjective קָטָן ("small"), as the verse contrasts a <u>weighty or difficult</u> <u>legal matter</u> with a minor case.[153] The connotation of קָשֶׁה in Exod 18:26 resembles that of Job 30:25, where the expression קְשֵׁה יוֹם refers to those whose <u>days</u> are <u>difficult</u>. The verse reads: "Did I not weep for those hard of day," my soul grieve for the needy?[154] In the Song of Songs, קָשֶׁה parallels the word עַז ("<u>strong</u>"), with the adjectives modifying the nouns "<u>passion</u>" and "love" (Song 8:6).[155] Similarly, קָשֶׁה depicts the <u>wind</u> in Isa 27:8, where the lexeme conveys a sense of <u>strength or severity</u>. Judges 4:24 characterizes the Israelites' <u>forceful</u> <u>military offensive</u> against the Canaanites, metonymically referred to as "the hand of the Israelites," by combining the infinitive absolute הָלוֹךְ with the adjective קָשֶׁה to express duration: "The hand of the Israelites proceeded ever harder (הָלוֹךְ וְקָשָׁה) against Jabin, king of Canaan."[156] In 2 Sam 2:17, the word applies to a <u>fierce</u> <u>battle</u> that ends in the rout of David's opponents. Isaiah 27:1 announces that God will punish the Leviathan with <u>God's sword</u>, which is touted as חַרְבּוֹ הַקָּשָׁה וְהַגְּדוֹלָה וְהַחֲזָקָה; the two other adjectives used in conjunction with קָשֶׁה signal <u>might and strength</u>.

The adjective takes on a different nuance in Judg 2:19 when it refers to the wayward behavior of the Israelites, who revert back to their "<u>stubborn</u> <u>ways</u>" after the death of their leader (לֹא הִפִּילוּ מִמַּעַלְלֵיהֶם וּמִדַּרְכָּם הַקָּשָׁה). The expression קְשֵׁה עֹרֶף, usually translated

---

[152] Similarly, see 1 Kgs 12:13 and 2 Chr 10:13. First Kings 14:6 refers to a harsh message; Isa 21:2 speaks of a harsh prophecy. In 2 Sam 19:44, a *qal* verb from this root depicts the harsh words of the men of Judah. Also see 2 Kgs 2:10.

[153] The verb קשה is used in a similar context in Deut 1:17 when God advises Moses how to handle a matter that is too difficult for him.

[154] Similarly, Ps 60:5 states: "You have shown your people hard things," implying difficulties or hardships.

[155] A similar parallelism appears in Gen 49:7, the verbs עַז and קָשָׁתָה describe the ferocity of Simeon and Levi's anger.

[156] See Paul Joüon, *A Grammar of Biblical Hebrew*, trans. T. Muraoka (Rome: Pontifical Biblical Institute, 1993), section 123s: "the hand of the Israelites went on becoming always heavier," with קָשֶׁה as a verbal adjective, "becoming hard," and *DCH*, s.v. הלך: "and the hand of the Israelites became harder and harder" (vol. 2, 553). In 1 Sam 5:7, the people of Ashdod exclaim: "Let not the Ark of the God of Israel stay among us, for His hand is hard upon us and upon Dagon our God."

as "stiff-necked," captures the same sense of obstinacy.[157] A verbal
form of this expression occurs more frequently, and often the charge
that people "stiffened their necks" appears alongside the accusation
that they did not listen to God. For instance, Jeremiah declares: "Yet
they did not hear or bend their ear, but they stiffened their neck,
not hearing and not taking correction" (Jer 17:23).[158] The root ק.ש.ה.
is used verbally and adjectivally with the noun לב or לבב ("heart")
to denote obduracy. Just as when the verb כבד ("to be heavy")
describes the condition of the heart, the expression means that "an
organ of perception . . . is no longer receiving outside stimuli."[159] For
example, Ps 95:8 cautions: "Do not harden your hearts (אל תקשו
לבבכם) as at Meribah," referring to the site where the Israelites'
rebelled against God, a place appropriately named "Strife." Similarly,
God warns Ezekiel: "But the house of Israel will refuse to listen to
you because they refuse to listen to Me; for the whole house of Israel
are tough-browed and hard-hearted (חזקי מצח וקשי לב)" (Ezek 3:7).[160]
Ezekiel utilizes these two roots in an earlier expression when he
teams the adjective קשה with the noun פנים ("face") to depict the
Israelites who have transgressed against God as "brazen-faced and
tough-hearted (קשי פנים וחזקי לב)" (Ezek 2:4). Moshe Greenberg
explains that "hard-faced" means that the exterior is "impassive, with
a face that shows no emotion or disconcertion when it should." He
points out a dichotomy between the first term, "brazen-faced," which
concerns the exterior and implies impudence and the second phrase,
"tough-hearted," which refers to the interior condition and suggests
obstinacy.[161]

In the preceding citations, the root ק.ש.ה. is used to describe the
condition of several body parts: the nape of the neck, the heart, and
the face. These expressions function figuratively as a way to char-

---

[157] Exod 32:9; 33:3, 5; Deut 9:6, 13; 31:27.

[158] Similarly, see 2 Kgs 17:14; Jer 7:26; 19:15; Neh 9:16, 17, 29; the expression
appears without the verb שמע in Deut 10:16; Prov 29:1; 2 Chr 30:8; 2 Chr 36:13.

[159] Robert Wilson, "The Hardening of Pharaoh's Heart," *CBQ* 41 (1979), 22.
According to Wilson, קשה differs from כבד and חזק in Exodus 4–14 in that it
"almost always has negative connotations" (23).

[160] Also see Exod 7:3, where God announces that He will harden Pharaoh's heart,
as well as Prov 28:14, which predicts that a person who hardens his heart will fall
into misfortune.

[161] Greenberg, 64. He notes that the adjectives are reversed in Ezek 3:7 (69). Cf.
עז פנים in Deut 28:50; Tigay notes that this expression refers to impudence or
shamelessness and, like Ezek 2:4, may be translated as "expressionless" (269).

acterize the attitude or behavior of the individuals who possess these body parts. On a number of occasions, as in 1 Sam 25:3, the adjective קשה applies more directly to human beings. In 1 Sam 1:15, Hannah calls herself "a woman hardened of spirit" (אשה קשת רוח). The surrounding context clarifies the meaning of this remark, which Alter translates as "bleak-spirited."[162] The narrator reports that Hannah is a "bitter" person (מרת נפש) who cries and cries (1 Sam 1:10). Hannah elaborates on her feelings in direct discourse, first when she asks God to look upon her "affliction" (1 Sam 1:11) and then when she admits to the priest Eli about her great "anxiety and grief" (1 Sam 1:16). Following Abner's death, David makes a concerted effort to prove to the people that he was not responsible for the murder of Saul's former commander. After he laments about Abner and fasts, David attempts to distance himself from the killers, Joab and Abishai, when he declares: "I am gentle (רך), and anointed king, and these people, sons of Zeruiah, are too hard for me (קשים ממני)" (2 Sam 3:39). Here, the adjective conveys a sense of severity and savagery. Isaiah 19:4 implies a similar nuance when the prophet predicts that the Egyptians will be delivered "into the hand of a hard master (אדנים קשה)"; here again, קשה parallels עז as the verse continues: "and a powerful ruler (מלך עז) will rule over them." The meaning of קשה differs in Isa 48:4. After Deutero-Isaiah reminds the Israelites: "I knew that you are hard (כי קשה אתה)," he depicts their stubbornness with the familiar imagery of the people as stiff-necked and brazen-faced: "an iron sinew is your neck, and your forehead bronze."

How do these data inform the interpretation of 1 Sam 25:3? In the interaction with David's men, Nabal certainly comes across as an obdurate person, stiff-necked and hard-hearted. On the one hand, unmoved by David's deferential request, he stubbornly refuses to part with his wealth. On the other hand, his behavior also can be characterized as harsh, for he treats David's men rudely and severely. In its imprecision, the adjective adeptly captures several aspects of Nabal's character.[163] While the preceding examination of patterns of

---

[162] Other translations vary, from the more literal "woman hardened of spirit" (Fox) to the more exegetical translations, like "a very unhappy woman" (*JPS*) and "a woman deeply troubled" (*NRS*).

[163] Additional considerations in the exegesis of this verse include the nature of the relationship between the expression "And the man was hard" and the statement that follows ("and evil in his deeds"), as well as the connection between the

usage for the root ק.שׁ.ה helps to elucidate the ways in which Nabal may be considered a "hard" man, determining the figurative status of this utterance proves more difficult.

If the adjective קשׁה were used primarily to label the tactile quality of concrete objects, such as a brick or a millstone, one could easily establish selection rules and thus identify an anomaly. However, the range of nouns that this adjective modifies and the various nuances the root conveys make such a process difficult. Out of the thirty-six times the adjective קשׁה appears, in four verses it directly describes a person or a group of people, nine times it modifies a part of the anatomy, and in the remaining twenty-three instances it mainly refers to actions or events, like a battle or labor, or to abstract entities, such as passion or a person's spirit. Thus, only in a limited number cases does קשׁה describe the physical properties of a concrete object. Only when modifying certain body parts—the neck, heart, and face—does the adjective purport to mean that the object is solid and firm to the touch, the opposite of soft;[164] and in these cases, the point of referring to these various body parts as "hard" is not to comment on their tangible, exterior features, but instead to communicate something about the inner nature of the particular individual. Given these statistics, can the concatenation of "the man" and "hard" be considered a semantic anomaly and thus some sort of figurative expression?

David Rumelhart ponders a similar statement in his article "Some Problems with the Notion of Literal Meanings." If the sentence "John is a cold person" is uttered in a context where it conveys the mean-

---

description of Nabal and that of Abigail. What degree of equivalence or contrast separates the two statements about Nabal? Like the comments about Abigail—which concern an interior quality, her intelligence, and an exterior feature, her physical appearance—do the observations about Nabal describe different aspects of his character? Or, instead, should the statements be viewed as near synonyms? Fokkelman notes that in contrast to the balanced pairs of differentiated qualities that praise Abigail, the statement that Nabal "is hard" lacks a counterpart, and he reads the second comment about Nabal as a continuation and explanation of the first (482). Both statements focus on Nabal's moral character, highlighting how he behaves and how he treats other people. David emphasizes the second aspect of Nabal's personality when he remarks: "He paid me back evil for good" (25:21). Elsewhere, other characters defame Nabal by calling him "worthless" and "foolish" (25:17, 25).

[164] In the case of the one other concrete object paired with קשׁה, God's sword, the accompanying list of adjectives clarifies that the verse focuses on the power of the weapon, not its firmness.

ing "John is unemotional," then "is this sentence *literally* true?"[165] He proposes three possible answers to this question:

1. No, it is not literally true, John is not actually *cold*, the sense in which he is cold is metaphorical, not literal.
2. Yes, cold is a word with several senses: one of these senses involves being unemotional, and in that sense of cold it is literally the case that John is cold.
3. Well yes and no. The use of cold to mean unemotional was originally metaphorical, but is now conventional. It is now merely an idiom. There is a sense in which idioms are *never* literally true, but it is not a figurative use either. Perhaps it is better so say that in our idiom John is literally a cold person, but were the words used according to their normal meanings, we would not say that he was cold, but that he was unemotional.[166]

As Rumelhart evaluates these positions, he finds fault with the second and third responses and concludes that the first provides the best answer. He observes:

> If we choose the first alternative, metaphor in language is absolutely ubiquitous . . . Nearly always, when we talk about abstract concepts, we choose language drawn from one or another concrete domain . . . It is quite possible that our primary method of understanding nonsensory concepts is through analogy with concrete experiences.[167]

One could substitute the utterance "The man was hard" for Rumelhart's example and ask: "Is this sentence literally true?" Rumelhart might respond: No, Nabal was not literally hard. Since the adjective does not describe the density of his body mass or the feel of his body to the human touch, the sense in which he was hard is metaphorical. In the *Theological Lexicon of the Old Testament* entry on קשׁה, the author asserts that verbal and nominal occurrences of this root always have a figurative meaning "and refer either to the severity of a matter that people perceive as oppressive or to the harshness that someone displays in interaction with others."[168] Quintilian

---

[165] David Rumelhart, "Some Problems with the Notion of Literal Meanings," in *Metaphor and Thought*, ed. Andrew Ortony, 2d ed. (Cambridge: Cambridge University Press, 1993), 80. Rumelhart approaches this subject from the perspective of a psychologist. He argues that "the distinction between literal and metaphorical language is rarely, if ever, reflected in a qualitative change in the psychological processes involved in the processing of that language" (72).

[166] Rumelhart, 80–81.

[167] Rumelhart, 81.

[168] A. S. van der Woude, *TLOT*, s.v. קשׁה, 1175.

cites this expression as an example of a "necessary metaphor," explaining that "we speak of a *hard* or *rough* man, there being no *literal* term for these temperaments."[169]

The question under consideration here does not concern whether or not the utterance is literally true, but, instead, whether or not the usage of קשה can be viewed as semantically anomalous. The focus centers on a linguistic, not an ontological, issue. Making a determination about the figurative status of this sentence depends in part on the operative notion of the term "literal," a disputed issue that surfaces frequently in the literature on metaphor. If figurative language is defined by distinguishing it from literal language, what conception of literal language is being implicitly or explicitly assumed? Some privilege literal language as "proper" and "superior" and denigrate figurative language as "improper" and "inferior."[170] Others conceive of literality as the "primary, matter-of-fact sense"[171] of a word or the "basic" meaning, in contrast to the "derived" figurative meaning.[172] Certain scholars define literal usage as "accustomed" or "lexicalized" usage,[173] while others perceive of literal as the "context-free"[174] meaning of an expression or "its meaning in a 'null' context."[175] Those who focus on the cognitive facets of metaphor tend to advocate a notion of literal language as semantically autonomous, meaning "directly meaningful" language[176] that is "under-

---

[169] Quintilian, 303.

[170] C. Barth, *TDOT*, vol. 7, s.v. כשל, 358. Barth challenges the feasibility of distinguishing between "a 'proper' literal usage" and "an 'improper' metaphorical usage" of the verb כשל ("to stumble"), pointing to the disproportionate number of figurative attestations of this verb. He concludes: "The dualism of a 'proper' and 'improper' meaning becomes unnecessary when the various usages are seen as ontologically equal concretions of a single symbol" (358).

[171] Caird, 133.

[172] Geoffrey Leech, *A Linguistic Guide to English Poetry* (London: Longman Group Limited, 1969), 151.

[173] Soskice, 71; also see Paul Ricoeur, *The Rule of Metaphor* (Toronto: University of Toronto Press, 1977), 291.

[174] Toolan, 25.

[175] Gibbs, 257.

[176] George Lakoff, "The Meanings of Literal," *Metaphor and Symbolic Activity* 1 (1986) 292. Lakoff outlines four different senses conveyed by the word "literal": conventional literality, subject matter literality, nonmetaphorical literality, and truth-conditional literality (292). Given the conflicting, confusing assumptions implied by this term, he advocates that "it is good policy to avoid the word *literal* as much as possible in discussions of metaphor" (293). If one must use the term, Lakoff argues that its meaning should be restricted to the third sense, "nonmetaphorical literality," which he defines as "directly meaningful language—not language that is understood, even partly, in terms of something else" (292).

stood and structured on its own terms—without making use of structure imported from a completely different conceptual domain."[177] A number of researchers posit that literal and figurative "are two ends of a scale, rather than clear-cut categories"[178] and propose moving away from the "limiting, binary, either/or conception" of speech as either literal or nonliteral.[179]

The aim of this section is not to resolve this complex and contentious issue, but to articulate some of the assumptions about literal language that undergird the present work. Because of the limitations inherent in the study of biblical Hebrew—primarily, the limited data available from a restricted, relatively small literary corpus—it is difficult to ascertain what constitutes the "usual" or "accustomed" usage of a word or expression in ancient Israel. The Tanakh and the paucity of extra-biblical Hebrew documents unearthed so far present a skewed picture of biblical Hebrew that hampers efforts to determine what might have been the "conventional" sense of a given term. For instance, as noted above, the verb עיט is only attested in metaphoric contexts, and statistics show that the root ק.ש.ה. most frequently conveys a figurative connotation. As a result, a working definition of literality cannot rest on calculations about frequency of usage.

Instead, the notion of literal language operative here involves "the basic, determinate, and context-free meaning of words and sentences."[180] Cristina Cacciari traces this "more common notion of literal language still used in linguistics as well as in psychological literature" to Katz and Fodor's "anonymous letter criterion": the meaning understood by a person who receives an anonymous letter containing only a single sentence.[181] Toolan points out that although the conceptualization of literal meaning as "context-transcending" is "necessary for standard linguistic treatments of the semantics and pragmatics of a language, in practice no such domain of context-free

---

[177] George Lakoff and Mark Turner, *More than Cool Reason* (Chicago: University of Chicago Press, 1989), 57. For other proponents of this position, see Steen, 24 or Macky, 25.

[178] Leech, 147; also see Nielsen, 64 and Jerrold M. Sadock, "Figurative Speech and Linguistics," in *Metaphor and Thought*, ed. Andrew Ortony, 2d ed. (Cambridge: Cambridge University Press, 1993), 55–57.

[179] Aaron, 4.

[180] Toolan, 25.

[181] Cristina Cacciari, "The Place of Idioms in a Literal and Metaphorical World," in *Idioms: Processing, Structure, and Interpretation*, ed. C. Cacciari and P. Tabossi (Hillsdale, NJ: Lawrence Erlbaum Associates, Publishers, 1993), 28.

meaning exists."[182] He notes that "the standard linguistic procedure is to concede that some kind of 'background' is a necessary frame for literal meaning but also to represent that background as neutral and inconsequential." He argues, however, "that literal meaning is itself a highly contextualized notion, that it is a cultural and ideological construct."[183] In spite of its shortcomings, this notion of literality seems to work best for the material at hand.

How does this definition of literal language apply to 1 Sam 25:3? If one assumes that the adjective קשֶׁה carries a basic, context-free meaning that describes the physical properties of a tangible object, then this implies certain selection restrictions. Note, however, that in the case of the biblical corpus, such an assumption may not be bolstered by attested citations. Nonetheless, the analysis of this lexeme depends on certain inferences about the word's basic meaning and the semantic norms dictated by this meaning. In a context where the adjective קשֶׁה describes the tactile attributes of a body builder's biceps, it would not be semantically anomalous to say that "the man was hard." In contrast, when the adjective is used to characterize an individual's personality, then it can be considered semantically incongruous to label the person as a "hard man." This incongruity tags the utterance as a trope. Having established that the collocation of lexemes in a given context constitutes a figurative application of this adjective, the next question to consider is whether or not the utterance qualifies as an example of the specific tropic device of metaphor. In the following chapter, this expression will be reevaluated in order to determine if it contains an underlying analogy, the second element involved in identifying a metaphor.

---

[182] Toolan, 25.

[183] Toolan, 25. Cacciari also acknowledges some of the criticism of the "zero context" assumption advocated by Katz and Fodor. She writes: "It has been argued that their proposal is deficient in many respects because it did not take into account linguistic presuppositions, background knowledge, and more broadly the role of world knowledge in comprehension processes" (28).

CHAPTER THREE

IDENTIFICATION AND INTERPRETATION OF BIBLICAL METAPHORS: ANALYZING THE ANALOGY INHERENT IN METAPHOR

I. Roger White's Approach to Metaphor

While a semantic anomaly helps to signal the presence of a metaphor, this feature in and of itself does not define a metaphor. Since all types of tropes involve some degree of deviation, what distinguishes metaphor from, say, hyperbole, irony, or metonymy? Unlike other forms of figurative language, metaphor entails an analogy. In his book *The Structure of Metaphor*, Roger White provides a novel approach that elucidates this aspect of metaphor. According to White, metaphor establishes an analogical comparison between two situations, the actual situation addressed in the metaphor and the hypothetical situation to which it is being compared. Interpreting a metaphor involves the reconstruction of these two situations, and White provides a technique to assist with the reconstruction process.

Whereas other scholars attribute the metaphorical status of a sentence to a single word within the sentence, White examines how a metaphor involves a combination of words in an utterance. He maintains: "In general, when we speak of a metaphor, we are referring to a sentence or another expression, in which some words are used metaphorically, and some are used non-metaphorically."[1] White regards a metaphor as a linguistic hybrid, an amalgam of two types of vocabulary. He explains:

> A metaphor contains two different kinds of vocabulary, a *primary* vocabulary, consisting of those words that would belong in a straightforward,

---

[1] White, 17. White admits that "talking of words being used metaphorically may be misleading, carrying with it overtones of 'words used in a metaphorical sense'"; yet he insists that "the *whole sentence* establishes the metaphor" (17). As noted earlier, White distinguishes himself from other scholars by offering an alternative to the standard word-based accounts of metaphor. He challenges the notion that every metaphor boils down to "an isolable word or phrase used metaphorically" (57).

non-metaphorical, description of the situation being metaphorically presented, and a *secondary* vocabulary that introduces the metaphorical
comparison into the sentence.[2]

For instance, analyzing a selection from Shakespeare's *Antony and
Cleopatra*, "I was a morsell for a Monarke" (I, v, 36), he asserts: "'I'
and 'a Monarke' belong to the primary vocabulary, and 'morsell'
belongs to the secondary vocabulary of the metaphor."[3]

In order to highlight the way in which a metaphor arises from the
combination of these two vocabularies, White presents a notational
system that utilizes various types of underlining. Marking the words
belonging to the primary vocabulary with a straight line and those
of the secondary vocabulary with a double line, the quotation from
Antony and Cleopatra appears graphically as follows:

I was a morsell for a Monarke.

White illustrates his approach with a quotation from Samuel Johnson's
Dictionary:

The spring awakes the flowers.[4]

This system separates the elements of the sentence that refer to the
primary or actual situation—in the Johnson example, the effect of
the spring on flowers—from the secondary or hypothetical situation
to which the actual situation is compared—in this case, the awaken-
ing of some sort of animate being.

White acknowledges that in certain cases some words may belong
to both the primary and secondary vocabularies of a metaphor, a
notion he labels "bifurcation." To illustrate this phenomenon, he
adds a third type of underlining, represented here with a dotted line.
White demonstrates the potential complexity of a metaphor by exploring how aspects of an utterance can apply to both the actual and
hypothetical situations, as seen in his treatment of the sentence
"Tolstoy was a great infant":

(1) Tolstoy was a great infant.
(2) Tolstoy was a great infant.
(3) Tolstoy was a great infant.

---

[2] White, 17.
[3] White, 17.
[4] White, 18.

In the first interpretation, "great" belongs to the secondary vocabulary and refers to the object described metaphorically, thus, the sentence compares Tolstoy to a great infant. The second interpretation considers "great" as part of the primary vocabulary, treating it as an adjective that modifies the subject, the great Tolstoy, who is compared to an infant. The third reading regards "great" as a case of bifurcation, meaning that the word belongs to both the primary and secondary vocabularies; the statement equates Tolstoy, the great novelist, with an overgrown infant.[5] White champions bifurcation as a widespread phenomenon, one that "makes possible some of the subtlest and most powerful effects achievable by the use of metaphor."[6] His analysis of the sentence about Tolstoy shows that even an "apparently simple metaphor permits a bewildering variety of readings,"[7] thereby supporting his contention that contrary to the "examples of extreme crudity and simplicity"[8] found in much of the literature on this topic, metaphor proves to be a complex and artful trope.

To help uncover this artistry and complexity, White has developed a technique for construing metaphors. First, he breaks up the original utterance into two open sentences, one containing only the primary vocabulary and the other, only the secondary vocabulary, with variables inserted in place of the missing elements. Next, he replaces the variables in each sentence, making appropriate substitutions to create two complete sentences: a primary sentence that describes the actual situation and a secondary sentence that describes the hypothetical situation to which the actual situation is being compared.[9] Using another example from Johnson's *Dictionary*, "He bridles his anger," step one of White's approach involves the separation of the primary and secondary vocabulary and the replacement of words or phrases that belong purely to the other type of vocabulary with a variable:

---

[5] White, 19–21.

[6] White, 22. White charges that in spite of its importance, this aspect of metaphor "is scarcely noticed at all in the theoretical explorations of metaphor." He speculates that scholars ignore the phenomenon of bifurcation partly because "the besetting sin of so many writers on metaphor is to develop their entire discussion with nothing but examples of extreme crudity and simplicity," and partly because "it is something whose presence is easily overlooked" (22).

[7] White, 18.

[8] White, 22.

[9] White, 78–79.

(1) Primary vocabulary: He *x* his anger.
    Secondary vocabulary: *Y* bridles *z*.

Step two entails filling in the blanks, substituting the variables with
fitting vocabulary in order to form two "quite straightforward literal
sentences."[10] The first sentence relates to the actual situation—a person controlling his anger—and the second sentence relates to the
hypothetical situation invoked as a comparison—a rider bridling a
horse.

(2) Primary sentence: He *checks* his anger.
    Secondary sentence: *The rider* bridles *his horse.*

The conflated metaphorical sentence reads: He bridles his anger.[11]

White applies this technique to a more complicated utterance, a
quotation by Iago in Shakespeare's *Othello*: "Heere he comes. / As
he shall smile, Othello shall go mad: / And his unbookish Ielousie
must construe / Poore Cassio's smiles, gestures and light behaviours
/ Quite in the wrong" (IV, i, 7ff). He argues that many Shakespeare
critics have been baffled by this metaphor or have misunderstood it,
for they "have tried to treat it primarily as a matter of the metaphorical use of the *word* 'unbookish.' "[12] Instead of assuming that the
metaphor "consists in the intrusion of the 'remote epithet', *unbookish*,
into an otherwise literal sentences,"[13] White examines the interplay
of language in this utterance and the way it develops the initial comparison at the heart of the metaphor. As he analyzes this passage,
he shows how Shakespeare plays with the comparison between someone's behavior and a book, an analogy found in other works by this
playwright:

> Shakespeare describes Othello (metonymically his jealousy) as 'unbook-
> ish', that is to say someone who is unskilled in the art of reading and
> interpreting books, and so prone to misconstrue them. The metaphor
> goes on to tell us that, as a consequence, there is one 'book' in par-
> ticular that he will be bound to misconstrue, namely 'Cassio's smiles,
> gestures and light behaviours.'[14]

---

[10] White, 79.
[11] White, 93.
[12] White, 62–63.
[13] White, 63–64.
[14] White, 64.

White begins to decipher the metaphor by establishing which words belong to the primary and secondary vocabulary, and which—those phrases marked with the dotted line—describe both the actual and hypothetical situations, "*both* Othello interpreting Cassio's behaviour, *and* the person translating a book with whom Othello is being compared."[15]

> His unbookish Ielousie must construe poore Cassio's smiles, gestures and light behaviours quite in the wrong.[16]

To gain a more precise understanding of the way this metaphor works, White then creates two open sentences, sentence I containing the primary vocabulary and sentence II the secondary vocabulary.

> (1) Open sentence I: His x jealousy must construe poore Cassio's smiles, gestures and light behaviours quite in the wrong.
> Open sentence II: The unbookish x must construe y quite in the wrong.[17]

Next, he replaces the variables based on his understanding of the two situations, thereby constructing two straightforward, nonfigurative sentences.

> (2) Primary sentence: His *uncultured* jealousy must construe poore Cassio's smiles, gestures and light behaviours quite in the wrong.
> Secondary sentence: The unbookish *schoolboy* must construe *The Illiad* quite in the wrong.[18]

White conceives of the metaphor as a conflation of these two grammatically analogous sentences, with enough of each type of vocabulary retained to allow the audience to reconstruct the actual and hypothetical situations.[19] He adds:

> As a result of such a conflation, we are invited to explore a network of similarities and dissimilarities between the two situations, and see the one situation in terms of the other situation, to see it as if it were the other situation.[20]

---

[15] White, 77.
[16] White, 77 (example slightly modified).
[17] White, 77.
[18] White, 78. Regarding the substitution of the specific text, *The Iliad*, White writes: "Anyone who grasps the role of this primary sentence in the analysis of this metaphor will recognise that this name has not been chosen because we are concerned with this book in particular, but purely because it may be taken as a typical representative of a range of objects, as a typical *text-that-needs-construing*" (112–113).
[19] White, 79.
[20] White, 80.

But precisely how does this process of reconstruction take place? How does one identify the hypothetical situation and make "appropriate" substitutions in the primary and secondary sentences? White addresses these questions in his discussion of Johnson's example "He bridles his anger." When forming his secondary sentence, White considers "horse" the natural candidate for the object of the verb "to bridle." He acknowledges, however, that other possibilities make sense: "Maybe someone in North Africa would detect an allusion here to a camel in the same automatic way that we detect the horse."[21] Furthermore, he recognizes that even if a number of people make the same substitution of "horse" in the secondary sentence, they might have in mind a number of different hypothetical situations:

i   A cowboy at a rodeo breaking an untamed horse.
ii A farmer harnessing a carthorse.
iii A jockey preparing a racehorse for a race.[22]

White argues that in the present context, (i) provides the best picture of a person restraining his anger. On the other hand, if the sentence read, "He bridles his imagination," (iii) would become a better choice, for "the idea of the powerful arab being brought under control so as to be enabled to complete its task becomes the most natural way to hear the metaphor."[23] White also considers another potential substitution, using "scold" instead of "horse" as the object of the verb "to bridle." He notes that a scold's bridle is a less familiar object of this verb, one which an interpreter would not immediately consider, unless alerted to the possibility by linguistic or other clues in the surrounding context.

From this discussion, White outlines a number of considerations that guide the construction of an appropriate secondary sentence:

i   We only accept as candidate secondary sentences such as seem to us to describe natural and familiar secondary situations. (We usually bridle horses, not turkeys.)
ii We further narrow down the possibilities by reflecting upon the point in comparing the resulting secondary situation to the actual situation. (Controlling one's anger is more aptly compared to taming a mustang than to harnessing a carthorse.)

---

[21] White, 94.
[22] White, 94.
[23] White, 95.

iii   We accept secondary sentences that accommodate the metaphor
to its immediate context, and in particular to its linguistic context.[24]

White admits that this interpretive process is not necessarily a successive procedure, nor a conscious one, for in many instances an
audience comprehends a metaphor immediately and automatically.[25]
Nevertheless, in order to explicate complicated or uncertain utterances, or to enhance the understanding of more simple metaphors,
this type of analytical technique proves valuable.

White qualifies his approach to metaphor with the acknowledgement that the notions of primary and secondary sentences "are con-
venient fictions, heuristic devices enabling us to give a simple *representation*
of the metaphorical process, but not actually *descriptive* of it."[26] In
other words, the "auxiliary construction" of the primary and secondary sentences provides a means of "*representing* the linguistic structure of the metaphorical sentence," but it does not directly depict
the metaphorical process.[27] Thus, with caution and precision, he
speaks about metaphor as a hybrid sentence that "may be regarded
as" or "viewed as"—but not *is*—the result of the conflation of two
distinct, grammatically analogous sentences.[28] White outlines two reasons why the description of metaphor as arising from the process of
conflation of two other sentences must be thought of as a heuristic
fiction. First, he stresses "that the metaphorical sentence does not
determine a unique pair of primary and secondary sentences, but
that we are permitted a range of legitimate variation in the construction of such sentences." He concludes: "We cannot strictly speaking describe the metaphor as the result of having conflated two
sentences, since there do not exist two specific, unique, sentences of
which it is a conflation."[29] Pointing out a second, more important
reason, he writes:

> It is surely incredible to suppose that the typical process that occurs
> when we use metaphor is one in which we *first* formulate sentences
> describing two different situations, which we *then* proceed to conflate
> in the manner outlined . . . Equally, when we hear someone else's
> metaphor, we will normally understand what they say directly, without

---

[24] White, 95.
[25] White, 95–96; also see 109–10.
[26] White, 80.
[27] White, 110.
[28] White, 79 and 105.
[29] White, 109.

taking the detour of deriving two conflated sentences from their words.
In the case of an obscure and difficult metaphor, we *may* interpret it
by producing such candidate primary or secondary sentences . . . But
that is not the normal case; the normal case is one in which the only
words that occur to both the speaker and the hearer of a metaphor
are the ones actually occurring in the text of the metaphor itself.[30]

While the technique of creating primary and secondary sentences
helps the interpreter understand the structure and significance of the
metaphor, White strives for an account of metaphor "that is faithful
to what actually occurs when we construct and understand metaphors."[31] As part of his theory, he regards a metaphorical utterance
as a "Duck-Rabbit," the type of ambiguous picture which can be seen
either as a picture of a duck or as a picture of a rabbit. He explains: "It
is a sentence that may simultaneously be regarded as presenting two
different situations; looked at one way, it describes the actual situation,
and looked at the other way, an hypothetical situation with which that
situation is being compared."[32] The words in a metaphorical utterance perform a "dual role" as they contribute to the description of
these two, superimposed situations. For White, constructing primary
and secondary sentences is a way of making explicit "the double life
enjoyed by the words within the metaphor itself, and is simply a
representation of an internal drama performed by the actual words
of the metaphor themselves."[33]

The interests of the present project lie less in White's more abstract
theory of metaphor and more in the practical technique he has
devised to help the interpreter unpack the underlying analogy and
analyze the connections between the actual and hypothetical situations. According to White, metaphors of any subtlety or complexity
continually make "creative demands upon the imagination of the
interpreter"[34] as they invite the reader to explore the connections
between the two, simultaneous situations at play in the "drama" of
a metaphor. White's approach will be applied to 1 Samuel 25 in
order to enrich our evolving understanding of the identification and
analysis of biblical metaphors.

---

[30] White, 109–10.
[31] White, 110.
[32] White, 115. He notes that the concept of a 'duck-rabbit' is familiar from the
work of Ludwig Wittgenstein, who took the idea from Joseph Jastrow (284, n. 7).
[33] White, 115.
[34] White, 108 and 105.

II. Application to 1 Samuel 25

A. *1 Samuel 25:14*—ויעט בהם *("He swooped down on them")*

The method outlined above involves a two-part process: (i) the determination of the actual and hypothetical situations and (ii) the formation of primary and secondary sentences. These two stages operate simultaneously, not sequentially, for each step informs and helps clarify the other. For example, the analysis of the statement, "He swooped down on them" (25:14), starts with an attempt to specify the actual situation addressed in the metaphor and the hypothetical situation to which it is being compared, both of which can be initially expressed in the following manner:

> Actual situation: Nabal acts harshly toward David's messengers.
> Hypothetical situation: A raptor swoops down upon an object.

Next, the utterance is dissected by separating the primary and secondary vocabulary.

> Primary vocabulary: He *x* them.
> Secondary vocabulary: *Y* swooped down on *z*.

The third step entails the creation of primary and secondary sentences by replacing the variables with fitting substitutions. In the secondary sentence, the nominal form of the root ע.י.ט. provides a natural substitution for the subject: raptor. Turning to the next gap in the secondary sentence, the bird of prey swooped down on some sort of object. Exactly what type of object might a raptor swoop down upon? Is it possible, or important, to determine a more specific substitution? Applying White's guidelines for selecting candidate secondary sentences to the verse at hand results in a number of considerations: (i) What is a natural and familiar secondary situation, given what we know about raptors in general and, more precisely, birds of prey mentioned in the Bible? (ii) What is the point of the comparison between the hypothetical and actual situations? (iii) What best fits the immediate context of the exchange between Nabal's servant and Abigail?

Addressing the first question leads to several avenues of investigation. First, what can we learn from other biblical passages that contain the root ע.י.ט. or use other vocabulary to refer to the activity of raptors? Secondly, what can we ascertain from existing scientific knowledge about the hunting habits of raptors, particularly those

likely to have been visible in ancient Israel? The initial line of inquiry
requires a survey of the relevant biblical citations. While only figurative
uses of the verb עיט have been preserved (1 Sam 14:32; 15:19), the
noun עיט is used in passages that describe raptors descending upon
or eating a number of items, including the nonspecific term "food"
(Ezek 39:4), branches with ripening grapes (Isa 18:5–6), and animal
carcasses (Gen 15:11). A larger number of biblical verses employ the
more general term עוף השמים ("bird of the skies") when depicting
carrion birds consuming corpses. For instance, Goliath and David
both boast that they will give their enemy's flesh to the birds of the
skies and the beasts of the field (1 Sam 17:44, 46). Similarly, Jeremiah
warns: "Yes, the dead bodies of this people will be food for the birds
of the skies and all the beasts of the earth, with none to frighten
them off" (Jer 7:33).[35] Passages containing the noun נשר, which may
designate either a vulture or an eagle, speak of this bird feasting on
blood of the slain (Job 39:30) or devouring eyes gouged out by a
raven (Prov 30:17). Overall, the majority of biblical verses that identify the specific object upon which the raptor descends refer to a
corpse or carcass. In comparison, scientific studies of raptors reveal
a far more varied diet. Forsman's study *The Raptors of Europe and the
Middle East* shows that the numerous species of raptors sighted in
modern-day Israel consume everything from insects, fish, and birds
to mammals, carrion, and organic litter.[36]

Given the dissonance between the information about raptors culled
from biblical sources on the one hand and from empirical research
on the other, how does one determine what constitutes a "natural
and familiar" secondary situation? Black addresses this issue when
he explains his notion of "associated commonplaces." Building upon
Richards' comment that a metaphor forces a reader to connect two
ideas, Black declares: "In this 'connexion' resides the secret and the
mystery of metaphor."[37] How does a person who encounters the

---

[35] Also see Deut 28:26; 2 Sam 21:10; 1 Kgs 14:11.

[36] Of the forty-three species listed in the book, thirty-two have been documented
in Israel, based on the photographs accompanying each species. Studies of animals
in the Bible tend to take information about birds of prey currently found in Israel
and extrapolate about the identification and characteristics of birds that "probably"
or "doubtless" existed in the biblical period. See, for example, Roy Pinney, *The
Animals in the Bible: The Identity and Natural History of All the Animals Mentioned in the
Bible* (Philadelphia: Chilton Books, 1964) or V. Møller-Christensen and K. E. Jordt
Jorgensen, *Encyclopedia of Bible Creatures* (Philadelphia: Fortress Press, 1965).

[37] Black, "Metaphor," 73.

statement "Man is a wolf" connect the "principle subject" (man) with the "subsidiary subject" (wolf) in order to uncover the intended meaning of the metaphorical sentence? Black argues that the interpretation of the metaphor depends not on scientific knowledge about the habits of wolves, but instead on the "set of standard beliefs about wolves (current platitudes) that are the common possession of the members of some speech community."[38] The interpreter constructs a "system of implications" about wolves—they are fierce, treacherous, carnivorous, and so forth—and then links this list with a corresponding "system of implications" about men. The overlapping sections of these lists become prominent and shape the interpretation of the metaphor, while those facets of wolves that do not connect with humans are pushed into the background.[39]

Darr emphasizes the importance of Black's notion of "associated commonplaces" for the study of figurative language in the Bible, yet she recognizes the challenges involved in reconstructing "standard beliefs" of ancient Israelites. She writes:

> How can we recover the complex associations surrounding a trope's terms in the world of ancient Israel? Unlike modern anthropologists doing fieldwork in extant cultures not their own, biblical scholars cannot ask ancient Israelites to explain their figurative uses of language. We have only texts, biblical and extra-biblical, to assist us. Our task is hindered by incomplete or unrecoverable data.[40]

In spite of the difficulties, she maintains that understanding biblical language and imagery requires "recovering, as best as we can, ancient Israel's complex webs of socially-and-culturally conditioned associations with a particular trope's terms."[41]

In the case at hand, raptors may be observed engaging in a range of different behaviors, such as hovering in the air for extended periods,[42] leisurely beating their wings to snatch a bird in flight,[43] or hopping around on the ground in search of insects.[44] However, a survey of the relevant biblical citations shows that biblical writers

---

[38] Black, 74.
[39] Black, 75.
[40] Darr, 41.
[41] Darr, 42.
[42] Behavior seen, for example, in the short-toed vulture (Forsman, 156), long-legged buzzard (291), or kestrel (443).
[43] Characteristic of the hobby (Forsman, 505).
[44] Pattern of behavior observed in the red-footed falcon (Forsman, 456).

focused primarily on two aspects of raptors' behavior: the way they soar at great heights with outstretched wings[45] or swoop down on their prey. The available biblical evidence suggests that upon hearing that Nabal "swooped down" on David's men, an ancient Israelite audience likely would have envisioned a bird of prey rapidly descending upon a corpse or carcass as the hypothetical situation invoked by this metaphor. These data point to the substitution of the more general term "prey" or the more specific "carrion" in the secondary sentence.

> Secondary vocabulary: Y swooped down on z.
> Secondary sentence: *The raptor* swooped down on *the prey.*[46]

Turning to the primary sentence, finding a fitting substitution proves more difficult. Phrased rather broadly, the actual situation concerns Nabal's reaction to David's messengers; but how, exactly, did Nabal react? Which aspect of the interaction does the metaphor attempt to capture: Nabal's demeanor, his choice of language, his tone of voice? Among White's guidelines, he advises taking into consideration the point of the comparison and the immediate context. Various aspects of the surrounding context contain the potential to provide clues regarding the precise nature of the interaction between Nabal and David's men: the narrator's depiction of the actual episode (v. 10), Nabal's words to the messengers (vv. 10–11), the reaction of David's men (v. 12), and other comments in the speech of Nabal's servant (vv. 14–17). Unfortunately, none of these avenues of information leads to a definitive understanding of the episode.

The narrator formulaically states that Nabal "answered . . . and said" (25:10), without offering any observations or judgments about Nabal's behavior. Nabal's response commences with two staccato questions that refer to David in a derogatory manner: "Who is David? And who is the son of Jesse?" (25:10), a startling contrast to David's obsequious remarks. David refers to himself as Nabal's "son" (25:8), yet Nabal professes no recognition of this individual. Equally unexpected in tone and content is Nabal's subsequent comment about

---

[45] See Jer 48:40; 49:22; Ps 18:1; Job 39:27. Forsman mentions a number of raptors noted for the way they soar high above their hunting grounds, including bonelli's eagle (404) and the booted eagle (416).

[46] Whereas White preferred a more specific substation in the example involving *The Illiad*, a more less specific option has been selected here.

the numbers of escaped slaves, a barb that questions David's status and adds to the boorish impression of Nabal. When he finally rejects David's request, Nabal does so indirectly, through a rhetorical question that emphasizes his sense of self-reliance and selfishness, conveyed through the accumulation of eight forms of the first person singular,[47] as well as through his arrogance and rudeness, expressed in the phrase "men who come from I don't know where" (25:11). After Nabal finishes speaking, the text states that the men turned around[48] and "told [David] all these words" (25:12). By using summarizing speech here instead of direct discourse, the author eliminates another potential opportunity to provide insight into Nabal's actions, through either an explicit statement by the messengers characterizing their conversation with Nabal or a more subtle suggestion of their impressions relayed through the repetition of Nabal's comments.

Of all the available means to explicate the metaphor, the most direct source of insight could have come from the speaker himself. The ambiguity about this metaphor would have been eliminated if Nabal's servant had supplemented his observation that "he swooped down on them" with a modifying clause specifying how Nabal resembled a raptor. Furthermore, he could have clarified the intended meaning of the utterance by placing a straightforward verb in parallelism with ויעט. However, the speaker withholds an interpretation of the metaphor. Another factor that complicates the interpretation of the metaphor concerns the speaker's role in the episode. When Nabal's servant selects a verb that elicits an image of a raptor swooping down on its prey, he expresses his own impression as a presumed witness to the exchange between Nabal and David's men. However, his choice of words is influenced by his personal opinion about his master, whom he later calls a "scoundrel" (25:17), as well as by his intent to motivate Abigail to take action and prevent the impending disaster. He is not an objective observer, but a participant in the drama, and his own life depends on his ability to persuade Abigail to intercede.

All of this leaves the audience with the exegetical task of determining where the associated commonplaces overlap. As White instructs,

---

[47] An observation made by Alter, *The David Story*, 154 and Bar-Efrat, *1 Samuel*, 315.

[48] Alter translates ויהפכו as "whirled around," suggesting that David's men physically responded to Nabal through their hasty retreat.

the point of the comparison also factors into the selection of a substitution for the primary and secondary sentences. In this case, the
hypothetical situation (a raptor swooping down on its prey) can intersect with the actual situation (a wealthy man rejecting a request for
a payback) in various ways. An author can make the point of the
analogy explicit through some modifying element, such as an adjective like "swiftly" or "aggressively." Here, however, the point of the
analogy remains ambiguous, allowing for a number of interpretive
possibilities. Raptors are well-known for their speed, particularly when
descending upon a desired target. For instance, hobbies can "appear
out of the blue . . . flying at tremendous speed," and the merlin "takes
prey by surprise, approaching in a fast, rocket-like flight low over
the ground." Similarly, when the booted eagle spots prey, it "stoops
at great speed with folded wings and long legs stretched forward."[49]
Job 9:26 compares days that pass swiftly to "an eagle rushing to its
food (כנשר יטוש עלי אכל)." Likewise, Hab 1:8 describes the approaching Chaldeans as "an eagle hurrying to eat (כנשר חש לאכול)." Perhaps
the metaphor implies that Nabal reacted quickly, refusing David's
request without stopping to consider the merit of the entreaty or the
potential ramifications of the rejection. This interpretation focuses
more on the outcome of the confrontation, the fact that Nabal rejects
David's request and does not give the messengers anything, even
though, as Nabal's lad goes on to explain, "they were good to us"
(25:15).

Mention of raptors also elicits images of a carnivore tearing into
its prey, ferociously ripping apart its victim: a pack of vultures rushing in to attack a carcass,[50] an eagle dissecting the limbs and organs
of a large mammal,[51] a falcon grabbing its prey with its talons and
then dismembering and eating it in flight.[52] Connecting this aspect
of the raptor's behavior with Nabal's treatment of David's men, the
metaphor suggests that Nabal verbally attacked the messengers, instinc-

---

[49] Forsman, 505, 495, 416 respectively.

[50] Brown, 119–120. Brown begins her chapter on hunting and feeding methods
with an interesting comment: "Considering that the way in which birds of prey kill
is perhaps the most spectacular and interesting aspect of their lives, it is surprising
how little we really know about how it is done . . . Most experienced observers of
birds of prey admit that they have seldom seen their subjects kill even by accident"
(105).

[51] Brown, 118–119.

[52] Forsman, 456. See previously cited biblical verses, like Job 39:30 or Prov 30:17.

tively or impulsively "tearing into" them. He takes his prey by surprise with the tone and tenor of his words. His haughty, derogatory
rhetorical questions function like talons, ripping apart the veneer of
politeness and camaraderie constructed by David. With his insults
and his refusal to give up any of his belongings to the "son of Jesse"
and the "men who come from I don't know where," Nabal delivers a crushing blow, an act that ultimately leads to his own demise.

After exploring the various possible points of intersection between
the actual and hypothetical situations, the task remains to complete
the substitution and create a primary sentence.

Primary vocabulary: (Nabal) x (David's men).[53]

In this case, replacing the variable proves more challenging than initially might be expected. Is there a "straightforward, literal" English
verb that can capture the different facets of the situation, the fact
that Nabal both rejects the men and speaks to them in a disdain-
ful fashion, and also convey the intended negative impression of
Nabal? Words like "attack" or "assail" are imprecise, for they encom-
pass both physical and verbal actions. A choice like "reject" or
"rebuff" refers too narrowly to one aspect of the multi-dimensional
episode. More colloquial expressions like "rip into" or "tear into" carry
figurative connotations, just like the metaphor being replaced.

Underlying the difficulty involved in selecting a fitting substitution
for the primary sentence is a debate about the paraphrasability of
metaphor. According to Johnson, from the time of the Greek philosophers to the mid-twentieth century, metaphor was viewed as "an
elliptical simile . . . which [could] be translated into a literal paraphrase
without any loss of cognitive content."[54] The renewed interest in
metaphor by modern-day scholars sparked a reconsideration of the
notion that metaphorical meaning "is reducible to literal paraphrase."[55]
John Searle, among others, asserts that "paraphrase is somehow inadequate." He concludes that something is lost when even "feeble
metaphors" like "Richard is a gorilla" or "Sally is a block of ice"
are translated into a paraphrase: "Richard is fierce, nasty, and prone
to violence" or "Sally is an extremely unemotional and unresponsive person." With more elaborate examples, he adds, "our sense of

---

[53] Parentheses indicate substitutions made for the unspecified subject and object.
[54] Johnson, 4.
[55] Johnson, 20.

the inadequacy of the paraphrase becomes more acute."[56] He poses the question: "Does every existing language provide us exact devices for expressing literally whatever we wish to express in any given metaphor?" Answering negatively, he concludes: "We often use metaphor precisely because there is no literal expression that expresses exactly what we mean."[57] Similarly, Lakoff and Turner reject the notion that a metaphor can be paraphrased in nonmetaphorical language, for such a position "fails to account for both the inferential and conceptualizing capacity of metaphor."[58]

The example at hand illustrates the challenges involved in trying to capture in nonfigurative language the nuances and complexity of both the actual situation and its various points of intersection with the hypothetical situation. This verse thus points out a weakness in White's methodology. In many cases, creating a primary sentence can become a frustrating or seemingly futile task, because often a single nonfigurative substitution fails to convey the suggestiveness and exegetical potential of the original metaphor. Nevertheless, in spite of its shortcomings, White's interpretive technique still provides a valuable heuristic device for unpacking the analogy embedded in the metaphor. The process demands precision in the analysis of the actual and hypothetical situations, as well as in the choice of language for the substitutions. These various steps force the interpreter to look closely at what is going on in the text and in the invoked image, and to scrutinize the interplay between the two. Upon what does a bird of prey descend and how does it consume its victims? How did Nabal react and how did his servant want to depict that reaction? White's heuristic procedure helps the interpreter gain a deeper understanding of the connection between the two elements in the analogy, the place where, according to Black, "the secret and the mystery of metaphor" reside.[59]

B. *1 Samuel 25:16*—חומה היו עלינו
("They were a wall around us both night and day")

The next metaphor seems, at first glance, fairly simple. However, as seen in the prior example, the steps of articulating the actual and hypothetical situations and creating primary and secondary sentences

---

[56] Searle, 87.
[57] Searle, 111.
[58] Lakoff and Turner, 120.
[59] Black, 73.

refine one's reading of the text, helping to uncover the potential richness and complexity found in even a simple metaphor. The procedure first involves drafting an initial sketch of the actual and hypothetical situations:

> Actual situation: David's men protected Nabal's shepherds continuously. Hypothetical situation: Some type of physical object or building material served as a wall around some other entity.

A process of refinement follows, as an attempt is made to determine what type of objects might have been employed to build a wall in ancient Israel. In order to ascertain this information, three resources present themselves: (i) Archaeology: What data have archaeologists uncovered about the types of building materials used for walls in ancient Israel? (ii) Textual evidence: Which biblical or extrabiblical passages provide information on walls in the biblical period? (iii) Context: Does the literary context offer explicit indicators or implicit clues about what would be the most appropriate substitution in this particular verse?

Archaeological evidence reveals a reliance on two main types of building materials, stones and sun-dried mud bricks, a choice dictated primarily by geographic and economic factors. Ronny Reich explains:

> Ancient Israel can be divided roughly into two regions as far as the use of building materials—stone and sun-dried brick—is concerned. This division is the result, in general, of the country's geomorphological division into mountainous regions, valleys, and wadi beds. Of course, stones can also be found in wadi beds, in the *kurkar* formations along the coast, and elsewhere beyond the mountain areas, and mud for bricks can be collected in the wadis of the mountainous areas as well. . . . A survey of the materials used to build buildings in various regions of the country shows that preference generally went to local resources, as people chose the most available and cheapest supplies.[60]

Walls, in particular, were constructed from either mud brick or stones, usually field stones or dressed stones with mortar applied to connect the building blocks.[61] Reflecting on the benefits of massive structures

---

[60] Ronny Reich, "Building Materials and Architectural Elements in Ancient Israel," in *The Architecture of Ancient Israel*, ed. Aharon Kempinski and Ronny Reich (Jerusalem: Israel Exploration Society, 1992), 1.

[61] Ehud Netzer, "Massive Structures: Processes in Construction and Deterioration" in *The Architecture of Ancient Israel*, ed. Aharon Kempinski and Ronny Reich (Jerusalem: Israel Exploration Society, 1992), 20.

in comparison to other structures like caves, tents, or huts, Ehud
Netzer writes that the function of a building "is to protect its inhabitants, man and livestock alike, from the elements . . . and offer physical protection against wild animals, thieves, etc."[62]

As discussed in the prior chapter, a survey of the biblical evidence
shows that the word חומה ("wall") in 1 Sam 25:14 usually refers to
city walls. The security of a city's inhabitants depended on the
strength and impenetrability of the lofty walls "in which [they] trust"
(Deut 28:52), though in times of tranquility a people might dwell
securely without walls, bars, or gates (Ezek 38:11). In spite of the
frequency with which the word חומה occurs, only a handful of verses
mention the building materials used for walls in ancient Israel. Most
notably, in Neh 3:34–35, Sanballat and Tobiah mock the attempt
to rebuild the walls of Jerusalem. One asks: "Can they revive those
stones out of the dust heaps, burned as they are?" The other replies:
"Also that which they are building, if a fox climbs it, he will breach
their stone wall."[63] Two citations containing the related term גדר
("wall" or "fence") also indicate the usage of stones for building an
enclosure: Prov 24:31 describes the ruined stone fence around a vineyard and Lam 3:9 speaks of God fencing in a person's way with
hewn stone. The word קיר ("wall") most often refers to the interior
or exterior wall of a building. Second Samuel 5:11 records that King
Hiram sent David cedar wood, carpenters, and stonemasons, "crafts-
men for the stone of the wall," to build his palace. Thus, whereas
archaeological evidence suggests that one plausibly could envision
David's men either as a wall of stone or mud brick, the biblical data
focus on stones, with no mention of bricks in connection with walls.

In terms of the literary context of 1 Samuel 25, the word "stone"
provides a fitting, clever substitution given the numerous references to stones in this chapter. For example, in v. 37, the narrator
states that Nabal "became a stone," and v. 29 speaks about a sling-

---

[62] Netzer, 17. He adds that buildings also maintain a comfortable temperature
and sometimes provide privacy.
[63] Nehemiah 2:8 refers to "a letter to Asaph, the keeper of the King's Park,
directing him to give [Nehemiah] timber for roofing the gatehouses of the temple
fortress and the city walls and for the house [he] shall occupy." Blenkinsopp speculates that the wood beams could have been used either as cross beams or rafters
for the roof or combined with ashlars in the building of the walls (*Ezra-Nehemiah*
[Philadelphia: The Westminster Press, 1988], 121–22). Jeremiah 1:18 and 15:20
envision Jeremiah as a bronze wall.

shot from which David's enemies will be flung, an implicit reference to stones. Thus, the information gathered from these three
avenues of investigation points to the following completion of the
secondary sentence:

> Secondary vocabulary: *Y* were a wall around us both night and day.[64]
> Secondary sentence: *The stones* were a wall around (Nabal's shepherds)
> both night and day.

At first glance, completing the primary sentence seems fairly easy, given
the primary function of walls to protect that which they surround.

> Primary vocabulary: They *x* us both night and day.
> Primary sentence: (David's men) *protected* (Nabal's shepherds) both night
> and day.

However, when one reexamines what David and Nabal's servant
actually say about the services performed by David's men on behalf
of Nabal's shepherds, questions arise as to whether "protect" proves
to be the most appropriate substitution.

    When David sends his messengers to Nabal, he prefaces his request
for some of Nabal's bounty with a recap of the way his men treated
Nabal's shepherds:

> A[Now, the shepherds who belong to you were with us.]
> B[We did not humiliate them,]
> C[and nothing of theirs was missing]
> D[all the time they were in Carmel.]
> E[Ask your servants, and they will tell you] (25:7–8).

Nabal's servant reiterates David's words, though he adds two statements, indicated with brackets, and he slightly alters and expands
the wording of the original message in other ways:[65]

---

[64] There are a number of different ways to distribute the primary, secondary,
and bifurcated vocabulary. For instance, the utterance could have been construed:
They were a wall around us both night and day. Such a division calls for a nominal substitution in the primary sentence, which is somewhat more limiting than
the present configuration. White does not provide detailed guidelines for separating the different types of vocabulary, though he acknowledges that a single utterance can be construed in a number of ways in his chapter on the "Ambiguity of
Construal" (37–55). For instance, as with the previously discussed sentence "Tolstoy
is a great infant," he shows how the following utterance can be construed in two
different ways: Language is a game with exact rules or Language is a game with
exact rules (55).

[65] Alter observes: "In keeping with the general practice of biblical dialogue, the

{And the men were very good to us,}
ʙ'[and we were not humiliated,]
ᴄ'[and we missed nothing]
ᴅ'[all the time we went around with them, during our being in the field.]
{They were a wall around us both night and day,}
ᴀ'[all the time of our being with them, tending the sheep.] (25:15–16)

Through the presence of two negative statements (B and C), David's speech emphasizes what did not transpire, but might have, when his men encountered Nabal's shepherds: They did not humiliate, or possibly harm,[66] Nabal's shepherds, and nothing was taken from the shepherds. While the passive wording of the second point (C) leaves the possible culprit unidentified, given the prior statement (B), the phrase insinuates that nothing was taken *by David's men*. So important is this point that David repeats it later, as part of his vow to decimate Nabal: "All in vain did I guard all that belonged to that fellow in the desert, and nothing was missing of all that he had" (25:21). According to Alter, "the message is that David's men did not permit themselves to take any of Nabal's flock, and perhaps also that as armed men they defended Nabal's people against marauders."[67] Nabal's servant supplements David's speech with two positive comments that frame the ambiguous central point: "and we were not humiliated, and we missed nothing" (25:15). Although the additional metaphor, "they were a wall around us both night and day" (25:16), implies that David's men protected the shepherds from outside bandits, neither speaker explicitly mentions any sort of threat from an outside force. Alter concludes about David's message: "But there is a certain ambiguity as to whether David was providing protection out of sheer good will or conducting a protection racket in order to get the necessary provisions for his guerilla band."[68]

---

servant recycles the language of David's message to Nabal . . . but amplifies it" (*The David Story*, 155).

[66] Interpretations of this verb vary, from verbs that imply a purely verbal interaction, such as "humiliate" (Alter), to those that suggest the possibility of a physical interaction, like "abuse" (McCarter), "harm" (*JPS, NRS*), "hurt" (Fox), or "molest" (*REB, NJB*).

[67] Alter, *The David Story*, 153.

[68] Alter, *The David Story*, 153. Berlin considers the implication of the verb נִפְקַד and posits that "perhaps the point is not that David did not steal from Nabal's shepherds, but that he did not demand payment from the shepherds for his services. Therefore his coming to Nabal for payment was appropriate and Nabal fails to see that" (personal communication).

Given the implications of the messages of David and the servant, does the substitution in the primary sentence, "They *protected* us," accurately capture the dynamics of the actual situation? While "protected" expresses the key function of walls in ancient Israel, does this verb best fit the narrative context? Is there another English term that will communicate the point that that David's men did not physically or verbally harm the servants themselves, as opposed to, or in addition to, preventing outsiders from doing so? Synonyms like "defend" or "guard" refer to the act of warding off assault or injury from another party, without conveying what Alter terms "the racketeering sense" of protection.[69] As noted above, it can be difficult to find a substitution for the primary sentence that expresses the multiple nuances of the metaphor.

A factor that complicates this discussion is the purpose of inserting the metaphorical utterance in the first place. When Nabal's lad supplements David's speech with this metaphor, he does not aim, necessarily, at a faithful description of the way David's men treated the shepherds. Instead, he seeks to influence Abigail's perception of the relationship. To paint a more positive picture of the encounter between David's men and Nabal's shepherds, the speaker begins with the straightforward remark, "And the men were very good to us" (25:15), a sentiment he echoes later with the metaphor, "They were a wall around us both night and day" (25:16). Thus, while the notion of "protection" may not precisely communicate the dynamics of the original episode, it does convey the speaker's intended point. Nabal's servant wants Abigail to believe that "they protected us both night and day." Although finding the ideal substitution may seem unattainable, sometimes requiring the exegete to settle for an inadequate paraphrase, the process proves valuable. Even in the case of a seemingly simple metaphor, White's approach prompts the reader to reexamine the text and refine one's interpretation of the metaphor and the larger narrative unit.

C. *1 Samuel 25:29b²*—*ואת נפש איביך יקלענה בתוך כף הקלע*
("*And He will sling the life of your enemies from the hollow of the sling*")

In this example, the hypothetical situation is clear and the secondary sentence can be constructed easily, in part because of the amount

---

[69] Alter, *The David Story*, 155.

of secondary vocabulary incorporated in the metaphor. In a case like v. 14 ("he swooped down on them"), the verb alone alludes to the hypothetical situation. Here, both the verb and the prepositional phrase point to the underlying analogy. When Abigail predicts the demise of David's enemies, she depicts God as a person flinging stones from a sling shot:[70]

> Conflated metaphor: He <u>will</u> <u>sling</u> the life of your enemies <u>from the hollow of the sling</u>.
>
> Hypothetical situation: A person slings stones from a slingshot.
>
> Secondary vocabulary: *Y* <u>will</u> <u>sling</u> *z* <u>from the hollow of the sling</u>.
> Secondary sentence: *A person* <u>will</u> <u>sling</u> *stones* <u>from the hollow of the sling</u>.

Had Abigail simply stated, "And the life of your enemies He will sling," the verb קלע in and of itself would have signaled this analogy, for the biblical passages containing the root ק.ל.ע. definitively link this lexeme with the act of hurling stones from a slingshot. The prepositional phrase confirms this interpretation and enhances the visual picture painted by the metaphor.

More difficult to determine, however, is the actual situation and the appropriate substitution for the primary sentence. When Abigail confidently declares that God will sling David's enemies from a slingshot, does she expect that God will eliminate the enemies altogether, by causing their deaths, or, instead, does she hope that God merely will harm or physically remove David's foes, thereby preventing them from being a menace to David? Clues to this query potentially may come from two sources: patterns of usage and narrative context. In the first case, is the root ק.ל.ע. used elsewhere in a way that makes the intended meaning in v. 29 clearer, perhaps through a parallel term or a comment that explicates the nuance of the expression? Only two verses use this root figuratively. In Jer 10:18, the verb refers to exile, not death, when God proclaims: "Look I am slinging out the

---

[70] William Propp sees a similar image in the exodus narrative. Commenting on the depiction of God hurling the Egyptian horses and drivers into the sea in Exod 15:1, Propp speculates: "In light of other similarities between 15:1b–18 and myths of divine combat, I would detect a variation upon a mythic motif: instead of subduing the Sea by shooting arrows into it, Yahweh subdues Egypt by shooting Egypt itself into the sea ... We might also assimilate the Egyptians, not to arrows, but to slingstones, since they are compared to stones in vv 5, 16" (*Exodus 1–18* [New York: Doubleday, 1998], 511).

dwellers of the land this time, and I will afflict them." Zechariah 9:15 describes how slingstones will "consume and conquer (וּאכלו וכבשו אבני קלע)," without specifying whether the image implies destruction or death. Secondly, does the surrounding context indicate the intended meaning of this utterance? Through two metaphors and the repetition of the word נפש, the verse sets up a contrast between the positive fate of David and the negative fate of his enemies. Abigail asserts: "When a person rises up to pursue you and to seek your life (נפשך), my lord's life (נפש) will be bound in the bundle of living with YHWH your God, and the life (נפש) of your enemies He will sling from the hollow of a sling" (25:29). The comment about David's fate carries its own uncertainties, as will be discussed in the next section, but it implies that David will survive the threat to his life posed by his foes. Since the utterance in v. 29b[1] expresses a hope that David will live, this suggests that v. 29b[2] concerns the death of the enemies. In addition, the presence of the noun נפש in the phrase "life of your enemies" points to the demise of David's foes. Nevertheless, to preserve the lingering ambiguity of the Hebrew, the English term "destroy" was selected as a substitute for the primary sentence. This verb carries a range of meanings, implying either death or ruin.

> Actual situation: God will eliminate David's enemies, by causing their death or by otherwise preventing them from menacing David.
>
> Primary vocabulary: (God) will *x* the life of your enemies.
> Primary sentence: (God) will *destroy* the life of your enemies.

D. *1 Samuel 25:29b[1]*—והיתה נפש אדני צרורה בצרור החיים את יי אלהיך
("May my lord's life be bound in the bundle of the living with/
by YHWH your God")

The other metaphoric utterance in v. 29 contains an even greater degree of uncertainty, for the actual situation remains rather vague. Abigail expresses the general hope that when a person rises up in pursuit of David, he will prevail over his foes and survive the threat to his life. In part, the ambiguity enters into the sentence through the prepositional phrase את יי אלהיך. What is the meaning of the preposition in this context, and how does the phrase function in relation to the rest of the utterance? If the preposition carries the standard sense of "with," denoting companionship, then the statement suggests that after David prevails over his enemy, he will be in the presence of or watched over by God.[71] On the other hand, if the preposition אֵת denotes agency, meaning "by," then the sentence implies that God is the subject, the One who will deliver David from his pursuers.[72] Or, instead of modifying the prior statement, the prepositional phrase may function in apposition to it, as a parallel or explanatory clause. In other words, perhaps being bound in the bundle of the living means that David will be "with YHWH." Do Abigail's words connote the sentiment: "May you be saved, i.e., placed *in the care of* YHWH your God,"[73] or "May you be saved *by* YHWH your God"?

Contributing to the confusion is the more significant conceptual crux: What does it mean to be "bound in the bundle of the living"? Scholars have proposed two hypotheses. In Job 14:16–17, Job hopes for the day when God will watch over him less vigilantly: "Then you would [not] count my steps, nor be alert for my sins. My guilt would be sealed in a bundle (חתם בצרור פשעי), you would coat over my iniquity."[74] In a 1967 commentary on Job, N. H. Tur-Sinai argues that צרור in Job 14:17 and 1 Sam 25:29 refers to a tied document. Marvin Pope explains:

> The "bundle" Tur-Sinai understood as relating to the tying and sealing of papyrus documents. Instruments thus bound and sealed were legally inaccessible to persons unauthorized to break the seal, and the content of the document could not be known until it was opened.[75]

Tur-Sinai's theory influenced McCarter's translation of v. 29: "my lord's life will be tied up in the Document of the Living." McCarter equates the expression "Document of the Living" with the "Book of

---

[71] *BDB* explains that the preposition אֵת denotes proximity and establishes proximity of companionship as the first category of meaning in the entry, meaning "together with." *DCH* lists 1 Sam 25:29 under section three of the entry for this preposition, meaning "under the control of, in the care of," as in Gen 43:8 or Jer 43:6. Section four lists Gen 5:22, 24 as an example in which אֵת carries the nuance of "in the presence of," as in the statement that Enoch walked "in the presence of" God.

[72] In Gen 30:33, אֵת with a passive participle indicates agency: גנוב הוא אתי, "stolen by me." Jöuon discusses "prepositions with a passive verb to indicate the author of the action"; he mentions ל, ב, מן in this regard, without including אֵת in the discussion (132c).

[73] A number of translations treat אֵת in a similar manner, as "in the care of the Lord" (*JPS*, *NAB*; cf. *NRS* and McCarter). Others translate אֵת as "with" (Fox, Alter).

[74] Translation from Marvin Pope, *Job* (New York: Doubleday & Company, Inc., 1973), 105.

[75] Pope, 109; N. H. Tur Sinai, *The Book of Job: A New Commentary*, rev. ed. (Jerusalem: Kiryath Sepher, 1967), 240–41.

the Living (ספר חיים)" in Ps 69:29 and notes: "This is the heavenly book in which all people are recorded; exclusion from it means death."[76]

A different interpretation incorporates A. Leo Oppenheim's discovery of an ancient Nuzi accounting system involving tally stones. In Kirkuk, archaeologists found an ovoid clay pouch with an inscription on the outside listing stones referring to the kind and condition of forty-eight sheep and goats; when originally unearthed, the pouch contained forty-eight small pebbles. Pope summarizes Oppenheim's conclusions:

> Oppenheim's study of the terminology applied to the stones referring to sheep and goats in the Nuzi documents indicates that the stones were "deposited," "removed," or "transferred" in, from, or to various receptacles to represent the actual movements or change in status of the animals in question. A series of receptacles must have been kept for pebbles representing every category of animals, so that when an animal died, was lost, or stolen, used for food, sacrifice, or transferred for shearing, pebbles representing each animal could be added, removed, or transferred to the appropriate containers. . . . By this simple operational device a constant and instant inventory would be available on the state and distribution of flocks.[77]

In a 1960 article, O. Eissfelt applied Oppenheim's research to the biblical references to the "bundle of the living," resulting in a new reading of v. 29:

> While there is no trace in the OT of the use of counting stones, which represented the living, or those destined for life, the words of Abigail to David, I Sam xxv 29, imply that the "bundle of the living" was thought of as containing stones which represented the living, or those destined for life . . . The figure is not of a bag of slingstones which are collected only to be hurled away, or of lots of stones to be shaken out, but rather of tally stones for accounting. The removal of stones from the bundle of the living . . . is the equivalent of blotting names from the book of the living, Ps 69:29.[78]

---

[76] McCarter, 399. Fox tentatively supports this hypothesis when he writes in a footnote to his translation, "bond of life," that " 'bond' here may mean a 'bundle,' i.e., a written document, as in the ancient idea of a 'Book of Life' " (126).

[77] Pope, 109–10. Pope notes that "various uses of this device still persist in the Near East" (110).

[78] Pope, 110, based on O. Eissfeldt, "Der Beutel der Lebendigen, alttestamentliche Erzahlungs und Dichtungsmotive in Lichte neuer Nuzi-texte," *Berichte uber die Verhandlungen der Sachsischen Akademie der Wissenschaften zu Leipzig*, Philologisch-historische Klasse, Band 105, Heft 6, Berlin, 1960. Theodor Gaster also cites Oppenheim's

Bar-Efrat and Alter adopt this interpretation. Explaining that the stones represent the living people listed in God's "book of life," Bar-Efrat concludes that the metaphoric expression means that David will enjoy long life.[79]

Each of these proposals yields a different hypothetical situation and secondary sentence, while the actual situation and primary sentence remain basically the same. The two interpretations agree on the basic message behind Abigail's imagery, restated as the actual situation:

> Actual situation: Abigail expresses confidence that David will survive the threat from his enemy and live.

The primary sentences below retain the ambiguity of the utterance through an indeterminate translation of the preposition; both contain the substitution, "to be saved" for the original "to be bound."

> Primary vocabulary—Interpretation 1: May my lord's life be x with/by YHWH your God.
> Primary vocabulary—Interpretation 2: May my lord's life be x with/by YHWH your God.
> Primary sentence—Interpretation 1: May my lord's life be *saved* with/by YHWH your God.
> Primary sentence—Interpretation 2: May my lord's life be *saved* with/by YHWH your God.

The main differences between the two readings of v. 29 manifest themselves in the hypothetical situations. The first interpretation envisions a person, likely a scribe, recording names on a scroll and then binding and sealing the papyrus document. Such an understanding equates the phrases "bound in a pouch" or "sealed in a pouch" in Job 14:17 with the notion of being inscribed in the "book of life," the scroll in which God records the names of the living. This line of reasoning assumes that the utterance in v. 29 in a sense functions elliptically: the statement, "to be bound in the bundle of life" presupposes that the person's name first has been recorded in the "book of life," a document called the "bundle of life" once it has been tied and sealed. Note, however, that references to the divine record of the living speak of people being inscribed or erased, but not bound.[80]

---

research, along with a few other proposals, in *Myth, Legend, and Custom in the Old Testament* (New York: Harper & Row, Publishers, 1969), 457–462.

[79] Bar-Efrat, *1 Samuel*, 321–22; also see Alter, *The David Story*, 158.

[80] Psalm 69:29 expresses the hope that the wicked will "be erased from the scroll

> Secondary vocabulary—Interpretation 1: <u>May my lord's</u> *y* <u>be</u> <u>bound in the bundle</u> of *a* <u>with/by</u> *z*.
> Secondary sentence—Interpretation 1: <u>May my lord's</u> *name* <u>be</u> <u>bound in the bundle</u> of *names* <u>by</u> *a scribe*.

The second interpretation conceives of God as a person using small stones to keep track of a particular object. More specifically, in line with Oppenheim's Nuzi artifact, the analogy invokes an image of a shepherd counting his animals by placing a pebble in a pouch for each living creature. Viewed in this manner, the verse resembles a number of biblical passages that depict God as a shepherd.[81]

> Secondary vocabulary—Interpretation 2: <u>May</u> *y* <u>be</u> <u>bound in the bundle of</u> *a* <u>with/by</u> *z*.
> Secondary sentence—Interpretation 2: <u>May</u> *stones* <u>be</u> <u>bound in the bundle of</u> *stones* <u>by</u>[82] *the shepherd*.

Given the other metaphors in this chapter that refer to stones, along with the weaknesses of the prior theory, this reading emerges as the more compelling hypothesis. Note, however, that no other biblical evidence corroborates the existence of such an accounting practice in ancient Israel.

Along with the difficulties involved in trying to reconstruct the hypothetical situation underlying this metaphor and the ambiguities in the actual situation, another challenge surfaces when applying White's method to this sentence: How does the construct phrase "bundle of the living" operate in this system? In the above analysis, "bound in the bundle of the living" was treated as one entity and replaced in the primary sentence with the variable *x*:

---

of life and not be inscribed with the righteous." In Exod 32:32–33, when Moses asks to be erased from the scroll God has written, God replies: "The one who has sinned against Me, him will I erase from My scroll." Isaiah 4:3 refers to those who remain in Jerusalem as "all who are inscribed for life in Jerusalem." Daniel 12:1 speaks about the rescue of "all who are found inscribed in the book." Malachi 3:16 describes a "scroll of remembrance (ספר זכרון)" written for God to record those who revere YHWH. For additional background on this subject, see Shalom Paul, "Heavenly Tablets and the Book of Life," *JANES* 5 (1973) 345–353.

[81] See Ps 23:1; 80:2; Isa 40:11; Hos 4:16; Gen 48:15; Mic 7:14; Ezek 34.

[82] In both cases, the prepositional phrase את ה' / אלהיך poses problems in the reconstruction of the secondary sentence. "With" implies that after the scribe records and seals the document or the shepherd places the stones in the pouch, the "bundle" is in his care; he may also have been the agent of these actions, but the syntax does not specify this, focusing more on possession. "By" designates the scribe or shepherd as the agent responsible for performing the act, a reading supported by Gen 30:33 and more logical in this context.

Primary vocabulary—Interpretation 2: <u>May</u> <u>my lord's life</u> <u>be</u> *x* <u>with/by</u>
<u>YHWH your God</u>.

Such a construal makes no attempt to separate the primary and secondary vocabularies woven together in the phrase "<u>bundle</u> <u>of</u> <u>the</u>
<u>living</u>," nor to incorporate its primary vocabulary, "the living," into
the surrounding primary sentence. In the secondary sentence below,
"the living" has been replaced by the variable *b*, but the phrase,
"the living," has not been retained in the primary vocabulary.

Secondary vocabulary—Interpretation 2: <u>May</u> *a* <u>be</u> <u>bound in the bun-</u>
<u>dle</u> <u>of</u> *b* <u>with/by</u> *c*.

A different approach would have been to parse the utterance as
follows:

Primary vocabulary—Interpretation 2a: <u>May</u> <u>my lord's life</u> <u>be</u> *x* <u>in the</u>
y <u>of</u> <u>the living</u> <u>with/by</u> <u>YHWH your God</u>.
Secondary vocabulary—Interpretation 2a: <u>May</u> *a* <u>be</u> <u>bound in the bun-</u>
<u>dle</u> <u>of</u> *b* <u>with/by</u> *c*.
Primary sentence—Interpretation 2a: <u>May</u> <u>my lord's life</u> <u>be</u> *saved* <u>in</u>
<u>the</u> *presence* <u>of</u> <u>the living</u> <u>with/by</u> <u>YHWH your God</u>.
Secondary sentence—Interpretation 2a: <u>May</u> *stones* <u>be</u> <u>bound</u> <u>in the</u>
<u>bundle</u> <u>of</u> *stones* <u>by</u> *the shepherd*.

While this approach creates two grammatically equivalent sentences
and preserves all the elements of the original sentence, the resulting
primary sentence proves awkward. What does it mean to "be saved
in the presence of the living"? More significantly, this reading distorts the metaphor's message. The point is not that other people will
witness as David is saved from his enemies, but that David will survive and be counted among the living. The challenges involved in
construing a construct expression surface in the following example
as well.

E. *1 Samuel 25:31*—ולא תהיה זאת . . . למכשול לב לאדני
("<u>Do not let</u> <u>this</u> <u>be</u> . . . a <u>stumbling block of the heart</u> <u>for my lord</u>")

Because of the questionable status of the first half of v. 31 ("let this
not be for you a tottering"), this discussion will focus on the second
half of the utterance: "Let this not be . . . an obstacle of the heart
for my lord." Here, Abigail subtly warns David that if he murders
Nabal and his men, then this act may prove detrimental when he
later becomes king (v. 30). As in v. 29, the actual situation proves

somewhat ambiguous, for the metaphor implies any sort of unspecified "downfall," such as loss of power, illness, or death. Relevant biblical citations do not clarify the situation, for while certain verses specify that those who stumble over an obstacle shall die[83] or fall and be injured,[84] most others leave the outcome of the person who stumbles uncertain.[85] In terms of the larger narrative context, at a later point in the David story, committing murder does prove fatal; but the murder of Uriah and the adulterous affair with Bathsheba result in the death of David and Bathsheba's child, not the loss of David's own life (2 Sam 12:13–14). The indeterminate nature of the actual situation necessitates finding an equally vague substitution for the primary sentence. "Detriment" proves a fitting selection because of its unspecified meaning, referring to any cause of loss or damage.[86]

> Primary vocabulary: Do not let (murder) be . . . a *x* for my lord.
> Primary sentence: Do not let (murder) be . . . a *detriment* for my lord.

In comparison to the ambiguities in the actual situation, the hypothetical situation evoked by this metaphor is fairly straightforward. The secondary vocabulary elicits the image of an individual walking on a pathway who encounters an object on the ground that temporarily impedes or blocks his forward movement on the pathway, causing the person to trip, stumble, and perhaps fall. What type of object might one encounter on the road as an obstacle? The majority of relevant citations do not mention the specific type of object that constitutes a מכשול.[87] A few verses describe one person stumbling

---

[83] Ezek 3:20 ("when I put a stumbling block before him, he shall die") and Jer 6:21 ("I am giving to this people stumbling blocks, and they will stumble on them; fathers and sons together, neighbor and friend shall perish").

[84] Isaiah 8:15; Prov 24:16 states: "Seven times the righteous person falls and gets up, but the wicked stumble with (one) misfortune."

[85] For instance, Ezek 44:12 states that the Levites "will bear their punishment" for their "stumbling block of iniquity"; Ps 119:165 contrasts the absence of a stumbling block with the presence of well-being.

[86] Other possibilities like "threat," "harm," or "peril" fit awkwardly in the sentence. Had the sentence been construed differently, as "Do not let (murder) *x* my lord," then more options would work, such as "threaten" or "jeopardize." Assigning the verb "to be," the article "a," and the preposition "for" to the secondary vocabulary, as opposed to marking these features as bifurcated, allows for more freedom in selecting potential substitutions; but such a construal is not grammatically analogous to the original utterance. The approach taken here has been to try to preserve the grammatical structure by construing as much of the sentence as possible in bifurcated form and then to alter the construal if difficulties develop when attempting to fill in the sentences.

[87] See, for example, Lev 19:14 or Ps 119:165.

over another person, dead or alive.[88] Another group of passages
points to rocks as a likely stumbling block. Isaiah 8:14 refers to a
צור מכשול ("rock of stumbling") which parallels אבן נגף ("stone of
striking"). Isaiah 57:14 contains instructions to clear a road by remov-
ing all obstacles (הרימו מכשול); Isaiah 62:10 specifies that clearing a
road involves the removal of stones (סקלו מאבן). Psalm 91 assures
the addressee that God will appoint guardian angels "to guard you
on all your paths" and to "carry you in their hands lest your foot
strikes a stone (פן תגף באבן רגלך)" (Ps 91:11–12). Such verses support the following substitution in the secondary sentence:

> Secondary vocabulary: Do not let y be . . . an obstacle of the z for my
> lord.
> Secondary sentence: Do not let *a rock* be . . . an obstacle of the z for
> my lord.

The complex part of this metaphor comes in the construal of the
phrase "obstacle of the heart," an issue encountered in the prior
example. Analyzing this phrase does not present difficulties in terms
of the hypothetical situation or secondary sentence, for the metaphor
clearly refers to an obstacle encountered by the feet:

> Secondary vocabulary: obstacle of the z
> Secondary sentence: obstacle of the *feet*

This substitution fits smoothly into the larger secondary sentence:

> Secondary sentence: Do not let *a rock* be . . . an obstacle of the *feet* for
> my lord.

However, filling in the primary sentence proves more challenging,
both when considering the phrase in isolation and when attempting
to incorporate it into the original primary sentence.

> Primary vocabulary: y of the heart

Given the range of meanings of the word לב ("heart"),[89] what is the
actual situation to which the primary sentence refers? Any number

---

[88] For instance, Jeremiah speaks of two warriors stumbling against each other
and falling down (Jer 46:12); also see Lev 26:37. Nahum depicts a gruesome scene
in which corpses pile up and "they stumble over bodies" (Nah 3:3).

[89] As will be discussed in greater detail in the following section, the word לב
("heart") denotes various parts of the anatomy as well as the seat of intelligence
and emotion.

of possible punishments might befall David should he kill Nabal. The vaguely worded warning could imply a physical ramification, an "illness of the heart," an emotional response, such as "grief of the heart," or a range of noncorporeal consequences, like loss of political power for David or his descendants. As seen in v. 29, construct phrases like "bundle of the living" or "stumbling block of the heart" do not operate easily in White's system. While this stands out as another weakness in the application of White's method to biblical narrative, the awkward integration of such phrases does not overshadow the insights uncovered in the process of employing White's approach to biblical metaphor.

F. *1 Samuel 25:37b[1]*—וימת לבו בקרבו
("And his heart died within him")

The diverse denotations of the noun לב ("heart") complicate the construal of this utterance. H. L. Ginsberg differentiates between the strictly anatomical senses and the not strictly anatomical senses of לב and the related noun לבב. The first category includes various body parts, such as the breast and throat, as well as cases where "more often it merely conveys the general idea of 'the insides, the interior of the body.'" Ginsberg notes: "Even where the word *lev* clearly refers to something inside the body cavity, it does not always mean specifically the heart."[90] Regarding the second category, he explains: "It is the *lev(av)* that figures most often in references to the inner life, both emotion and—and this is its special sphere—intellectual."[91] As a result of the dominant use of these terms to denote "mind, thinking, intention, understanding" and "feelings,"[92] Ginsberg contends that "a faithful English translation" should substitute "mind" or sometimes "spirit" for "heart," or often "not render the noun at all."[93]

In what sense is the word לב being used in the verse under consideration? Bar-Efrat understands לב as a reference to the brain, which suffers from paralysis after Nabal hears what transpired at

---

[90] H. L. Ginsberg, "Heart," *Encyclopaedia Judaica* 8:8.
[91] Ginsberg, 8.
[92] *DCH* article (s.v. לב) divides its entry into five categories: (1) mind, thinking, intention, understanding; (2) feelings, such as joy, grief, fear, courage, and anger; (3) will, inclination, disposition, personality; (4) physical heart, chest; (5) middle.
[93] Ginsberg, 8.

night and results in silence.[94] Alter also interprets the noun anatomically, as a reference to the cardiac muscle or possibly the brain. He posits that "the terrifying information that David had been on his way . . . with four hundred armed men intent on mayhem triggers a paralyzing heart attack, or perhaps, a stroke."[95] Ginsberg acknowledges that "when *lev(av)* is mentioned alone it is often hard to decide whether the underlying physical concept is specifically the heart or the inwards generally." However, he points out that "the Bible never mentions about the *lev(av)* anything that is literally physical, such as a heartbeat; neither does it ever mention any literal pain or ailment of it."[96] Thus, while the narrative context allows an anatomical rendering of לֵב, the usage of this noun elsewhere in the Tanakh suggests that the expression may refer to a psychic response, meaning that Nabal "lost all his nerve" and "was defeated."[97] The man who previously displayed such bravado when he glibly dismissed David's request now falls silent,[98] not because he is physically incapacitated, but because he is stunned to learn of the ramifications of his actions.

Can the application of White's heuristic device provide insight into this expression? The readings reviewed above result in different translations of the noun לֵב:

1. His <u>brain</u> <u>died</u> <u>within him</u>.
2. His <u>heart</u> <u>died</u> <u>within him</u>.
3. His <u>courage</u> <u>died</u> <u>within him</u>.

These translations yield variant primary sentences, but a single secondary sentence:

Primary sentence 1: <u>His brain</u> *malfunctioned* <u>within him</u>.
Primary sentence 2: <u>His heart</u> *stopped* <u>within him</u>.
Primary sentence 3: <u>His courage</u> *ceased* <u>within him</u>.

Secondary sentence 1–3: *The human being* <u>died</u>.

---

[94] Bar-Efrat, *1 Samuel*, 324.

[95] Alter, *The David Story*, 160. He surmises: "Abigail gives the distinct appearance of counting on her husband's cowardice and on a bad heart she might have been aware of from previous manifestations of ill health. If this assumption is correct, she would be using her knowledge of his physical frailty to carry out the tacit contract on his life—bloodlessly, with God Himself left to do the deed" (160).

[96] Ginsberg, 8.

[97] This reading was suggested by Berlin (personal communication) and is reflected in the *JPS* and *NAB* translations, "his courage died within him."

[98] Silence is indicted by the following remark, "And he became a stone."

All three cases involve personification, which Lakoff and Turner characterize as "metaphors through which we understand other things as people." They explain:

> As human beings, we can best understand other things in our own terms. Personification permits us to use our knowledge about ourselves to maximal effect, to use insights about ourselves to help us comprehend such things as forces of nature, common events, abstract concepts, and inanimate objects.[99]

Recognizing this utterance as an instance of personification confirms its identity as a metaphor, but does not resolve the exegetical ambiguity. Regardless of the perceived denotation of the noun לב, the expression involves an analogy, for it compares an actual situation (either the blockage of blood flow to the heart or brain or the abrupt absence of courage) to a hypothetical situation (the complete and permanent cessation of life).

G. *1 Samuel 25:37b²*—וְהוּא הָיָה לְאָבֶן (*"And he became a stone"*)

Does Nabal experience a debilitating, but not fatal, medical condition that results in a stillness of the body, such as a heart attack, stroke, or coma? Or, instead, does he find himself bereft of the confidence and verve exhibited earlier, as manifested by his silence? These two interpretations yield two slightly different primary sentences:

> Primary sentence 1: (Nabal) became *still.*
> Primary sentence 2: (Nabal) became *silent.*[100]

In either case, finding an appropriate substitution for the secondary sentence proves challenging. The transformational element of the utterance poses part of the problem. What "becomes" a stone? One could complete the secondary sentence as follows:

> Secondary vocabulary: *Υ* became a stone.
> Secondary sentence: *Minerals* became a stone.

However, this sentence does not capture the thrust of the analogy. In terms of the hypothetical situation, the utterance compares Nabal to a stone, something motionless and unresponsive.

> Hypothetical situation: A stone is inert.[101]

---

[99] Lakoff and Turner, 72.

[100] Note that the substitution is not exactly grammatically analogous since "still" and "silent" are adjectives, not a noun.

[101] A number of biblical verses highlight this aspect of a stone. When Habakkuk

The focus of the comparison is not on the transformational aspect, which is introduced through the bifurcation of the verb "became"; instead, the point of the statement is that Nabal resembles a stone.[102]

The dissonance between the hypothetical situation and the secondary sentence raises a question as to how effectively White's approach applies to metaphorical predications, metaphors in the form "*A* is a *B*." White addresses this issue in an appendix entitled "Metaphorical Predication." Convinced that any complete account of metaphor should be able to account for metaphorical predications just like any other metaphors, he insists on the need to show that his method of constructing primary and secondary sentences works with such simple metaphors. He continues:

> What is more, such argument would need to show not only that it was technically possible to apply it, but that using this particular device for bringing out the structure of the metaphor provided the most fruitful way to explicate its significance. The demonstration that it was possible to display a metaphorical predication as a result of conflating primary and secondary sentences would be empty unless such a demonstration also showed that such a display in some way reflected the actual ideas that gave rise to the metaphor.[103]

To test his approach, White examines Aristotle's statement, "Achilles is a lion," which Homer expands and develops in the *Iliad*. Noting that this metaphorical predication rests on the analogy: "Achilles is to the human race as a lion is to the animal kingdom," he claims:

> At the linguistic level, this is tantamount to seeing the metaphorical predication as the result of conflating the primary and secondary sentences, "Achilles is a ruthless man of war," say, and "Ferdinand is a lion."[104]

White concludes with a confident assertion that even metaphorical predications fit with in the scope of his theory of metaphor.[105]

---

chastises those who worship idols, he declares: "Woe, you who say to wood, 'Wake up,' 'awaken' to inert stone (לְאֶבֶן דּוּמָם)" (Hab 2:19). Similarly, Exod 15:16 speaks of the nations who are "still as stone (יִדְּמוּ כָּאָבֶן)" when they witness God's might. Job 41:16 describes the Leviathan's heart as "cast (hard) as stone, and cast (hard) as the nether millstone." Twice Ezekiel contrasts a heart of stone (לֵב הָאֶבֶן) with a heart of flesh (Ezek 11:19; 36:26).

[102] If the verb is not retained in the secondary sentence, then the sentence reads: *x* <u>a stone</u>. Such a construal does not retain enough of a syntactic structure to reconstruct a hypothetical situation or a secondary sentence.

[103] White, 236.

[104] White, 245.

[105] White, 245.

Nevertheless, his comments do not provide practical suggestions for dealing effectively with a case like the narrator's statement, "And he became a stone."

H. *1 Samuel 25:3*—קשה והאיש *("The man was hard")*

In order to fit the working definition of a metaphor, the narrator's statement that Nabal "was hard" must exhibit an anomalous quality as well as an underlying analogy. To evaluate this aspect of the utterance, White's method will be employed to uncover and analyze possible comparisons. Taken out of context, one could argue that the utterance, "The man was hard," refers to a myriad of objects: a water jug, a metal tray, a tree trunk; all of these, and more, could be regarded as "hard." Given the lack of specificity, how can one identify a specific analogy invoked by this verse? In this particular literary setting, one hypothetical situation naturally comes to mind:[106]

> Primary vocabulary: The man was *x*.
> Secondary vocabulary: The *y* was hard.
>
> Primary sentence: The man was *obdurate*.
> Secondary sentence: The *stone* was hard.

Given the fact that Nabal "becomes a stone" at the end of this episode (v. 37), and considering the explicit and implicit references to stones in other verses (vv. 16, 29, 31), a stone stands out as an appropriate substitution. Thus, while the sentence, on its own, proves too vague to evoke a distinct analogy, the other metaphors in the chapter color its interpretation and point to an underlying comparison.

In a different context, however, one might analyze the statement differently and reach a contrary conclusion about its metaphoric status. For example, if the sentence appeared in the midst of a passage that repeatedly used the phrase ערף קשה ("hard-necked") to describe a stubborn individual, one would likely read the utterance "The man was hard" as a reference to the person having a hard or stiff neck. In that case, the statement functions metonymically, not metaphorically. Instead of comparing the man to something else, the exterior posture of the body signals an interior trait or condition.[107] The contrast between these two different interpretations shows the

---

[106] Unlike v. 39, the predicational form of this utterance does not hinder the construal of the sentence.

[107] Chapter five addresses the distinction between metaphor and metonymy.

importance of applying a text-based approach to metaphor, one that considers how a figurative utterance functions in a specific context.

III. CONCLUSION: THE HOW AND WHY OF METAPHOR

So far, this study has explored how metaphors operate. Through a close reading of 1 Samuel 25, chapters two and three have presented a means of identifying metaphor by establishing the presence of a semantic anomaly and unpacking its underlying analogy. The next chapter confronts the question of why writers and speakers utilize metaphor. If one can say, "God will destroy the life of your enemies" instead of "God will sling the life of your enemies from the hollow of the sling" or, "They protected us" instead of "They were a wall around us," why not communicate the desired sentiment in a more direct manner? Since even a seemingly simple metaphor can entail a considerable degree of complexity and ambiguity, why not speak in primary sentences instead of metaphoric utterances? Why introduce uncertainty or multiplicity of meaning and thus risk miscommunication?

CHAPTER FOUR

INTERPRETATION OF BIBLICAL METAPHORS:
THE EFFECT OF METAPHOR

I. Investigating the Effect of Metaphor

Starting with the earliest discussions of metaphor, writers have addressed the issue of its potential effects. In *The Art of Rhetoric*, Aristotle considers the potential impact of the orator's use of language on a given audience. He provides two explanations for the "pleasantness" inherent in metaphor. First, he ascribes to metaphor an "exotic" quality, since metaphors should be drawn "from related but not obvious things."[1] He observes: "Men in fact are affected in the same way by [rhetorical] style as by foreigners and compatriots. So the discourse must be made to sound exotic, for men are admirers of what is distant."[2] Secondly, the pleasantness of metaphor comes from its instructional aspect, for a speaker "produces understanding and recognition through the generic similarity" established between two elements, such as old age and a reed.[3] Aristotle contrasts a well-crafted metaphor, which can provide clarity, knowledge, wit, and vividness,[4] to an inappropriate metaphor, which can cause "frigidity" and prove "unpersuasive."[5]

Subsequent scholars have highlighted similar features, noting that metaphor can enhance the intellect, influence attitudes, and aesthetically please the audience. For instance, Peter Newmark identifies two main purposes of metaphor. The first "is to describe entities (objects or persons), events, qualities, concepts or states of mind more comprehensively, concisely, vividly, and in a more complex way than is possible by using literal language."[6] The second "is to

---

[1] Aristotle, 239. He cautions that metaphors "are also unclear if they are drawn from too far afield" (223).

[2] Aristotle, 218.

[3] Aristotle, 235.

[4] Aristotle explains that "vividness is produced by things that indicate actuality," by "making the inanimate animate" (238).

[5] Aristotle, 223.

[6] Peter Newmark, "The Translation of Metaphor," in *The Ubiquity of Metaphor*, ed. R. Dirven and W. Paprotte (Amsterdam: John Benjamins, 1985), 295.

please, sometimes aesthetically, to entertain, to amuse."[7] Similarly, Toolan discusses a number of benefits achieved through the skillful use of metaphor, including the fact that "in appropriate circumstances it may be entertaining and carry more influence."[8] He introduces an additional element when he asserts that metaphor can enhance the interpersonal affinity between the speaker and addressee. He concludes that people utilize creative metaphors "for purposes of enhanced expressivity, rapport, and understanding—in short, precisely the reasons for using language generally."[9]

Likewise, Agha approaches metaphor as a rhetorical figure, an instrument for acting upon or interacting with people and a means for conveying information in an engaging and persuasive way. He observes that metaphor "creatively transforms the hearer's sense of the situation described or denoted." Metaphor produces an interactional effect that can be seen subsequently in a text, "both in the represented dialogue and at the level of the effects on the reader." He insists that "the real task of analysis is not merely to catalogue the cases of metaphor, but to understand the dramatic and rhetorical effects of the implicit meanings conveyed by tropes."[10]

A number of biblical scholars also emphasize the rhetorical effects of metaphor. For instance, Nielsen outlines two functions of imagery in the Bible, one "informative" and the other "performative." In the first case, she views metaphor as "a tool to pass on information."[11] In the second, she asserts that imagery "helps influence the hearer's attitude and (if successful) his actions."[12] Darr adopts Nielsen's notion of a dichotomy between the informative and performative aspects of figurative language, explaining that not only does imagery communicate ideas, but it also "elicit[s] participation on the part of the readers or hearers."[13] She describes figurative language as "strategic speech," meaning language that "invit[es] readers to different perceptions of reality"[14] and persuades them to change their attitudes and actions.[15] Darr links her approach to figurative language to that

---

[7] Newmark, 295.
[8] Toolan, 66.
[9] Toolan, 92.
[10] Agha, personal correspondence.
[11] Nielsen, 56.
[12] Nielsen, 56.
[13] Darr, 43.
[14] Darr, 36.
[15] Darr, 43.

of J. Cheryl Exum, who emphasizes that literary tropes and rhetorical figures "are not just embellishments but rather mediums of persuasion." Exum adds: "They are forceful ways of making a point; they center attention and involve the listener in making essential connections necessary for interpretation."[16]

To what extent do these writings correlate with the analysis of 1 Samuel 25? Can a close reading of this chapter confirm that the metaphors in this narrative unit produce the types of effects proposed by the preceding scholars? When considering the potential impact of figurative language in a narrative, one must evaluate the interactional consequences that operate in several spheres: within the story and between the text and its receptors.

II. The Effects of the Metaphors in 1 Samuel 25

A. *Metaphor in Dialogue and Its Effects on the Characters*

When used in dialogue, one can examine the impact of a particular metaphor on the other characters in the narrative. Indications of tropic effect can be determined by studying subsequent turns of the dialogue as well as the narrator's description of resultant responses and ensuing action. Five of the eight metaphoric utterances in 1 Samuel 25 occur in the context of direct discourse: in the speech by Nabal's servant to Abigail and in Abigail's lengthy plea to David. In both cases, the surrounding narrative context provides sufficient evidence to demonstrate the effectiveness of the speakers' use of metaphor.

In the first speech, the text does not contain a verbal response by Abigail; she answers the speaker through her actions. According to Alter, a common practice in biblical narrative "is simply to cut off one speaker in a dialogue without comment," as seen in 1 Sam 25:18.[17] Instead of positioning the addressee as the speaker in a subsequent turn of the dialogue or summarizing the remaining exchange between Abigail and the servant, the storyteller speeds the drama along by switching to a narrative account of Abigail's hurried preparations. Through the alacrity of her motions[18] and the quantity of

---

[16] Exum, 331. She observes that the study of the effects of tropes is a neglected aspect of biblical studies (331).

[17] Alter, *The Art of Biblical Narrative*, 79.

[18] Responding quickly is a hallmark of this biblical character. The verb מהר ("to

goods she gathers, the narrator signals that Abigail has heeded the servant's words and decided "what [she] must do" (v. 17) to prevent the unspecified evil from transpiring.

In this case, the metaphors fulfill both informative and performative functions. They provide background knowledge about the prior events, informing Abigail about Nabal's harsh treatment of David's messengers and the favorable role of David's men in the wilderness. In addition, the metaphors influence Abigail's attitudes and actions, as seen in her decision to intervene and in the negative way she characterizes Nabal when speaking to David (vv. 25–26).

After Abigail finishes speaking to David, he responds verbally, making it clear in two successive speeches that she has convinced him not to fulfill his vow of revenge. First, he blesses her for restraining him (v. 33). Next, he declares to Abigail, who earlier had flung herself on her face (v. 23): "I have lifted up your face" (v. 35), meaning that he has granted her petition.[19] Emphasizing his determination not to carry out his previous plans, and alluding to the risk inherent in Abigail's daring actions, David boasts that had God not kept him from harming Abigail, "there would not have been left to Nabal by morning's light a single pisser against the wall" (v. 34). David reaffirms the persuasiveness of the speech and its speaker later in the narrative when he seeks to make Abigail his wife (vv. 39–40). David's response, in words and deeds, proves that Abigail's speech achieved its performative aims. In terms of its informative function, instead of simply communicating data, she uses her metaphors to predict future events and warn David of the potential ramifications of his actions. Since the chapter ends with Abigail becoming David's wife (v. 42), the story supports Toolan's claim that metaphor can enhance the "interpersonal affinity" and "rapport" between speaker and addressee.

In both of these exchanges, the speakers use multiple metaphors, two in the first speech and three in the second, in conjunction with a range of other rhetorical devices. Nabal's lad marshals a number of more subtle rhetorical strategies intended to convince Abigail to

---

hurry") occurs in 25:18, as well in vv. 23, 34, 42, including when Abigail first greets David and when she later departs to become his wife. In contrast, she does not rush to speak to Nabal, but patiently waits until morning to inform Nabal of her encounter with David (v. 36).

[19] Here David uses a familiar metonymic expression, the type of utterance that will be explored in chapters five and six.

try to avert disaster. For instance, he sets up a stark contrast between David, who sends messengers to "greet" his master (לברך, from the root meaning "to bless"), and Nabal, who "swoops down" on them (v. 14). Whereas David's men "were very good" to the shepherds (v. 15), Nabal "is a scoundrel" (v. 17). In order to emphasize the praise-worthy nature of the treatment by David and his men, he supple-ments David's message with both a straightforward positive assessment ("They were very good to us") and a metaphor ("They were a wall around us"). Through these additions, the servant bolsters the merit of David's request for compensation, mention of which he omits from his speech. The more he makes David's request seem reason-able and well-deserved, the more he makes Nabal's reaction seem unfair and outrageous. Furthermore, he does not dictate to his mas-ter's wife how to eliminate the impending evil; instead, he leaves it up to the woman with "a good mind" (v. 3) to find her own solution.

When Abigail finally meets up with David, she too executes a well-crafted rhetorical plan. Before she even begins speaking, she communicates her submissive attitude through her obsequious ges-tures. Whereas Nabal figuratively "swoops down" on the messengers, Abigail literally flings herself at David's feet and bows low to the ground (vv. 23–24). She continues this deferential posture through her language, by repeatedly referring to David, often in the third person, as her "lord" and herself as David's "servant."[20] Alter praises the rhetorical tactics found in the first two verses of her remarks:

> The shrewdness of her extraordinary speech begins with the very first syllable she utters. She immediately takes all the blame on herself, though in the next breath she will be sure to transfer it heartily to her contemptible husband . . . It is hard to think of another instance in literature in which a wife so quickly and so devastatingly interposes distance between herself and her husband. She rapidly denounces her spouse and then counterposes herself ("And as for me," *wa'ani*) as a person who has no part in the rude rejection of David's emissaries.[21]

After initially assuming all blame and then absolving herself of any responsibility for her husband's behavior, Abigail indirectly tells David how to act. For example, as part of an oath, she praises "YHWH who

---

[20] She repeatedly uses deferential language when she calls David "lord" twelve times in eight verses (25:24–31) and figuratively refers to herself as "servant" six times: אמה five times (25:24, 25, 28, 31) and שפחה once (25:27).
[21] Alter, *The David Story*, 156.

kept you from coming into blood guilt with your own hand deliv-
ering you" (v. 26),[22] phrasing what she hopes will transpire in the
future in the past tense, as a completed deed. Further on, she turns
a plea for forgiveness into a prediction of God's imminent benefac-
tions, which she claims will given in part because "no evil will be
found in you" (v. 28). Similarly, at the end of her speech, Abigail
diplomatically disguises a warning of what is at stake should David
seek revenge as an expression of confidence that blood "shed for no
cause" will not stain the career of the future monarch (v. 31).[23]

Given the array of rhetorical devices used by both speakers, to
what extent can the effectiveness of their speeches be tied directly
to their use of metaphors? Although the metaphors work in concert
with a number of other tropes and literary devices, they stand out
as the more prominent rhetorical features. First of all, both speakers employ multiple metaphors in their discourses. Secondly, and
more significantly, metaphors like these appear fairly infrequently in
biblical narrative, which is marked by its terse, "conventionally delimited language."[24] In light of the norms of narrative style in the Bible,
such metaphors assume greater prominence and exert a more forceful rhetorical effect.

B. *The Effect of Metaphor on the Narrative Audience*

1. *Assumptions about Audience*

Metaphors found in dialogue and narration produce interactional
effects on the audience as well. The notion of a biblical audience
involves two main components: an ancient Israelite audience con-

---

[22] The subsequent chapters discuss the metonymic use of hands in biblical
narrative.

[23] David also employs a variety of rhetorical devices in his message to Nabal. For
instance, in his greeting to Nabal he repeats the word שלום three times, expressing
the hope that Nabal, Nabal's house, and all that is Nabal's will "fare well" (v. 6).
In doing so, he not only commences his speech in a solicitous manner, but he also
calls attention to the reason for his mission: Nabal's present prosperity. David
reminds Nabal of the prior services provided by his men, the basis upon which he
makes his request. Like Abigail, David uses deferential language, referring to his
messengers as Nabal's "servants" and to himself as Nabal's "son" (v. 8). Yet several key differences distinguish David's speech from that of Nabal's lad and Abigail.
Most notably, David does not speak to Nabal directly, and he does not utilize any
metaphors. Given the negative reception to his request, one can only wonder if
David's efforts might have proven more persuasive if he had added a cleverly crafted
metaphor.

[24] Alter, *Genesis*, xxv.

temporaneous with the author and a later reader. How might the average Israelites listening to the story of David, Nabal, and Abigail have responded to its figurative language? How would they have understood Abigail's mention of the "bundle of the living" (v. 29)? What associated commonplaces would have come to mind upon hearing that Nabal "swooped down" on David (v. 14)? How would they have envisioned the scene in which Nabal's "heart died within him and he became a stone" (v. 37)? Darr stresses the importance of trying to "recover the complex associations surrounding a trope's term in the world of ancient Israel" using biblical and extrabiblical sources.[25] While such tools can provide some perspective on how language was employed and understood long ago, answers to questions about tropic interpretation and effect upon the biblical audience remain rather speculative.

When speaking of a later, modern audience, scholars generally assume the existence of a fairly skilled and knowledgeable reader, someone familiar with the larger David story and other key biblical passages. To gauge the effects of figurative language on such an audience, one can explore how metaphors shape the readers' evolving perception of the characters, plot, and the meaning of the story as a whole.

2. *Metaphor and Narrative Connections*

As previously noted, many of the metaphors in 1 Samuel 25 involve stones. What effect does this type of metaphoric repetition produce? The metaphors create a sense of narrative unity, for they connect various aspects of the chapter and link this episode with other segments of the larger David story. For instance, Abigail assures David that God will sling his enemies from a slingshot (v. 29), implying an image of his foes as stones. In v. 37, this prediction comes to pass in a sense, for David's enemy Nabal figuratively becomes a stone. Mention of stones flung from a slingshot also recalls David's memorable slaying of Goliath (1 Samuel 17). Just as David's first foe was vanquished with a slingshot, so his present and future enemies will suffer a similar fate, not literally killed by David's slingstone, but figuratively defeated by God. Likewise, the portrayal of Nabal as a bird of prey prompts a connection between v. 14 and the two other

---

[25] Darr, 41; also see the more detailed description of her methodology in chapter one.

passages in 1 Samuel that metaphorically compare soldiers taking booty in a military campaign to raptors swooping down on their prey (1 Sam 14:32; 15:19).

Since the term "stumbling block" in v. 31 likely evokes an image of rock, Abigail's warning takes on greater specificity in light of v. 37. She cautions David not to jeopardize his career by stumbling over the person who becomes a stone, Nabal. The noun לב ("heart") further links these two verses. Because David restrains himself from carrying out his vow of revenge, Nabal does not become a מכשול לב ("stumbling block of the heart") for the future king. In the end, God accomplishes David's desired goal. One day, "Nabal's heart was of good cheer" (v. 36), but the next morning his heart figuratively "died with in him" (v. 37); ten days later, "**YHWH** smote Nabal and he died" (v. 38).

The metaphor in v. 37 also functions as an inclusio of sorts, connecting the conclusion of Nabal's story with the introduction. The man who initially was described somewhat ambiguously as a "hard" person (v. 3), in the end metaphorically becomes a hard object (v. 37). The connection between vv. 3 and 37 sparked by these metaphors gives rise to a reconsideration of an enigmatic aspect of the story, the third comment about Nabal in v. 3: the *ketib* stands as כלבו, whereas the *qere* reads, כלבי. Radak outlines three possible interpretations of this phrase: (i) The word can be read as the gentilic, כָּלְבִּי, indicating Nabal's ancestry: "He is a Calebite." (ii) The sentence can be explained according to the *ketib*, כְּלִבּוֹ, meaning "He was like his heart"; as Radak explains: "The appearance of his deeds was evil as his heart was evil." (iii) An alternative exegesis of the *qere* treats the phrase as a simile comparing Nabal to a dog, כְּלִבִּי ("dog-like"), "because of the inferiority of his deeds."[26] Most modern translators accept the *qere* reading, rendering the phrase as a reference to Nabal's Calebite background, which fits the geographical setting of this story.[27] A few commentators add a note about the possible "double mean-

---

[26] Radak on 1 Sam 25:3. Rashi explains: "from the house of Caleb." Ralbag comments: "because of the cruelty of his deeds, his character was like that of dogs." Abravanel proposes two possibilities: the *qere* as a comparison of Nabal to a dog and the *ketib* כלבו, meaning that his appearance resembles the nature of his heart. The Targum reads the words as a gentilic, whereas the Septuagint states *kynikos*, "dog-like."

[27] McCarter explains that the Calebites "were a people of non-Israelite origin later incorporated into Judah" whose "territory included the region around Hebron, where the present story takes place" (396).

ing"[28] or "play" on words[29] present when כלבי is construed as "dog-like." Fokkelman elaborates on this notion when he explores the denotative and connotative content of the statement:

> The denotative content . . . is a very natural element in introducing a character. In our case the tribal aspect reminds us of the district where the two formidable men have their possessions and, shortly, their conflict and it implies that the Judean David is not up against a clansman. But the connotative content is more exciting. This Nabal, who has just been disqualified by the narrator in advance by means of a black-and-white picture, is "a cur" and his "evil deeds" will lead him, via harsh egoism against David and debauchery on his own part (v. 36), back to the dead dog which remains of him in v. 38 . . . The semantic balance of the form *klby* (the Qere) makes a show of abstruseness about the Ketib *klbw* unnecessary . . . [T]his man is a Calebite dog.[30]

As Fox reminds his readers, the suggestion that Nabal is "dog-like" conveys "a negative image that recurs a number of times in Samuel."[31] In the prior chapter, David asks Saul: "After whom are you chasing? After a dead dog?" (1 Sam 24:15). Earlier on, Goliath taunts David: "Am I a dog that you come against me with sticks?" (1 Sam 17:43).[32]

Only a few scholars recognize the potential of reading this statement as a simile, "and he was like his heart." In an 1899 commentary on Samuel, Henry P. Smith notes that the *ketib* "is possibly an attempt to be witty—*he was like* or *the name* was like *his heart.*"[33] Jon Levenson considers the narrator's remark an example of the "process of deliberate, overt characterization" that marks this chapter. He asserts:

> The *ketib*, *kelibbo*, "he was like his heart," is probably an example of scribal sarcasm which alludes to the well-known verse, "The fool (*nabal*) has said in his heart (*belibbo*), 'There is no God'" (Ps 14:1 = 53:1). If so, then the *ketib* alludes to the prideful and ultimately stupid character of this man, who seems to have recognized no authority other than his own.[34]

---

[28] Alter, *The David Story*, 153.

[29] Fox, 122.

[30] Fokkelman, 482–83.

[31] Fox, 122.

[32] Also see 2 Sam 3:8; 9:8; 16:9, as well as 2 Kgs 8:13.

[33] H. P. Smith, *A Critical and Exegetical Commentary on the Books of Samuel* (New York: Scribner, 1899), 222–223. Cf. 1 Sam 13:14, where Samuel tells Saul that God seeks "a man after his own heart (איש כלבבו)."

[34] Jon Levenson, "1 Samuel 25 as Literature and as History," *CBQ* 40 (1978) 14–15.

Reading כלבו as a simile not only makes sense orthographically and grammatically, but also in terms of the larger literary context. The "hard" man is like his heart, just as "like his name he is" (v. 25); and, in the end, "his heart dies" and he resembles an inert stone.

On one level, כלבו simply supplies the routine expository information expected in the opening verses of a biblical story. On another level, it functions in a Janus-type manner, for its ambiguity allows it to connect with elements before and after this verse. Looking back to earlier episodes in the David saga, the suggestion that Nabal is "dog-like" calls to mind the dog metaphors in the book of Samuel and the overall, negative impression of dogs as lowly, despicable creature. Looking ahead, the simile "like his heart" foreshadows Nabal's nearly fatal condition at the end of the tale. Together, these two interpretations enhance the narrative cohesion created through metaphor, uniting elements within the narrative unit and between this episode and other parts of the David story.

3. Metaphor and Relationships of Equivalence and Contrast

The numerous references to stones also set up various relationships of equivalence and contrast. Assuming that the interpretation of the "bundle of the living" is correct, then the metaphors in v. 29 enhance the opposition Abigail sets up between the fate of David, whose stone will be placed in the bag signifying life, and the destiny of Nabal, who will be flung in the air like a stone and killed. Bar-Efrat perceptively notes that צרור not only means "pouch" (from I צרר), but also "pebble" (from III צרר).[35] He asserts: "Both meanings of צרור— pouch and stone—are made use of here in order to sharpen the contrast between the fates of David and the fate of his enemies."[36] Whereas stones have a negative connotation when they become an obstacle that can cause a person to trip and totter, they can be used positively to build a wall and provide protection. While it is praiseworthy for David's men to be described as a wall and implicitly compared to stones, the explicit depiction of Nabal as a stone signals his demise.

These metaphors contribute, along with other literary devices, to the contrast the author sets up between Nabal and the other two

---

[35] 2 Sam 17:13 and Amos 9:9.
[36] Bar-Efrat, *1 Samuel*, 322.

protagonists. The narrator spells out the antithesis between Abigail and Nabal in the third verse of the story, and the ensuing events only confirm the virtuous nature of the wife and the contemptible impression of her husband. The real drama in the story resides in the relationship between David and Nabal. Will David behave like, and therefore end up like, Nabal? Will he respond to Abigail's pleas in a stiff-necked and hard-hearted manner, "swooping down" on her and rejecting her attempt to mitigate the situation? Or will he allow himself to be swayed by a wise and beautiful woman, even after he has made an impulsive oath before God and his troops? The first word of David's response in v. 32, ברוך ("blessed"), signals his positive reception of Abigail and his commendable character. Unlike Nabal, David proves himself able to listen to reason and alter a determined course of action, qualities that will serve him well when he becomes "prince over Israel" (v. 30).[37]

III. Conclusion: Metaphor and Understanding

From the time of Aristotle to the present day, scholars have stressed the "informative" aspect of metaphor. However, if a speaker's only goal were to convey information, that aim could be accomplished in a more direct and reliable fashion. The narrator could have introduced Nabal with a nonfigurative adjective or described his reaction to Abigail's news in a more straightforward manner, such as with a statement like, "he was afraid and could not speak." Nabal's servant could have informed Abigail that Nabal "rejected" David's messengers or that David's men "protected" the shepherds. Abigail could simply have promised David: "God will save you and defeat your enemies." In exchange for such precision, these speakers gain other valuable communicative benefits. While metaphor often entails a degree of ambiguity, metaphoric utterances paint a graphic, memorable image that engages the audience's imagination and attention. One can envision David's men forming a barricade around the shepherds, picture David stumbling over a large obstacle, or imagine God flinging David's foes from a sling shot. Metaphors also involve a certain conceptual economy, allowing the speaker to convey nuanced, multifaceted

---

[37] David displays these same qualities in chapters 24 and 26, when he refrains from killing Saul though presented with opportunities to do so.

messages through a single, vivid utterance. For instance, the characterization of Nabal as a "hard" man encompasses several aspects of Nabal's personality, just as the depiction of him "swooping down" on David's messengers introduces various dynamics of the exchange. Metaphors like these not only provide data, but they also color the hearer's perception of the actual situation, a key component in the persuasive power of metaphor.

CHAPTER FIVE

METAPHOR AND OTHER TROPES

I. INTRODUCTION TO 2 SAMUEL 16:16–17:14

Following the encounter between David and Abigail in Carmel, David continues to solidify his power base, and he eventually succeeds Saul as king (2 Samuel 5). Shortly thereafter, the focus of the narrative shifts from warfare and political in-fighting to domestic dramas: David's affair with Bathsheba and its deadly aftermath (2 Samuel 11–12), the rape of David's daughter, Tamar, by her half-brother, Amnon (2 Sam 13:1–22), the vengeful murder of Amnon by his half-brother, Absalom (2 Sam 13:23–33), and a familial *coup d'état* after Absalom "stole the hearts of the men of Israel" (2 Sam 15:6) and usurped the throne from his father (2 Sam 15:7–12). As the deposed king flees from Jerusalem, David encounters a series of individuals, including Hushai the Archite. After learning that his trusted advisor, Ahitophel, has joined Absalom in the conspiracy, David enlists Hushai to return to Jerusalem and infiltrate the royal court: "If you cross over with me, you will be a burden to me. But if you return to the city and say to Absalom, 'Your servant will I be, O king. I was your father's servant, and now I will be your servant,' you can subvert Ahitophel's counsel for me" (2 Sam 15:33–34). Hushai adeptly fulfills his mission by employing numerous rhetorical techniques to influence Absalom and his supporters.

Because of the rhetorical richness of the confrontation between Ahitophel and Hushai, 2 Sam 16:16–17:14 provides an apt setting for the continued study of metaphor in biblical prose narrative. Whereas the prior chapters of this study concentrated on the identification and interpretation of metaphor, the present chapter endeavors to better understand metaphor by comparing it to other tropes, namely metonymy and simile.[1] This section aims to enhance our

---

[1] From the time of Quintilian through the eighteenth century, writers maintained a strict division between the terms "trope" and "figure." The term "trope," which includes metaphor, "is said to involve a provisional change ('alteration' or 'turning')

insight into how metaphor operates by exploring the elements it shares with other forms of figurative language and the facets that make it unique.

II. Metaphor and Metonymy in 2 Samuel 16:16–17:14

A. *Research Review: Approaches to Metonymy*

In *The Poetics*, Aristotle conflates two tropes under the rubric of "metaphor." Applying a more precise classification, "the transference of a term . . . from genus to species, species to genus, species to species"[2] describes metonymy, while transference "by analogy" characterizes metaphor. The eclipsing of metonymy by metaphor in Aristotle's early definition reflects the relationship between these two tropes in subsequent scholarship. Hugh Bredin begins his article "Metonymy" by stating that "one of the distinguishing marks of modern literary culture is the dominance given to metaphor over all the other figures and tropes."[3] Perplexed by this phenomenon, he observes: "Metonymy may in fact be more common than metaphor . . . yet it is seldom subjected to the detailed and lengthy investigations that metaphor undergoes."[4] Jonathan Culler addresses this issue as he imagines how delighted "our illustrious forbears in the field of rhetoric," like Quintilian and Fontanier, would be at the recent renewed interest in rhetoric; yet he wonders how they would react to the imbalanced attention to metaphor. He speculates:

> But they would be puzzled, I believe, at the extraordinary privilege accorded to metaphor. 'Why metaphor?' they might ask. Why not organize a symposium on the simile or synecdoche, on metalepsis or meiosis, or on such complex figures as anadiplosis, alloiosis, or antapo-

---

in the nature of a linguistic entity"; the term "figure" is "defined in terms of a logic of supplementarity as involving the 'adding' of a superfluous ornament to a linguistic entity already complete in itself" (Shirley Sharon-Zisser, "A Distinction No Longer of Use: Evolutionary Discourse and the Disappearance of the Trope/Figure Binarism," *Rhetorica* 11 [1993] 323). In this interesting article, Sharon-Zisser demonstrates how, since the nineteenth century, the terms "trope" and "figure" have been used interchangeably as "synonymous signifiers" (324).

[2] Aristotle, *The Poetics*, 67.

[3] Hugh Bredin, "Metonymy," *Poetics Today* 5 (1984) 45.

[4] Bredin, 45. He adds: "And not only is it not widely studied, but most accounts of it are unsatisfactory."

dosis? Metaphor is an important figure, they would concede, but by no means the only figure. Why should it usurp the attention of modern students of rhetoric?[5]

The research reviewed below shows that this tendency has started to change as scholars now are paying greater attention to metonymy.

The word "metonymy" comes from the Greek phrase "change of name," whereas the related term "synecdoche" means "act of taking together" or "understanding one thing with another." Both tropes share the common feature of "understanding one thing with another"; the main difference between the two lies in the connection between the elements involved. In the first century c.e. work, *Institutio Oratoria*, Quintilian defines metonymy as a trope which involves "the substitution of one name for another."[6] The author of the first century B.C.E. *Rhetorica Ad Herennium* explains that this is accomplished by substituting the name of the greater thing for that of the lesser, the thing invented for that of the inventor, the instrument for the possessor, cause for the effect or effect for cause, the content for container or container for content.[7] In contrast, "synecdoche occurs when the whole is known from a small part or a part from the whole" or when "the plural will be understood from the singular" or the singular from the plural.[8] Both authors agree that these tropes are found frequently not only in the words of poets and orators, but in everyday speech as well.[9]

Subsequent writers on metonymy and synecdoche closely adhere to their classical antecedents, focusing on substitution as the central

---

[5] Jonathan Culler, "The Turns of Metaphor," in *The Pursuit of Signs: Semiotics, Literature, Deconstruction* (Ithaca: Cornell University Press, 1981), 188. He writes: "Today metaphor is no longer one figure among others but the figure of figures, a figure for figurality (and I mean this quite literally) . . . metaphor is not just the literal or proper name for a trope based on resemblance but also and especially a figure for figurality in general" (189). According to Wallace Martin, the prevalence of metonymy helps to explain why scholars have tended to neglect this trope. He asserts: "Because metonymies are common in ordinary usage and new ones are often easy to decipher, they have attracted less critical attention than metaphor" ("Metonymy," in *The New Princeton Encyclopedia of Poetry and Poetics*, ed. Alex Preminger and T. V. F. Brogan [Princeton: Princeton University Press, 1993], 783).

[6] Quintilian, *Institutio Oratoria*, vol. 3, trans. H. E. Butler (London: William Heinemann, 1921), 313.

[7] *Rhetorica Ad Herennium*, 335–37. Quintilian complies a nearly identical list (335).

[8] *Rhetorica Ad Herennium*, 341.

[9] Quintilian, 313; *Rhetorica Ad Herennium*, 337.

feature of these two tropes. For example, in a 1777 lecture on oratory and criticism, Joseph Priestly declared:

> These terms [metonymy and synecdoche] are applied when, instead of the proper name of any thing or attribute, a name is borrowed from another object, which stands in any other relation to it than that of actual *resemblance*, which is referred to as *metaphor*.[10]

Although Priestly admits that "it is almost endless to enumerate all the relations of things which afford a foundation for this figure of speech," he nevertheless complies a list of relations similar to the one in *Rhetorica Ad Herennium*: cause and effect, agent and instrument, and so forth.[11] Similarly, many contemporary works emphasize the "borrowing," "transference," or "substitution" of one word for another based on some material, causal, or conceptual relation.[12] Such definitions typically specify the types of relations involved and provide illustrations, the kind of information found in the following table:[13]

Metonymical Relations		*Examples*
1. Cause	Effect	War is sad.
2. Inventor	Invented	She was reading Virgil.
3. User	Instrument	A hired gun.
4. Doer	Thing done	Crime must be punished.
5. Passion	Object of passion	She is my true love.
6. Container	Contained	A boiling kettle.
7. Place	Object in place	Wall Street panicked.
8. Time	Object in time	The age of science.
9. Possessor	Possessed	The smart money is in computer software.
10. Sign	Signified	Crown (for monarchy).
11. Concrete	Abstract	Youth is giddy and irresponsible.

While such lists coincide to a large degree, no consensus exists about the identity of the metonymical relations or the interpretation

---

[10] Joseph Priestly, *Lectures on Oratory and Criticism*, ed. V. M. Bevilacqua and R. Murphy (Carbondale: Southern Illinois University Press, 1965), 231; quoted in Wendell V. Harris, *Dictionary of Concepts in Literary Criticism and Theory* (Westport, CN: Greenwood Press, 1992), 232.

[11] Priestley, 231; Harris, 232.

[12] Martin, 783. For other examples, see Harris, 231 or *The Oxford English Dictionary*, 2nd edition, s.v. "metonymy": "(A figure of speech characterized by) the action of substituting for a word or phrase denoting an object, action, institution, etc., a word or phrase denoting a property or something associated with it."

[13] Bredin, 48 (his chart contains two examples of each category).

of the examples cited. For instance, Martin classifies "'the crown' for the king" under the heading of "associated object for its possessor or user," whereas Bredin categorizes this expression as an illustration of "sign for signified."[11] Peter Schofer and Donald Rice cite an altogether different approach to this example:

> The trope *crown* for *king* can be read either as a metonymy or a synecdoche, depending on whether the crown is simply associated with the king (part to the rest, i.e., metonymy) or whether it is considered an integral part of the concept of monarch (part for the whole, i.e., synecdoche).[15]

These sorts of catalogs can be helpful, for they lay out some of the possible ways to explain the relationship between the words used in a given utterance and the interpreted referent, the two elements in metonymy. However, as this example illustrates, such lists prove neither exhaustive nor definitive.

Lakoff and Johnson group their inventory of metonymic examples into seven divisions, starting with a category "the part for the whole," which others classify as the separate trope, synecdoche.[16] Their treatment of synecdoche as a subsidiary of metonymy reflects another area of disagreement among contemporary scholars. Some, like their classical counterparts, distinguish metonymy and synecdoche as separate tropes,[17] while others consider synecdoche a "subset"[18] or "special case"[19] of metonymy. Comparing these two tropes, Raymond Gibbs writes:

> Metonymy is related to synecdoche in that both tropes exploit the relationship of larger entities and lesser ones. Synecdoche substitutes the part for the whole as in
> They're taking on new hands down at the factory.
> where the term *hands* stands for men. Metonymy also substitutes the token for the type or a specific instance, property, or characteristic for the general principle or function. For instance, in

---

[14] Bredin, 48 and Martin 783. Martin's list of eight kinds of metonymical relations differs from Bredin's list of eleven in a number of ways, including the addition of the category of "parts of the body for states of consciousness associated with them" (783).

[15] Peter Schofer and Donald Rice, "Metaphor, Metonymy, and Synecdoche Revis(it)ed," *Semiotica* 21 (1977), 128.

[16] Lakoff and Johnson, 38. As an example, they cite the sentence, "The Giants need a *stronger arm* in right field."

[17] See, for instance, Bredin (54) or Schofer and Rice (137–142).

[18] Martin, 783.

[19] Harris, 231; Lakoff and Johnson, 36.

> They prefer the bullet to the ballot box.

where the term *bullet* represents armed conflict, while *ballot box* refers to peaceful democratic processes. Some linguistic expressions involve both synecdoche and metonymy. For instance, consider

> General Schwartzkopf had 400,000 fatigues at his command.

Here *fatigues*, the specific type of uniform worn by common soldiers, refers to soldiers, reflecting a part-whole relationship, or to warlike power, reflecting a token-for-type relationship.[20]

Given the essential commonalities between metonymy and synecdoche, and for the sake of simplicity, in the present work both figures will be collapsed under the single heading of "metonymy."

In their 1977 article, "Metaphor, Metonymy, and Synecdoche Revis(it)ed," Schofer and Rice also comment on the way that metaphor has "overshadowed and engulfed" other tropes. They note, however, that after the publication of works by several French theorists in the early 1970's, "it appeared for a moment that a palace revolution had overthrown metaphor with synecdoche and metonymy rushing in to fill the void, each proclaiming its supremacy over the two."[21] The catalyst that precipitated this apparent takeover was the work of the linguist Roman Jakobson. In an article originally published in 1956,[22] Jakobson links metaphor and metonymy to Ferdinand de Saussure's concept of syntagmatic and paradigmatic axes. He contends:

> Any linguistic sign involves two modes of arrangement: (1) Combination. Any sign is made up of constituent signs and/or occurs only in combination with other signs. . . . (2) Selection. A selection between alternatives implies the possibility of substituting one for another.[23]

Metonymy entails combination or contiguity, whereas metaphor is associated with selection. Schofer and Rice summarize the binary opposition at the core of Jakobson's theory:[24]

---

[20] Raymond W. Gibbs, Jr., "Speaking and Thinking with Metonymy," in *Metonymy in Language and Thought*, ed. Klaus-Uwe Panther and Günter Radden (Amsterdam/Philadelphia: John Benjamins Publishing Company, 1999), 63.

[21] Schofer and Rice, 121.

[22] Roman Jakobson, "Two Aspects of Language and Two Types of Aphasic Disturbances," in *Fundamentals of Language*, co-authored with Morris Halle (The Hague: Mouton, 1956), 53–82. Later, the article was published in French: "Deux aspects do langage et deux types d'aphasie," in *Essais de linguitique générale* (Paris: Editions du Seuil, 1963), 43–67. The article has been reprinted on numerous occasions and in various other languages. The edition cited here is Roman Jakobson, "Two Aspects of Language and Two Types of Aphasic Disturbances," in *Language and Literature*, ed. Krystyna Pomorska and Stephen Rudy (Cambridge: Belknap Press), 95–114.

[23] Jakobson, 98–99.

[24] Schofer and Rice, 127.

Metaphor	*Metonymy*
paradigmatic	syntagmatic
selection	combination
substitution	juxtaposition
in absentia	*in praesentia*[25]
internal relationship of similarity	external relationship of contiguity

Jakobson speaks about metaphor and metonymy broadly, considering these tropes as two fundamental processes that can be aligned not only with different forms of aphasia,[26] but also with Romanticism and Realism, as well as poetry and prose.[27]

Jakobson's 1956 article proved enormously influential, as becomes clear from a 1984 bibliography that catalogs ninety-five studies that develop, apply, or challenge Jakobson's binary model of metaphor and metonymy. The bibliography demonstrates how researchers in an array of fields have applied his theory, including linguistics, literary theory, film, and folklore.[28] Jakobson's influence is particularly pronounced in the structuralist school of French literary critics,[29]

[25] Jakobson explains: "In order to delimit the two modes of arrangement we have described as combination and selection, de Saussure states that the former 'is *in praesentia*: it is based on two or several terms jointly present in an actual series,' whereas the latter 'connects terms *in absentia* as members of a virtual mnemonic series'" (99).

[26] Jakobson associates different forms of aphasia with the metaphoric and metonymic poles. He observes that metonymy "is widely employed by aphasics whose selective capacities have been affected" (105). In contrast, aphasiacs with an impaired ability to "combine simpler linguistic entities into more complex units," what Jakobson labels as "the contiguity disorder," tend to use quasi-metaphoric expressions (106–107).

[27] Jakobson links Romanticism with metaphor and Realism with metonymy. Because "the principle of similarity underlines poetry," he considers poetry metaphoric, whereas prose aligns with metonymy, since it "is forwarded essentially by contiguity" (114).

[28] William Bohn, "Roman Jakobson's Theory of Metaphor and Metonymy: An Annotated Bibliography," *Style* 18 (1984) 534–50. Interestingly, in spite of the pervasive influence of Jakobson's work, almost no mention of Jakobson or his followers can be found in the cognitive research on metaphor or metonymy discussed below. René Dirven confirms this observation: "In the latest very rich literature on metaphor or on metonymy one finds very few references to the epoch-making short paper by Roman Jakobson, 'The Metaphoric and Metonymic Poles'" ("Metonymy and Metaphor: Different Mental Strategies of Conceptualisation," in *Metaphor and Metonymy in Comparison and Contrast*, ed. René Dirven and Ralf Pörings [Berlin: Mouton de Gruyter, 2002], 76). By including Jakobson's article in the collection, *Metaphor and Metonymy in Comparison and Contrast*, Dirven and Pörings seek to rectify this situation and integrate Jakobson into the conversation on metaphor and metonymy taking place among cognitive linguists.

[29] Maria Ruegg offers an interesting observation about the interest in classical rhetoric among French structuralists. She writes: "Despite their repeated insistence that the new theoretical age—inaugurated by Saussurian linguistics, Freudian analysis,

whose writers responded to Jakobson and proposed different ways to realign the relationships between these tropes.[30] Yet, in spite of the renewed interest in metonymy sparked by Jakobson's article, Schofer and Rice claim that in the end, "the muted struggle for the understanding and conquest of the terms" resulted in a return to the status quo, with metaphor again enthroned in its privileged position.[31]

A number of more recent publications signal another resurgence of interest in metonymy: *By Word of Mouth: Metaphor, Metonymy and Linguistic Action in a Cognitive Perspective* (1995),[32] *Metonymy in Language and Thought* (1999),[33] *Metaphor and Metonymy at the Crossroads: A Cognitive Perspective* (2000),[34] and *Metaphor and Metonymy in Comparison and Contrast* (2002), part of the "Cognitive Linguistics Research" series.[35] The titles of these four volumes testify to the fact that a "cognitive turn" has taken place in the study of metonymy. In an introduction to the cognitive theory of metaphor and metonymy (abbreviated in the field as CTMM), Antonio Barcelona explains:

Nietzschean 'symptomology' and Mallarmean poetics—constituted a 'radical epistemological rupture' with the 'pre-scientific' past, a large number of structuralists were, at the same time, strangely attracted to the antiquated, elaborately constructed system of tropes and figures offered in classical manuals of rhetoric. And what is even more surprising, they not only admired such works, but freely adopted, within their own 'revolutionary' discourse, a good many terms directly, and uncritically, derived from the most traditional of rhetorical texts" ("Metaphor and Metonymy: The Logic of Structuralist Rhetoric," *Glyph* 6 [1979] 141).

[30] For instance, Gérard Genette stresses the importance of recognizing synecdoche as a separate trope and he outlines various distinctions between synecdoche and metonymy ("La Rhétorique restreinte," *Figures III* [Paris: Edtitions du Seuil, 1972], 21–40; Schofer and Rice critique his work, 127–129). The group of scholars known as the Groupe de Liege places even greater emphasis on synecdoche, which they consider the central trope. They explain metaphor and metonymy, each in its own way, as a combination of two synecdoches (Jacques Dubois, et al., *Rhétorique générale* [Paris: Larousse, 1970]; their work is discussed in Schofer and Rice, 130–132 and Bredin, 49–51). Umberto Eco takes a different tack: he ignores synecdoche and "goes so far as to propose the primordality of metonymy" (Schofer and Rice, 129, referring to Umberto Eco, "Sémantique de la métaphore," *Tel Quel* 55 [1973] 25–46).

[31] Schofer and Rice, 121. They posit that Paul Ricoeur's *La Métaphore vive* (Paris: Editions du Seuil, 1975) helped to the reestablish metaphor in its privileged position.

[32] Louis Goossens, et al., eds., *By Word of Mouth: Metaphor, Metonymy and Linguistic Action in a Cognitive Perspective* (Amsterdam/Philadelphia: John Benjamins Publishing Company, 1995).

[33] Klaus-Uwe Panther and Günter Radden, eds., *Metonymy in Language and Thought* (Amsterdam/Philadelphia: John Benjamins Publishing Company, 1999).

[34] Antonio Barcelona, ed., *Metaphor and Metonymy at the Crossroads: A Cognitive Perspective* (Berlin: Mouton de Gruyter, 2000).

[35] René Dirven and Ralf Pörings, eds., *Metaphor and Metonymy in Comparison and Contrast* (Berlin: Mouton de Gruyter, 2002).

It should suffice here to enunciate the overriding assumption shared by all these researchers, i.e. that the so-called "language faculty" is just a reflection, in some cases a specialization, of general-purpose cognitive abilities, and is governed by general neural processes. Thus, in their view, there is a continuum between all sorts of cognition . . . and language.[36]

The link between language and cognition shapes the understanding of metaphor and metonymy, both of which "are regarded in cognitive linguistics as *conventional mental mechanisms*, not to be confused with their expression, linguistic or otherwise."[37] Lakoff and Johnson articulate a similar notion in their seminal book, *Metaphors We Live By*:

> [Metonymy] is also like metaphor in that it is not just a poetic or rhetorical device. Nor is it just a matter of language. Metonymic concepts . . . are part of the ordinary, everyday way we think and act as well as talk.[38]

They stress that, like metaphors, metonymic concepts structure our thoughts and actions, not just our language.[39]

Barcelona's conception of metonymy differs considerably from the definitions cited above that emphasize the substitution of one word for another. His definition exemplifies the interest in "mental activation" shared by cognitive linguists. He writes:

> Metonymy is a conceptual projection whereby one experiential domain (the target) is partially understood in terms of another experiential domain (the source) included *in the same common experiential domain*.[40]

---

[36] Antonio Barcelona, "Introduction: The Cognitive Theory of Metaphor and Metonymy," in *Metaphor and Metonymy at the Crossroads*, 2.

[37] Barcelona, 5.

[38] Lakoff and Johnson, 37.

[39] Lakoff and Johnson, 39.

[40] Barcelona, 4. How do cognitive linguists define a "domain"? Barcelona introduces the understanding of a cognitive domain used by most cognitive linguists as "an 'encyclopedic' domain (i.e. it includes all the entrenched knowledge that a speaker has about an area of experience)." He acknowledges that this encyclopedic notion means that a domain "will normally vary in breadth from person to person, and in many cases, it has no precise boundaries" (8–9). Given this definition, he raises an important question: "How can, then, the neat distinction between two domains be used to distinguish metonymy from metaphor? (9)." To address this issue, he proposes a modified definition of metaphor that specifies that the "source and target have to be treated as being in separate domains by the conventional conscious classification of domains prevailing in a given culture" (10). For a fuller discussion of this topic, see William Croft, "The Role of Domains in The Interpretation of Metaphors and Metonymies," in *Metaphor and Metonymy in Comparison and Contrast*, ed. René Dirven and Ralf Pörings, (Berlin: Mouton de Gruyter, 2002), 161–205.

A hallmark of the cognitive approach to metaphor, built upon the work of Lakoff and Johnson, is the notion that metaphor involves two cognitive domains. According to this theory, metaphor is considered the cognitive mechanism whereby one experiential domain is projected or "mapped" onto another experiential domain; as a result, the second domain is understood in terms of the first. Whereas metaphor involves two domains belonging to different superordinate domains, the mapping in metonymy takes place within one common cognitive domain. For instance, in the oft cited example, "love is a journey," cognitive linguists claim that the domain of journeys, which is a subdomain of movement, is "mapped" or "superimposed" on the distinct domain of love, which is a subdomain of emotions. In contrast, in the metonymic expression, "The ham sandwich is waiting for his check," the mapping takes place within one common superordinate domain, the restaurant, which includes both customer and food.[41]

Much of the recent interest in metonymy among cognitive linguists has centered on its interaction with metaphor. Several scholars argue against the notion of a binary opposition between metaphor and metonymy and instead insist upon a continuum between the two. For instance, Louis Goossens claims: "Although in principle metaphor and metonymy are distinct cognitive processes, it appears to be the case that the two are not mutually exclusive."[42] He even invents the neologism "metaphtonymy" in order to "increase our awareness of the fact that metaphor and metonymy can be intertwined."[43]

---

[41] Barcelona, 3–5. He takes this example from Lakoff and Johnson (35) and classifies it under the heading of "consumed goods for customer" (4).

[42] Louis Goossens, "Metaphtonymy: The Interaction of Metaphor and Metonymy in Figurative Expressions for Linguistic Action." in *By Word of Mouth: Metaphor, Metonymy and Linguistic Action in a Cognitive Perspective*, ed. Louis Goossens, et al. (Amsterdam/Philadelphia: John Benjamins Publishing Company, 1995), 159.

[43] Goossens, 159. Just as Goossens advocates the exploration of the "continuum from metonymy to metaphor," Dirven posits that "it may be more logical to see the various instances of metonymy and metaphor as points on a continuum, with non-figurativeness at one end and complex figurativeness at the other." See Louis Goossens, "From Three Respectable Horses' Mouths: Metonymy and Conventionalization in a Diachronically Differentiated Data Base," in *By Word of Mouth: Metaphor, Metonymy and Linguistic Action in a Cognitive Perspective*, ed. Louis Goossens, et al. (Amsterdam/Philadelphia: John Benjamins Publishing Company, 1995), 178 and René Dirven, "Metonymy and Metaphor: Different Mental Strategies of Conceptualisation," in *Metaphor and Metonymy in Comparison and Contrast*, ed. René Dirven and Ralf Pörings, (Berlin: Mouton de Gruyter, 2002), 93.

What light can these three general conceptions of metonymy—
the traditional "substitution" view, Jakobson's contiguity model, and
the cognitive theory—shed on metonymy in the Bible? In spite of the
burgeoning literature on metonymy, none of the works surveyed
above seems to fit particularly well with the goals of this study and
the conception of metaphor explored in the prior chapters. For the
present project, these approaches exhibit a number of shortcomings.
Cognitive studies have generated important insights about metonymy,
such as the contrast between mapping across two distinct domains
versus a single domain and the continuum between metaphor and
metonymy. Yet, as stated in chapter one, the relevance of this type
of research for the study at hand is limited, since the focus here
remains on figures of speech, not on the cognitive processes behind
them. For similar reasons, the applicability of Jakobson's ideas is also
limited. As a number of critics have pointed out, Jakobson oversimplifies
metaphor and metonymy so that the terms refer primarily to fundamental processes; he then "proceeds to leave the domain of words
for other extralinguistic fields."[44] Schofer and Rice charge: "His use
of the term 'contiguity' in so many senses—verbal, spatial, causal—
renders the term so general that it loses much of its value."[45] As a
result, Jakobson's writings do not help tremendously when trying to
understand how metaphor and metonymy operate in a particular literary context.

The traditional view of metonymy proves problematic for a different
reason, one discussed in chapter one: the substitution theory conceives of metonymy as a trope comprised of one isolable word that
can be extracted from an utterance and replaced with another, related
word. Like metaphor, metonymy is created from the combination of
words in a contiguous chain of lexemes embedded within a larger
text structure. With a bit of rewriting, White's previously quoted
insight about metaphor holds true for metonymy as well: The key
to understanding the way metonymy works is to understand the way
words have been combined in the metonymical utterance.[46]

As we turn from theories of metonymy to examples of this trope
found in biblical narrative, a text-based approach will be applied to

---

[44] Schofer and Rice, 127.
[45] Schofer and Rice, 127. For additional critiques, see Ruegg (146–147) and the
works listed in Bohn's bibliography.
[46] Sentence adapted from White, 4.

2 Sam 16:16–17:14.[47] In opposition to a word-level notion of language, a text-based approach views each separate element in a text as an integral part of various text-in-context relationships. Whereas a word or utterance may have a particular presupposed meaning in isolation, when situated within the other co-occurring parts that constitute a text, the word or utterance takes on an entailed construal, the meaning derived from understanding the text segment within its dependent context. The meaning in isolation, also referred to as the localizable or decontextualizable meaning, may coincide with the text-in-context construal, the sense assumed when an element is placed in a larger context; on the other hand, the two meanings may diverge. The disparity between the decontextualizable meaning and the text-in-context construal creates a feeling of incongruity that marks a trope. In the following section, two types of tropes will be examined, the instances of metaphor and metonymy in the story of Ahitophel and Hushai.

B. *2 Samuel 16:21b[1]*—כי נבאשת את אביך
("You have made yourself stink to your father")

After David flees Jerusalem, the upstart Absalom settles into the capital city and his new position of power. To Ahitophel, his co-conspirator and counselor, Absalom asks: "What shall we do?" (2 Sam 16:20). Ahitophel advises him to commit a brazen act that will allow him to flaunt in public the fact that he has usurped his father's royal prerogatives: "Come to bed with your father's concubines whom he has left to watch over the house, and let all Israel hear that you have made yourself stink to your father" (16:21). What does this expression mean? How does it operate as a trope? Does it qualify as an instance of metaphor or metonymy?

There is nothing grammatically or semantically anomalous about the statement: "You have made yourself stink to your father." If Ahitophel had suggested that Absalom roll around in manure so as to make himself malodorous to his father, the utterance would not trigger a tropic construal. In 2 Samuel 16, however, the larger context signals the presence of a trope. The sense that this verse con-

---

[47] This general approach and its application to metaphor and metonymy were introduced by Asif Agha, through classroom instruction and his valuable personal guidance on this chapter.

tains an incongruity arises from the disparity between the localized meaning of the text segment and the broader topic of the embedded text structure. The sentence under examination states that Absalom will cause himself to develop some sort of malodorous scent that David will smell. Yet the preceding and subsequent utterances concern the ramifications of the public discovery that Absalom has had sexual relations with David's concubines. How will David react to the news? How will this affect his relationship with Absalom? What impact will David's reaction have on the population in general and on Absalom's supporters in particular? The clues provided in the larger narrative context make it apparent that Ahitophel does not mean that having sex with the concubines will produce a body odor that David will find offensive; rather, he predicts that David will be repulsed by the act, leading him to sever all ties with his son.

To gain insight into this expression, standard biblical scholarship would advocate an examination of how the root ב.א.ש. is used in other biblical passages. Such a study shows that in half of the attested citations, this verb describes the rancid smell of various objects or entities. For instance, the plague of blood causes the Nile to stink (Exod 7:18, 21), just as the land of Egypt starts to stink from the accumulation of dead frogs (Exod 8:10). Other verses refer to the stench of manna infested with worms (Exod 16:20), dead fish (Isa 50:2), wounds (Ps 38:6), and perfumer's ointment spoiled by dead flies (Eccl 10:1). In the other instances, the verb is used in a manner similar to that of 2 Sam 16:21, to characterize the negative reaction that one individual or group has to another as a result of some egregious event. For example, after the Ammonites humiliated David's men, they realized that they "had made themselves stink to David" (2 Sam 10:6; 1 Chr 19:6).[48]

While this information provides a certain perspective on the root ב.א.ש., when employing a text-based approach to tropes such a survey does not inform the exegesis of a specific utterance. To explicate a particular text segment, one must examine the clues uncovered from the referents of the surrounding lexemes and from the prior and subsequent discourse. In isolation, nothing about the verb "to make oneself stink" allows the reader to figure out the tropic referent in this passage. The interpretation depends on the text structure of the larger narrative whole in which this verb is situated.

---

[48] Also see Gen 34:30; Exod 5:21; 1 Sam 13:4; 1 Sam 27:12; Prov 13:5.

Translations of this verse illustrate a tendency seen in the analysis of 1 Samuel 25, the inclination to disguise figurative language by providing an exegetical gloss instead of a more literal translation. Most translators render the verb as a more abstract assessment of David's feelings toward Absalom: "thou art abhorred by thy father" (*KJV*), "you have made yourself odious to your father" (*NRS* and McCarter), "you have become repugnant to your father" (Alter).[49] The *JPS* translation strays even farther from the Hebrew: "you have dared the wrath of your father." These translations assume that the proposed course of action, Absalom's public sexual conquest of the royal concubines, will elicit an emotional reaction, causing David to despise his son.

How does this sort of entailed interpretation, the interpretation derived from examining the text segment in context, relate to the presupposed meaning, the meaning of the utterance known independently of this particular literary passage? In the decontextualized construal, the verb implies that the body has produced a foul odor or that the individual has done something to his or her body that results in a stench of some sort. Either because of some internal bodily function, such as perspiration, or some external occurrence, such as the handling of dead fish, the individual emits an odor that another person perceives as offensive. Both interpretations posit a cause and effect relationship between these two individuals:

	Decontextualized Meaning	*Text-in-Context Construal*
Person[1] (cause)	Emits an offensive body odor	Performs an offensive action
Person[2] (effect[a])	Experiences physical repulsion to the odor	Experiences emotional repulsion to the action
Person[2] (effect[b])	Shuns contact with Person[1]	Severs ties with Person[1]

[49] In a comment on the use of this expression in 1 Sam 13:4, Alter justifies his translation: "The literal meaning of the Hebrew idiom is very much like 'to be in bad odor with,' but that antiquated English idiom has a certain Victorian fussiness not suitable to this narrator" (71). As expected, only Fox translates the verb literally, yet he treats the indirect object as the direct object: "you have made your father reek."

Does the relationship between these two columns constitute an instance of metaphor, metonymy, or some other trope? After detecting a dissonance between the text-in-context construal of an utterance and its decontextualized meaning, the next step involves an attempt to identify the precise nature of the trope. What type of relationship links the entailed understanding of the utterance and the presupposed construal? In this case, how can one characterize the connection between the decontextualized meaning, "You have made yourself stink to your father," and the text-in-context construal, the sense that Absalom's actions have caused an irreconcilable rift between father and son? The chart above shows that there are various points of similarity and difference between these two interpretations, with common aspects marked with a solid underline and contrasting features with a dotted line. The construals exhibit elements of both resemblance and contrast, displaying a complexity that makes labeling the trope difficult.

If the relationship between being malodorous and being odious constitutes a metonymy, then does the connection between the scent a person emits and the illicit sexual act a person performs fit within one of the categories of metonymic relations discussed above? One could argue that there is some sort of part-whole relationship between one person rejecting another because he is morally repulsive and because he is physically repulsive; yet, overall, this example does not fit easily into any of the standard metonymic categories. This conclusion suggests that the utterance may better qualify as a metaphor. Applying White's heuristic device, it is difficult to separate the utterance into primary and secondary vocabulary and then create primary and secondary sentences, because the sense of incongruity that motivates the tropic interpretation comes not from within this particular utterance, but from the relationship between the utterance and its surrounding context. The statement that "you have made yourself stink to your father" does not violate any selection restrictions, for the referents of the subject, reflexive verb, and indirect object do not infringe upon established patterns of usage. Just as an inanimate, concrete entity or object, like land or ointment, can stink, so can animate beings, like fish or human beings.

Although this utterance does not display the type of semantic anomaly witnessed in the metaphors in 1 Samuel 25, nevertheless, it does contain an underlying analogy:

> Hypothetical Situation: Absalom somehow develops a foul body odor that David will detect and presumably find offensive.
> Actual Situation: Ahitophel predicts that after Absalom has sex with David's concubines, David will find out, respond with indignation, and irreconcilably reject Absalom.

The main comparison operating here does not involve Person[1], rather Person[2]. The analogy does not arise from similarities between emitting a foul body odor and having sexual intercourse with the king's concubines. Instead, the expression equates the reaction a person has to an offensive odor to an individual's response to an offensive action. Given this analogical element, the utterance appears to align more toward the metaphoric end of the spectrum than the metonymic side, though the utterance defies easy categorization.

C. 2 Samuel 16:21b[2]—וחזקו ידי כל אשר אתך
("And the hands of all who are with you will be strengthened")

Ahitophel predicts that David's negative reaction to Absalom ultimately will have positive repercussions for Absalom's supporters: "and the hands of all who are with you will be strengthened" (16:21). Just as with the prior example, this utterance lacks any grammatical or semantic anomalies. In the context of an advertisement for an exercise class devoted to enhancing the hand muscles, the statement, "And the hands of all who are with you will be strengthened," would not exhibit any sort of incongruity. However, given the larger frame of this sentence, the anomaly become obvious. The next step entails trying to figure out the intended construal. Several possible referents seem plausible, including power, confidence, courage, or loyalty. How does one figure out the precise text-in-context construal of this utterance?

Decontextualized Meaning	Text-in-Context Construal
The muscles in the hands of all who are with you will become stronger.	The power/confidence/courage/loyalty of all who are with you will become stronger.

For a biblical scholar, one potential means of understanding this statement would be to examine how the language here is used elsewhere in the Tanakh. Earlier in the book of Samuel, David charges the men of Jabesh-gilead: "And now, may your hands be strengthened and may you be men of valor (ועתה תחזקנה ידיכם והיו לבני חיל)"

(2 Sam 2:7). In one prophetic book, God's command to "strengthen your hands" follows the negative dictate, "do not fear" (Zech 8:13). In another, two figurative expressions are juxtaposed: "Will your heart stand fast, will your hands be strong in the days when I deal with you? (הֲיַעֲמֹד לִבֵּךְ אִם תֶּחֱזַקְנָה יָדַיִךְ לַיָּמִים אֲשֶׁר אֲנִי עֹשֶׂה אוֹתָךְ)" (Ezek 22:14).[50] While these citations imply that having a strong hand involves possessing courage, other citations associate the hand with power through poetic parallelism. For instance, Jer 16:21 parallels יָד ("hand") and גְבוּרָה ("might"), so that the former has been translated as "power" and the latter as "might."[51] Other verses contain the collocation, בְּכֹחַ גָּדוֹל וּבְיָד חֲזָקָה, indicating that God acts with "great power" and "a strong hand" (Exod 32:11; Neh 1:10).

As noted previously, this type of investigation contributes to a general understanding of broader patterns of usage for the lexemes in this verse; however, such a study cannot resolve the ambiguities inherent in this particular utterance. In this case, a close reading of the discourse segments preceding this statement provides insight. Interestingly, the remark, "and the hands of all who are with you will be strengthened," does not directly follow the recommendation to sleep with the concubines. While this act surely functions as an assertion of Absalom's royal power and a visual, symbolic reinforcement of the fact that Absalom has replaced his father as king, Ahitophel does not state explicitly that either Absalom or his supporters will benefit from the sexual conquest of the concubines. Instead, Ahitophel calls attention to the ramifications of David's anticipated negative reaction to Absalom. It is the public hearing about David's response, not the sexual act itself, that will bolster Absalom's supporters in some way: "Come to bed with your father's concubines . . . and let all Israel hear that you have made yourself stink to your father" (16:21).

The remaining ambiguity concerning the precise implication of the statement "you have made yourself stink to your father" further complicates the construal of the present utterance. What are the conceivable consequences that might transpire after David learns about his son's actions? David might be so enraged that he fights against

---

[50] Greenberg translates the first, "unusual expression," as, "Will your heart be stout?" (456). Seven times the *qal* verb חֹזֶק appear with the subject יָד (also see Judg 7:11; Ezek 3:14; Zech 8:9). Nine times the *pi'el* חֹזֶק occurs with the object יָד (Judg 9:24; 1 Sam 23:16; Isa 35:3; Jer 23:14; Ezek 13:22; Job 4:3; Ezra 1:6; Neh 2:18; 6:9), as does the *hip'il* הֶחֱזִיק three times (Gen 21:18; Ezek 16:49; Zech 14:13).

[51] See *JPS* translation and Lundbom, 766.

Absalom all the more fiercely, a scenario Hushai suggests further on
(17:8); such a reaction certainly would not benefit Absalom's men.
Or, as various commentators have proposed, David might respond
by permanently severing all ties with his son.[52] Although the king
took Absalom back after he murdered his brother Amnon (2 Sam
14:33), the current deed promises to be so flagrant as to make a
future reconciliation inconceivable. Since Absalom's supporters will
no longer need to worry about being left in a vulnerable, despised
position should father and son reunite, they will have more confidence
in their leader or perhaps more courage to defend the new king.
Had the assurance about Absalom's supporters followed the instruction to sleep with the concubines, the reference to the strengthening of the hands might have conveyed the notion that the political
power of those with Absalom had been bolstered by Absalom's brazen
act. However, given the existing sequence of statements by Ahitophel,
the utterance appears to refer more to a heightened degree of
confidence, loyalty, or resolve.

As seen in other verses, an interpretative gloss replaces this figurative
remark in a number of biblical translations.[53] Various translators conclude that the expression, "to strengthen the hands" means, in more
abstract terms, that Absalom's men "will be encouraged" (*JPS*) or
"will take courage" (*NAB*). These renderings eliminate the lexeme,
"hands," and specify that the phrase "the hands of all who are with
you" refers to "all who support you" (*JPS*), "everyone on your side"
(McCarter), or "all your partisans" (*NAB*). Such translations read the
word "hands" metonymically, as an instance in which a body part
stands for the whole person. Others render "hands" as "resolution,"
which will be "confirm[ed]" (*REB*) or "strengthened" (*NJB*) by
Absalom's followers. In these cases, a physical body part is associated
metonymically with a mental state. According to Barcelona, one type
of metonymic relationship links "body part for person," which explains
the interpretation of hands as a symbol for Absalom's supporters.
Another type of metonymic relationship correlates "body part for
intellectual attributes conventionally associated with it,"[54] a fitting
category for the connection between resolve or courage and the hand.

---

[52] See Rashi; Joseph Kara; Alter, *The David Story*, 295; Bar-Efrat, *2 Samuel*, 179.
[53] For a more literal translation of this utterance, see Alter, Fox, *KJV*, and *NRS*.
[54] Barcelona labels the utterance, "There are a lot of good heads at the University,"
under both headings (4).

The attempt to label the metonymic relationship raises a question about what leads to the association between two entities. It is not difficult to account for the connection between hands and power. Hands engage in combat or perform other actions that demonstrate an individual's physical power. Hands also wield items like weapons and scepters, objects associated with military and political power. Since hands are used to swear oaths in the Bible,[55] hands could conceivably become associated with loyalty. In a society like our own in which a firm handshake marks the conclusion of a deal or the establishment of some sort relationship, one could understand how a strong hand might connote resolve or confidence. Because of the chronological and cultural distance that separates contemporary interpreters from the writers of the Bible and the limitations on our knowledge of ancient Israel, it may not always be possible to reconstruct the evolution of a metonymic connection or identify the precise metonymic relationship.

D. *2 Samuel 17:2*—וְהוּא יָגֵעַ וּרְפֵה יָדַיִם
("And he will be tired and droopy handed")

Complying with Ahitophel's counsel, Absalom's men pitched a tent for him on the roof and "he came to bed with his father's concubines before the eyes of all Israel" (16:22). The narrator does not record how David or the general public actually responded to this act.[56] Instead, as the story continues, Ahitophel speaks up and presents Absalom with a second course of action. Ahitophel takes the initiative, both in offering further advice and in executing his plan, an observation illustrated by the preponderance of seven first-person verbs in his concise, three-verse speech (17:1–3). Ahitophel volunteers to muster a contingent of troops and pursue David immediately, so as to attack him "when he is tired and droopy handed" (17:2). He anticipates that the startled troops will flee, allowing him to defeat the king. In both pieces of advice (16:21 and 17:1–3), Ahitophel mentions "hands," thus creating a contrast: unlike the first plan, which was devised to make the hands of Absalom's supporters strong, the second presupposes that David's hands will be weak.

---

[55] See, for instance, Gen 24:2.

[56] Later, when David returns to Jerusalem and resumes his position as king, the narrator notes that David placed the ten concubines "in a house under watch, but he did not come to bed with them" (2 Sam 20:3).

For several reasons, the expression "droopy handed" proves less ambiguous than the two prior examples. First, the preceding verb specifies in straight-forward, nonfigurative language David's expected condition: "when he is tired (ינע אוהו)" (17:2). The subsequent statement, "and droopy handed," supplements the initial assertion. Secondly, the connection between drooping hands and tiredness is more transparent than in the prior two cases. Here, the decontextualized meaning and the text-in-context construal exhibit a clear part-whole relationship in which a posture or gesture functions as an external manifestation of an internal condition. Barcelona classifies this type of utterance as an instance of an "effect for cause" metonymy, similar to the sentences "He walked with drooping shoulders" and "John has a long face."[57] Others might consider this an example of a "concrete for the abstract" metonymy, since a perceptible demeanor signals an abstract emotion.

Nevertheless, questions remain about the precise nuance of the expression. Does the remark about David being "droopy handed" semantically echo the comment that "he is tired"? Or, instead, do the two statements exhibit a greater degree of contrast: the first predicts that David is physically exhausted while the second suggests that he is emotionally weary and demoralized as well. A number of translations adopt the second approach. For instance, McCarter renders the clause, "when he is weary and his guard is down," interpreting the drooping hands as a sign of vulnerability.[58] Others substitute the comment about David's hands with various adjectives characterizing his emotional condition: "while he is weary and disheartened" (*JPS*), "discouraged" (*NRS, NAB*), or "dispirited" (*REB, NJB*).[59] The disparity between what is actually said in the Hebrew text and the construal of the utterance incorporated into these English translations marks this utterance as a trope.

What motivates the assumption that the expression "droopy-handed" means that David is "disheartened" or "discouraged"? To what extent is this interpretation generated by a close reading of the utterance in its surrounding literary context, or to what extent has this understanding been influenced by the other biblical passages in which this

---

[57] Barcelona, 4–5.
[58] Note that McCarter interprets the utterance through his translation (378), not through an exegetical comment.
[59] In contrast, Alter translates as "slack handed" and Fox as "slack of hands."

expression occurs? The plural noun ידים ("hands") is used with the verb רפה ("to droop") ten times[60] and with the adjective from the same root (רפה) three times.[61] In most of these cases, the expression appears as part of a cluster of phrases that depict the stereotypical fear and panic experienced after the reception of bad news.[62] Yet in 2 Samuel 17 does Ahitophel intend to suggest that slack hands indicate fear or fatigue? Given the fact that the narrator has already noted that David and his men are "exhausted (עיפים)" (2 Sam 16:14), and considering that Ahitophel's plan depends upon David being weary and unable to fight effectively against him, a text-in-context reading recommends the latter option. In this particular context, the metonymic expression "droopy-handed" seems to mirror the preceding verb and connote a lack of physical energy, not a lack courage.

How does this expression operate as a trope? Imagine an individual who happened to sight David and his troops in the wilderness, right after they fled Jerusalem. If that person ran back to Ahitophel and reported what he had observed, he might offer his assessment of David's condition, perhaps stating that he seemed tired and demoralized. Or he might recount how David acted, perhaps describing how he leaned against a rock with his eyes closed, his breathing loud and labored, his shoulders slumped, his hands hanging limply at his side, his armor strewn about on the ground. In this imaginary context, these statements accurately depict David's visible physical conduct; but at the same time, individually and collectively, they also indicate his physical conditional or emotional state. In such a scenario, the descriptions of David's demeanor exemplify White's concept of bifurcation. The observations function not only on a nonfigurative level, but they also signal the condition conventionally associated with these actions. In the literary context under discussion, 2 Samuel 17, Ahitophel speculates about David; he does not deliver an eye-witness report. Although he correctly assumes that

---

[60] 2 Sam 4:1; Isa 13:7; Jer 6:24; Jer 50:43; Ezek 7:17; 21:12; Zeph 3:16; Ezra 4:4; Neh 6:9; 2 Chr 15:7.

[61] 2 Sam 17:2; Isa 35:3; Job 4:3.

[62] For a fuller discussion of these texts and their Ugaritic parallels, see D. R. Hillers, "A Convention in Hebrew Literature: The Reaction to Bad News," *ZAW* 77 (1965) 86–90. This expression is also attested in Lachish letter 6, which states: "The [official's] statements are not good—they are of a kind *hrpt ydyk*" (line 6). Dennis Pardee translates the expression "slacken your hands" as "to slacken your courage" (*Handbook of Ancient Hebrew Letters* [Chico: Scholars Press, 1982], 100–101).

the king will be tired after such a journey, he does not know with certainty that David's hands will be hanging lax at his side. He utilizes this expression in order to reiterate his contention that David will be weary, and thus to help convince Absalom to adopt his suggested strategy.

E. 2 Samuel 17:10a² — הָמֵס יִמָּס ("it/he will surely melt")

In spite of the shrewdness of Ahitophel's counsel, and the approval it receives from the elders (17:4), Absalom solicits a second opinion from Hushai: "Like this has Ahitophel spoken. Shall we act on his word?" (17:6). Bar-Efrat outlines the challenges facing Hushai as he sets out to counter Ahitophel's plan with a proposal designed to surreptitiously save the deposed king:

> The mission with which Hushai was charged—to argue against Ahitophel's advice—was extremely difficult for two reasons. First of all, Ahitophel was regarded as an authority . . . while Hushai's advice, though valued by Absalom—as indicated by the fact that he was asked to give his opinion—was far less esteemed than Ahitophel's . . . Secondly, the advice Hushai had to counter was not only extremely good, but had also been acknowledged as such by Absalom and all the elders of Israel (v. 4). In consequence, Hushai had to use very sophisticated tactics in order to induce his audience to change its mind, to dismiss the good plan as bad and accept the bad plan as good.[63]

When Hushai points out several flaws in Ahitophel's assessment of the military situation, he warns that if they execute Ahitophel's proposal, David's troops will rout Absalom's forces. He envisions the following scenario: when one of Absalom's soldiers hears about the defeat, "though he be a man of valor whose heart is like the heart of a lion, it/he will surely melt" (17:10).

As this translation indicates, the Hebrew text is indeterminate, for the third person, masculine singular verb יִמָּס can refer to either antecedent: the masculine singular word "heart" (לֵב) in the prior clause or the masculine singular subject introduced at the beginning of the verse, "he" (הוּא). While most translations of Samuel specify that the verb refers to the person,[64] a number of biblical dictionar-

---

[63] Bar-Efrat, *Narrative Art in the Bible*, 223–224.
[64] See, for instance, Alter, Fox, McCarter, *JPS*, *NRS*, or *KJV*.

ies identify the heart as the subject.[65] Either way, the general sense of the sentence is clear: Even a brave warrior will react with fear when faced with the news of an impending defeat. Translators respond to this statement in various ways. Some, like Fox, insist on a more literal rendering of the Hebrew: "He will melt, yes, melt away."[66] Others treat the verb more exegetically: "he will surely quail" (Alter);[67] "he will be shaken" (*JPS*);[68] "he'll grow faint with fear" (McCarter); "even the valiant . . . will be demoralised" (*NJB*). Some take a different approach and interpret "heart" metonymically as "courage," thereby linking a bodily organ with an emotion associated with it. Thus the *NAB* translation of Hushai's comment reads: "Then even the brave man . . . will lose courage" (2 Sam 17:20).[69] While some translations retain a figurative element, others transform the phrase into a straightforward comment about the soldier's anticipated emotional condition.

What tags the Hebrew utterance as a trope? The decontextualized meaning of the verb "to melt" involves the process whereby certain physical objects become liquefied by heat. For instance, uncollected manna melts in the sun (Exod 16:21), heat melts ice (Sir 3:15), and wax melts when exposed to fire.[70] Whether one understands the subject of the verb in 2 Sam 17:10 to be the heart or the person in general, the collocation of either noun with the verb "to melt"

---

[65] *DCH* and *BDB*, s.v. מסס. The *DCH* entry translates and explicates 2 Sam 17:10: "*and even if he be a valiant person, whose heart is like the heart of a lion, it will indeed be melted,* i.e. he will be discouraged" (367).

[66] Fox attempts to replicate the Hebrew syntax, which combines the infinitive absolute המס with the imperfect ימס to convey an emphatic nuance. The *KJV* and *NRS* translate the verb as "utterly melt," but *NRS* adds "with fear" for clarification.

[67] Alter includes a note explaining that "the literal meaning of the Hebrew is 'he will surely melt'" (298).

[68] This translation may have been influenced by the semantically similar root מוג. In his comment on Ezek 21:20, Greenberg sites Rashi's observation that מוג "means both 'be agitated, waver' (// 'quake' in Nahum 1:5, and cf. Arabic *mawj* 'wave') and 'melt'" (425).

[69] Similarly, *DCH* explains in a gloss that the expression means that "he will be discouraged" (s.v. מסס). Also see the *JPS* translation of Deut 20:8, "lest the courage of his comrades flag like his." Elsewhere, the *JPS Tanakh* renders this expression with the English idiom "to lose heart" (Josh 2:11; 5:1) or with the verb, "to sink," as in Isa 13:7: "all men's hearts shall sink" (also see Josh 7:5; Isa 19:1; Ezek 21:12; cf. Nah 2:11).

[70] Various passages use the melting of wax in similes to describe other phenomenon, such as the way the wicked will perish (Ps 68:3) or mountains will react to God's presence (Mic 1:4; Ps 97:5). Judges 15:14 compares the dissolution or "melting" of the rope on Samson's arms to flax that catches fire.

constitutes the type of selection restriction violation that marks this assertion as semantically anomalous. In contrast, if the masculine singular verb referred to a liquefiable substance like wax (דוֹנג) or ice (קרח), no incongruity would exist in the sentence, "It will surely melt."

The tendency for biblical dictionaries to read the heart as the subject in 2 Sam 17:10 likely reflects the frequency with which the noun "heart" is described as "melting" in the Bible and in texts from Qumran, with approximately a dozen citations in each body of literature.[71] For instance, Rahab uses these words to evoke the fear of the Israelites felt by the Canaanites. She tells the spies: "Dread of you has fallen upon us, and all the inhabitants of the land are shaking (נמגו) before you" (Josh 2:9); after hearing about the wonders performed by God, "our hears melted and there was no spirit left standing in anyone because of you" (Josh 2:11). The Israelites experience a similar response when defeated by the forces of Ai: "The people's heart melted and turned to water" (Josh 7:5). In a number of passages, this phase appears as part of a sequence of stereotypical indicators of alarm, as in Isaiah's portrayal of the impending the day of YHWH: "Therefore all hands will drop and the heart of every person will melt. And they will be terrified, pangs and throes will seize them, they will writhe like a woman in labor" (Isa 13:7–8).[72] In Ps 22:15, the image depicts illness and suffering: "Like water, I am poured out. All my bones are out of joint. My heart is like wax, melted in my bowels."[73]

In addition, similes involving melting objects occur in a number of Akkadian and Hittite magical texts and treaties. In the Hittite Soldier's Oath, wax and mutton fat are thrown onto a pan while the speaker invokes a curse that threatens the melting of the offender: "Just as this wax melts and just as this mutton fat dissolves,—whoever breaks these oaths, [shows disrespect to the king] of the Hatti [land,] let [him] melt lik[e wax], let him dissolve like [mutton fat]!"[74]

---

[71] לב or לבב appears as the subject of the nip‘al מסס ten times (Deut 20:8; Josh 2:11; 5:1; 7:5; 2 Sam 17:10; Isa 13:7; 19:1; Ezek 21:12; Nah 2:11; Ps 22:15); the noun is found once as the object of מסס hip‘il (Deut 1:28) and once with מסה hip‘il (Josh 14:8). The verses that use this expression figuratively exceed the attested nonfigurative citations. For a list of the Qumran citations, see *DCH*, s.v. מסס, nip‘al and hip‘il, and s.v. the adjective, מס.

[72] For similar passages, see Hillers, 87–89.

[73] Also see Ps 6:7, which describes how the psalmist melts his bed with tears.

[74] Translation by A. Goetze, *ANET*, 353; quoted in Delbert Hillers, "The Effective Simile in Biblical Literature," *JAOS* 103 (1983) 183.

The Esarhaddon vassal-treaties contain a similar curse: "Just as one burns a wax figurine in fire, dissolves a clay one in water, so may they burn your figure in fire, submerge it in water."[75] Delbert Hillers explains how melting operates in the Akkadian Maqlû texts:

> Thus the benevolent witch-doctor in the Maqlû series, intending to rid a victim of a black-magic spell, makes images of tallow, copper, dough, asphalt, clay, or wax. These figures are identified with the sorcerer or sorceress who has laid the spell on the victim. Then they are burned as the magician recites the spell, containing a simile: "As these figures melt, dissolve, and run down, so may sorcerer and sorceress melt, dissolve, and run down!"[76]

Hillers labels these examples "effective" similes, meaning that the "speech is intended to produce an effect in the world beyond ordinary discourse."[77] He differentiates the "effective" similes found in various ancient Near Eastern texts and in biblical prayers and prophetic oracles from the type of "descriptive"[78] similes encountered in 2 Samuel 17.

What does it mean for the heart to melt? The hypothetical situation involves a substance like wax or ice that becomes liquefied when exposed to heat and drips in a downward motion. The actual situation involves a person in a state of fear, who, in a moment of panic after hearing that his fellow soldiers have been defeated, feels as if his heart has dropped.[79] Applying White's heuristic device, the metaphor in 2 Sam 17:10 can be construed as followed:

Primary Vocabulary: [The heart] will surely x.
Secondary Vocabulary: The y will surely melt.

Primary Sentence 1: [The heart] will surely *drop*.
Secondary Sentence: The *wax*[80] will surely melt.

According to this construal, an extremely frightful situation produces a sensation whereby one's internal organs seem to sink to the pit of one's stomach, thus resembling a quickly dissolving piece of wax or ice.

---

[75] Translation by Erica Reiner, *ANET*, 540; quoted in Hillers, 183.
[76] Hillers, 181.
[77] Hillers, 181.
[78] Hillers, 183.
[79] For this insight, I thank the Lower Merion police officer who pulled me over and issued me a citation for a burnt out headlight.
[80] While numerous substances could have been substituted in this sentence, wax was selected since it is referred to most often in the Bible.

An alternative approach, similar to one explored in connection
with 1 Sam 25:37, would be to understand לב in a nonanatomical
sense as a reference to courage. The dissolving or softening of one's
courage signals the opposite of the strengthening of the heart (אמץ לב),
which denotes an exhibition of courage.[81] Such an interpretation
yields the following construal:

> Primary Sentence 2: [The courage] will surely *disappear.*
> Secondary Sentence: The *wax* will surely melt.

While the identification of the subject in 2 Sam 17:10 as the "heart"
appears reasonable given the frequent combination of the noun לב
("heart") and the verb מסס ("melt"), one also could argue that in
the particular context of Hushai's remarks the focus of the sentence
seems to be on the response of the soldier. The sentence emphasizes the main subject, the soldier who will hear that Absalom's forces
have been routed, by placing masculine singular pronoun והוא ("and
he") in the frontal position: "And he, even though he is a man of
valor . . . it/he will surely melt." In addition, the simile in the relative clause "whose heart is like a lion's heart" modifies the "man of
valor," after which the sentence returns to the initial subject when
Hushai predicts that the soldier "will surely melt." How does this
third interpretation alter the analysis of the analogy?

> Primary Sentence 3: [The man] will surely *collapse.*
> Secondary Sentence: The *wax* will surely melt.

Here, the verb is understood as a description of the man's physical
response to news of the rout of Absalom's troops. Just as wax drips
down while melting, so the soldier will collapse to the ground in
fear and dismay.[82] In other words, like the disintegrating wax, he
will "fall apart" and prove incapable of mounting a successful attack.

F. *2 Samuel 17:11b*—ופניך הלכים בקרב
("And your face will walk into battle")

After criticizing Ahitophel's strategy, Hushai then offers his own proposal. He advises Absalom to muster a large army in order to over-

---

[81] Ps 27:14; 31:25. This interpretation was suggested by Jeffrey Tigay (personal
correspondence).
[82] McCarter suggests a similar interpretation in his translation: "He'll grow faint
with fear" (379).

whelm David's experienced band of fighters. In contrast to Ahitophel's plan, which envisions giving Ahitophel all the responsibility and the subsequent glory, Hushai emphasizes Absalom's role in the attack: "and your face will walk into battle"[83] (17:11). In this easily interpreted metonymy, one body part, the face, stands for the larger individual, Absalom.

Only two other passages utilize a similar syntactic construction, both in reference to God's actions on behalf of the Israelites. Using the same subject and verb, God promises to accompany the Israelites as they travel through the wilderness: "And He said: 'My face will go (פָּנַי יֵלֵכוּ) and I will give you a rest.' And [Moses] said to Him: 'If Your face does not go (אִם אֵין פָּנֶיךָ הֹלְכִים), do not bring us up from here'" (Exod 33:14–15). Elsewhere, Moses states: "And because He loved your fathers and chose their seed after them, His face brought you out, with His great might, from Egypt" (Deut 4:37). Jeffrey Tigay notes that this expression, sometimes translated with the appropriate pronoun[84] or the word "presence"[85] serves as the Hebrew equivalent of "in person." In his commentary on Deut 4:37, he explains: "The idiom emphasizes that God used no intermediary (such as an angel) in freeing Israel but, as a sign of His favor, freed them personally."[86] By using a fairly rare construction otherwise reserved for the Divine, Hushai crafts a fitting scenario for the new king. Bar-Efrat reflects on the effectiveness of his choice of words:

> The effort to give prominence to Absalom reaches its culmination in the solemn pronouncement, 'and that your presence (literally, your face) go to battle'.... Hushai plays on Absalom's desires and aspirations, directing his words towards the delusions of grandeur and excessive self-love of the ambitious prince.[87]

---

[83] Some understand the text as meaning בְּקִרְבָּם ("among them") instead of בְּקֶרֶב ("into battle"), a reading reflected in the Septuagint (McCarter, Fox). McCarter argues that בְּקֶרֶב "is probably an Aramaism and late" (382).

[84] For example, *JPS*: "I will go in the lead" (Exod 33:14) and "He Himself ... led you out of Egypt" (Deut 4:37).

[85] See the translation of Exod 33:14–15 and Deut 4:37 in Everett Fox, *The Five Books of Moses* (New York: Schocken Books, 1995).

[86] Tigay, 57. As Tigay explains, other passages in the Bible describe an angel serving as God's agent; see, for instance Exod 32:34, which promises Moses that God's angel will go before him (מַלְאָכִי יֵלֵךְ לְפָנֶיךָ).

[87] Bar-Efrat, *Narrative Art in the Bible*, 233.

G. *Reflections on Metaphor and Metonymy in 2 Samuel 16:16–17:14*

As Bar-Efrat's comment illustrates, metaphor and metonymy both possess the ability to produce rhetorical effects. Alter notes a sharp contrast between "the pointedly unmetaphoric, businesslike character of Ahitophel's language" and "Hushai's elaborately figurative rhetoric of persuasion."[88] However, closer examination shows that Ahitophel's advice in 2 Sam 16:21 and 17:1–3 is not devoid of figurative language. He, too, employs tropes to try to persuade the inexperienced, impressionable king. While he succeeds the first time, he fails the second, the results of which prove deadly for him and Absalom.[89] Ahitophel's terse second speech, containing only one fairly familiar tropic expression, proves no match for Hushai's artfully crafted speech, suffused with a variety of rhetorical devices.[90]

The preceding analysis shows that both metaphor and metonymy contain an anomaly, the crucial element that triggers a tropic construal. In metaphor, the sense of an incongruity sometimes arises from a selection restrictions violation, as in the depiction of the melting individual or heart in 2 Sam 17:10. In other cases, the anomaly results from the dissonance between the decontextualized meaning of an utterance and its text-in-context construal. The examples of metonymy in this narrative unit exhibit the latter form of anomaly.

Of the utterances examined above, some easily fit within the distinct categories of metaphor and metonymy. What distinguishes the two? Metaphor is marked by the existence of an analogy. In such instances, White's analytical techniques of articulating the actual and hypothetical situations and constructing primary and secondary sentences help the interpreter to identify and refine the analysis of the underlying comparison. With metonymy, connection, not comparison, links the decontextualized meaning and the text-in-context construal. The various lists of metonymic relations aid the reader in evaluating some of the potential ways a metonymic connection may manifest itself. However, as with any heuristic device, such lists are

---

[88] Alter, *The David Story*, 296–297.

[89] Ahitophel hangs himself when he discovers that his council was not acted upon (2 Sam 17:23). Absalom dies in battle as he executes Hushai's imprudent military strategy (2 Sam 18:9–15).

[90] In addition to the metonymic and metaphoric expressions analyzed above, Hushai employs a number of similes and hyberbolic statements, which will be discussed in the second half of this chapter.

restricted in their usefulness; they cannot enable the exegete to definitively label and explain every instance of metonymy. Likewise, in certain cases, the broader taxonomical attempt to categorize every type of trope can prove to be a futile endeavor. Some statements, like Ahitophel's comment that Absalom will make himself stink to his father (16:21), resist the neat classifications rhetoricians have defined over the centuries, for the creativity of human language expands beyond the confines of labels like metaphor or metonymy. Yet that which may frustrate scholars contributes to the delight and expressive potential of writers and readers, speakers and listeners.

III. SIMILES IN 2 SAMUEL 16:16–17:14

A. *Research Review: Studies of Similes*

One of the most distinctive features of Hushai's speech is its abundance of similes, four in an eight-verse discourse segment. Although the topic of simile has not generated nearly the volume of literature that has been produced on metaphor and metonymy, from the classical period until the present day scholars have compared metaphor and simile. Aristotle perceived simile as a less pleasant form of a metaphor, though he stressed that both rhetorical devices involve an analogy.[91] Classical rhetoricians like Quintilian reversed the order and defined metaphor as "a shorter form of simile."[92] Many contemporary scholars minimize the differences between the two and insist that the distinction "seems extremely unimportant,"[93] for metaphor and simile are practically "interchangeable,"[94] with "no fundamental difference" between them.[95]

Black disagrees with this approach. While he acknowledges that a metaphor "is grounded in similarity and analogy," he cautions that this does not mean that metaphor and simile differ only in form. In certain contexts, he admits, a simile "may still be figurative, and hardly more than a stylistic variant" upon a metaphor. For instance, he argues that little semantic difference separates the metaphor, "My

---

[91] Aristotle, *Rhetoric*, 224.
[92] Quintilian, 305.
[93] Booth, 53.
[94] Caird, 144.
[95] Nielsen, 61.

Love is a red, red rose," from the simile, "My Love is like a red, red rose."[96] Nevertheless, Black heralds the distinctive features that make metaphor a superior trope. He writes:

> But to suppose that the metaphorical statement is an abstract or précis of a literal point-by-point comparison, in which the primary and secondary subjects are juxtaposed for the sake of noting dissimilarities as well as similarities, is to misconstrue the function of a metaphor. In discursively comparing one subject *with* another, we sacrifice the distinctive power and effectiveness of a good metaphor. The literal comparison lacks the ambience and suggestiveness, and the imposed "view" of the primary subject, upon which a metaphor's power to illuminate depends.[97]

Soskice criticizes the position of Black and his followers. First, she argues that the claim that simile cannot rival the impact or meaning of metaphor only holds "if one takes as examples uninspiring similes."[98] She asserts that certain similes appear "flat" or "prosaic not because they are similes but because the insights they embody are prosaic" or "because the parallels drawn seem trite." In contrast, with a more striking simile in which the comparison "is in no way obvious or boring," deleting the word "like" does not alter the impact.[99] Furthermore, Soskice charges that Black has mistakenly suggested that all similes are point-for-point comparisons. She stresses that while some similes involve the comparison of similars, others entail the comparison of dissimilars. She adds that in the latter case, "simile shares much of the imaginative life and cognitive function of its metaphorical counterparts."[100]

Others have used different terminology to discriminate between various types of comparisons. In an influential article, Ortony distinguishes between "ordinary comparisons" or "ordinary similarity statements," as in the sentence, "Encyclopedias are like dictionaries," and similes, as in the statement, "Encyclopedias are like gold mines." He labels the former "literal comparisons," since encyclo-

---

[96] Black, "More about Metaphor," 30.
[97] Black, 30–31.
[98] Soskice, 58.
[99] Soskice, 58–59.
[100] Soskice, 59. Seeking to further refine the differences between similes, Soskice distinguishes between "illustrative" and "modelling" similes. Whereas an "illustrative" simile "compares, point for point, two known entities," the "modelling" simile uses "a subject that is reasonably well known to us to explain or provide schematization for a state of affairs which is beyond our full grasp" (60).

pedias do in fact resemble dictionaries, and the latter "nonliteral comparisons," since encyclopedias are not really like gold mines.[101] A number of scholars have adopted and refined Ortony's distinction. For instance, Kittay writes that "literal comparison takes place within fixed, common, or given categories," as when a hippopotamus is compared with an elephant, whereas "comparisons in metaphor and simile cross categorical boundaries," as when a hippopotamus is compared to a religious institution.[102] Building upon Kittay's work, Gary Long conceives of similes as figurative, "cross-categorical comparisons" that involve two different semantic fields. In contrast, he labels as "nonfigurative comparisons" inner-categorical comparisons that are restricted to a single semantic field. To illustrate the difference, he opposes the simile, "An education is like a stairway," to the nonfigurative comparison, "A scalpel is like a razor."[103]

How does this research comport with the examples encountered in the Bible? In Terry Brensinger's study, *Simile and Prophetic Language in the Old Testament*, he observes that "similes are far more at home in biblical poetry than in narrative."[104] While similes, like metaphors, do not appear with the same frequency in prose as in poetry, 2 Samuel 17 shows that similes operate effectively in biblical narrative.

As part of a discussion of "The Style of the Royal Counselor's Discourse," Robert Polzin attempts to understand the "predilection for simile" seen in this chapter by studying all the similes found in 1–2 Samuel. "Why," he wonders, "are so many voices in this chapter . . . addicted to comparisons?"[105] He calculates that 1–2 Samuel

---

[101] Andrew Ortony, "Similarity in Similes and Metaphors," in *Metaphor and Thought*, 2d edition, ed. Andrew Ortony (Cambridge: Cambridge University Press, 1993), 347.

[102] Kittay, 18–19. The inspiration for these examples comes from T. S. Elliot's poem, 'The Hippopotamus,' which juxtaposes descriptions of the Church and a hippopotamus.

[103] Gary Alan Long, "Dead or Alive? Literality and God-Metaphors in the Hebrew Bible," *JAAR* 62 (1994), 516.

[104] Terry Lee Brensinger, *Simile and Prophetic Language in the Old Testament* (Lewiston, NY: The Edwin Mellen Press, 1996), 9.

[105] Robert Polzin, *David and the Deuteronomist* (Bloomington: Indiana University Press, 1993), 172. In addition to Hushai's four similes, Polzin counts a fifth simile, for he adopts the Septuagint reading of 2 Sam 17:3. The Septuagint renders the enigmatic concluding verse of Ahitophel's advice: "as a bride comes to her husband." Bar-Efrat and Alter insist that such a reading does not fit with the tenor of Ahitophel's speech, for "it would violate the pointedly unmetaphoric, businesslike character of Ahitophel's language, which stands in sharp contrast to Hushai's elaborately figurative rhetoric of persuasion" (Alter, *The David Story*, 296–297; also see Bar-Efrat, *2 Samuel*, 179–180). Alter translates the verse: "And let me turn back all the troops to you, for it is one man you seek."

contains about ninety instances in which the narrator or a charac-
ter uses explicit comparisons with k^e, $ka^{\,\flat a}sher$, or *ken*, and he attempts
to differentiate between the various types of comparisons found in
this corpus. He classifies one segment of the examples as follows:

> Roughly one-third of these explicit comparisons in 1–2 Samuel (about
> twenty-eight out of ninety occurrences) are temporal or diachronic, like
> Hushai's words to Absalom, "As I have served your father, so I will
> serve you" (2 Sam 16:19) . . . Such temporal statements most often
> relate the past to the present or future in a "as then, so now" com-
> parison, yet lack the graphic imaging that belongs to simile as a figure
> of speech.[106]

The remaining two-thirds of the explicit comparisons display such
graphic images, as in the description of the shaft of Goliath's spear:
"like a weaver's beam" (1 Sam 17:7). According to Polzin, the presence of this type of "pictorial image" qualifies a comparison as a
simile "in the technical sense of the term."[107] He concludes that the
"bold" and "colorful" similes in 2 Samuel 17 serve a persuasive function, helping the characters to "convince by rhetoric alone."[108] A
close reading of the four similes in Hushai's speech will permit an
evaluation of Polzin's findings and other claims about similes and
their relationship to metaphor.

B. *2 Samuel 17:8*—כדב שכול בשדה
("like a bear bereaved in the field")

As Hushai begins to undermine Ahitophel's plan, he reminds Absalom
that David and his men are seasoned fighters. He predicts that David
will hide out by himself at night, thus making it more difficult to
capture him than Ahitophel anticipates. In 2 Sam 17:8, Hushai presents a sequence of phrases depicting David and his soldiers, with a
simile positioned in the center. First, he establishes their general pro-
fessional qualifications: "You yourself know your father and his men,
that they are warriors (נבֹרים המה)." Secondly, he characterizes their
current emotional status: "and that they are bitter of spirit (ומרי נפש
המה)." Next, he introduces a simile: "like a bear bereaved in the
field (כדב שכול בשדה)." Finally, he refers to David specifically, com-

---

[106] Polzin, 172.
[107] Polzin, 172.
[108] Polzin, 178.

menting on his prior experience and his expected present behavior: "And your father is a man of war (וְאָבִיךָ אִישׁ מִלְחָמָה) and he will not spend the night with the troops (וְלֹא יָלִין אֶת־הָעָם)." While the surface structure of the simile makes the presence of a comparison explicit, it does not necessarily make the statement unambiguous or simple to decipher.

Hushai does not elaborate on the conduct or emotions typically associated with a bereaved bear, nor does he specify what a she-bear who has lost her cubs and a warrior have in common. Presumably, an audience in the biblical period would have possessed a greater degree of familiarity with bears, either from first-hand sightings of the animal or from the characteristics imparted through commonly used expressions or well-known lore.[109] For a contemporary audience, however, the simile may require some explication and background knowledge. A nearly identical simile appears in Hos 13:8, part of a series of similes depicting God's punishment of the Israelites: "And I will be to them like a lion, like a leopard on the road I lie in wait. I confront them like a bereaved bear, and I rip open the enclosure of their heart, and I devour them there like a lion; the beast of the field will tear them apart" (Hos 13:7–8). Commenting on this passage, Francis Andersen and David Noel Freedman label the comparison to the she-bear a "hackneyed" simile in which the bear exacts vengeance on those who snatched her cubs because "her rage is blind."[110] Hans Walter Wolff describes this as a "gruesome" image that depicts the rage of the "voracious animal."[111] Other references to bears in the Bible also pair the bear and the lion, which suggests that bears were known as powerful, violent, and dangerous animals. The provocation involved in taking the female bear's cubs only further exacerbated these qualities.[112]

---

[109] Oded Borowski reports that "the Syrian brown bear (*Ursus syriacus*; Heb. *dob*) was quite common in Palestine during biblical times" (*Every Living Thing: Daily Use of Animals in Ancient Israel* [Walnut Creek: Altamira Press, 1998], 201).

[110] Andersen and Freedman, 635.

[111] Hans Walter Wolff, *Hosea* (Philadelphia: Fortress Press, 1974), 226.

[112] References to bears and lions appear in 1 Sam 17:34, 36, 37; Hos 13:8; Amos 5:19; Prov 28:15; Lam 3:10. Other passages that mention bears include 2 Kgs 2:24; Isa 11:7; Isa 59:11; Prov 17:12. Borowski notes: "In general, bears do not molest humans unless they are surprised or attacked, and then they are more dangerous than any of the great cats" (201–202). Also see A. Caquot, *TDOT*, vol. 3, s.v. "דֹּב *dobh*," 70–71. Caquot asserts that the biblical passages mentioning bears "give the impression of being literary cliches rather than zoological observations" (70–71).

Bar-Efrat claims that the simile in v. 8 cleverly supplements both of the two previous adjectives used to characterize David and his men: "The word 'bear' in the image illustrates and reinforces the quality of 'mighty men', while 'robbed of her cubs', emphasizes 'enraged'."[113] In addition, several features link David, in particular, with the image of a bear. In 1 Samuel 17, David recounts how, as a shepherd, he would chase after any lion or bear that attacked his sheep and rescue the sheep from the predator's clutches (1 Sam 17:34–35). He confidently proclaims: "Both lion and bear your servant has struck down, and this uncircumcised Philistine will be like one of them . . . YHWH who rescued me from the lion and the bear will rescue me from the hand of the Philistine" (1 Sam 17:36–37). Alter remarks that by recapitulating earlier points in the David story, Hushai "is invoking the legend of the heroic David, who as a boy slew bear and lion . . . and who gathered round him bitter men, warriors, seasoned fighters."[114] In opposition to 1 Samuel 17, where the bear is depicted in a negative light and compared to David's enemy, 2 Samuel 17 evokes the bear in positive manner, in order to enhance the portrayal of the heroic warrior.

Given the power and ferociousness associated with bears, the simile aptly supports Hushai's contention that David and his men will prove a formidable adversary when attacked by Absalom's forces. But what makes the image of a *bereaved* bear, as opposed to an ordinary bear, especially appropriate for this particular narrative context? Commentators have noted that a bereaved bear connotes rage and an impulse for revenge, thus supplementing Hushai's portrayal of Absalom's opponents. However, insufficient attention has been given to another important aspect of this simile. Just as the bear has lost her cubs, David has lost the kingship. At this point in the story, David is compared figuratively to one who has lost children, for he has lost his royal power. More importantly, the image also recalls Amnon's murder and foreshadows the upcoming death of Absalom, two instances in which David actually becomes a bereft parent. In the latter episode, the experience of losing a child elicits sorrow, not rage (2 Sam 19:1–9). As seen in the analysis of the metaphors in 1 Samuel 25, this simile intersects with several other parts of the David story, thus contributing to a sense of narrative cohesion.

---

[113] Bar-Efrat, *Narrative Art in the Bible*, 227.
[114] Alter, *The David Story*, 297.

How does this simile differ from previously examined metaphors? To understand the differences better, consider how the simile would read if recast as a metaphor: "You yourself know your father and his men, that they are warriors and that they are bitter of spirit, a bear bereaved in the field." This reconfiguration yields the following conflated sentence: "Your father and his men are a bear bereaved in the field." This formulation brings to the fore the dissonance between the plural subject, David and his men, and the singular predicate, the bereaved bear. In addition, such a sentence creates a semantic incongruity by equating human beings with a wild animal. In its original expression, the simile lacks this anomalous element since the sentence explicitly compares the men to a bear, without equating the two.

While anomaly distinguishes metaphor from simile, analogy unites the two. Because of this common comparative feature, White's notion of an actual and hypothetical situation can be applied to a simile. In this case, the simile centers upon a hypothetical situation in which the bear's cubs have been killed or taken. In terms of the actual situation, David and his men have fled Jerusalem following Absalom's *coup d'état*; David has lost the kingship and his men have been ousted from their official positions in the royal court. These two situations intersect in a number of respects. Both creatures, the bear and the warriors, are known for their might and ferocity. Both have been robbed of something precious, bear cubs on the one hand and political power on the other. Both presumably respond with anger and an instinct to avenge their loss. Both are located "in the field," far from the royal residence David normally inhabits. Hushai does not spell out any of these associated commonplaces in his remarks. Instead, he relies on his listeners to understand the commonalities and infer the various implications of the analogy.

C. *2 Samuel 17:10a[1]*—אשר לבו כלב האריה
("whose heart is like the heart of a lion")

As Hushai continues to dissuade Absalom of the possibility of being able to quickly and easily defeat David, he creates a vignette of sorts, a scenario in which Absalom's forces will "fall from the first," presumably overpowered by David and his forces hiding out in the wilderness. He predicts: "The one who hears of it will say, 'There was a rout among the troops who follow after Absalom.' And though he be a man of valor, whose heart is like the heart of a lion, it/he

will surely melt" (17:9–10). This sequence of statements contains two
figurative expressions, a simile juxtaposed to the previously discussed
metaphor. As in v. 8, a more straightforward description of the individual precedes the simile. Also like the prior simile, no explanation
accompanies the simile specifying the particular qualities shared by
the two components of the comparison. What do a lion and a soldier have in common? Similar to the case of the bereaved bear, the
interpretation of the simile requires a familiarity with the characteristics
of a lion, through either first-hand observation or well-known lore.

References to lions abound in the Tanakh, with more than half
a dozen different terms used to designate this animal. Reflecting on
the repeated mention of lions, Blenkinsopp concludes:

> As biblical records and Assyrian records and iconography attest, lions
> lived in close proximity to human settlements on both sides of the
> Euphrates during the Iron Age; in fact, lions are attested in Palestine
> up to the Middle Ages and in Iraq into the early years of the twen-
> tieth century. The real and dangerous proximity of these splendid ani-
> mals combined with their symbolic potential will explain why they
> occur so frequently in the literature.[115]

Greenberg observes that "the poetic figure of a ravaging lion under-
went a metamorphosis" in the Bible.[116] Whereas the lion appears as
a "heroic emblem" in certain sections of the Torah,[117] in Psalms,
lions function as "an emblem of the wicked enemy;"[118] in the prophetic
books, the lion is used "as a figure of fierce cruelty."[119] A survey of
lion imagery found throughout the Tanakh shows that

> the various facets of the lion's existence, as hunter and hunted, as bold
> and strong or stealthy and ruthless, as all powerful or savage, permit
> it to represent a nation in its prime or in decline, both the wicked
> and the righteous, both the Almighty and evil.[120]

Which of this array of characteristics does Hushai refer to in 2 Sam
17:10? Several features of this verse and its larger context help the
interpreter narrow down the options. First, Hushai compares the

---

[115] Blenkinsopp, 221 (comment on Isaiah 5:26–30).
[116] Greenberg, 357 (comment on Ezek 19:1–14).
[117] Jacob's blessing of Judah (Gen 49:9), Moses' blessing of Gad and Dan (Deut
33:20, 22), and Balaam's praise of Israel (Num 23:24; 24:9).
[118] E.g., Ps 7:3; 17:12.
[119] E.g., Ezek 19:1–9; Nah 2:12–13.
[120] Leland Ryken, James Wilhoit, Tremper Longman III, eds., *Dictionary of Biblical Imagery*, s.v. "Lion," 514.

heart of the soldier to the *heart* of the lion, which places the focus on their inner nature.[121] Whereas other passages concentrate on the behavior of the lion, such as its roar[122] or the way it devours its prey,[123] this verse suggests a connection between the temperament of man and beast. Secondly, the preceding description of the soldier as a בן חיל (literally a "son of might") also helps to clarify the comparison. Although the word חיל designates human strength, the collocation בן חיל often connotes courage, not physical might. For instance, in 2 Sam 13:28, Absalom charges his men as he sends them off to kill his brother, Amnon: "Fear not . . . and act as men of valor (והיו לבני חיל)."[124] Finally, the main point of Hushai's fictional scenario is the contrast he sets up between the usual nature of the soldier and how he will respond in this particular instance. Under most circumstances, the soldier resembles the lion, who "is mightiest among beasts and does not turn back before anything" (Prov 30:30);[125] but when he hears that David's forces have routed Absalom's men, even the most courageous fighter will react with fear. These various facets of the passage clarify the implicit link that motivates the simile: courage. Furthermore, the articulation of the actual situation and the hypothetical situation helps to explicate the analogy:

> Actual situation: The imaginary soldier who hears about the rout is a valiant warrior.
> Hypothetical situation: A lion is a fearless, mighty beast.

D. *2 Samuel 17:11a—*כחול אשר על הים לרב
("like the sand that is by the sea in abundance")

Bar-Efrat observes that Hushai's speech contains two parts. The first section (vv. 8–10) "is devoted to exposing the weak points in Ahitophel's advice" and the second (vv. 11–13) "elucidates the alternative plan, which is supposedly better."[126] When he shifts to the second part, Hushai attempts to convince Absalom that David and his men pose

---

[121] Contrast 1 Chr 12:9, which focuses on exterior appearance when it characterizes David's followers as having the "faces of lions."

[122] E.g., Jer 12:8; Ezek 22:25; Prov 28:15.

[123] E.g., Ezek 19:1–9; Nah 2:13; Ps 7:3.

[124] Also see 2 Sam 2:7.

[125] For another depiction of the courage of the lion, see Isa 31:4, which describes how the lion is not frightened by the shepherds called to scare the lion away from its prey.

[126] Bar-Efrat, *Narrative Art in the Bible*, 225.

such a threat that the only way to defeat them is to muster an immense army: "And so I advise you, let there surely be gathered around you all Israel, from Dan to Beersheba, like the sand that is by the sea in abundance, and your face will walk into battle" (17:11). The simile helps to allay fears of a defeat—fears Hushai fans in his earlier remarks—for it conveys "the idea that only overwhelmingly superior numbers . . . can prevail against so formidable a foe as David."[127]

Unlike the two prior similes, this utterance leaves no doubt about the point of intersection between the two elements of the analogy. In this case, the addition of the prepositional phrase לרב ("in abundance") makes the connection explicit. Hushai encourages Absalom to amass a vast army, as numerous as the multitudinous granules of sand on the seashore. Darr asserts that the presence or absence of such modifying statements, which she terms "explicit secondary predicates," plays an important role in the analysis of a simile. She defines a "secondary predicate" as "the complex of concepts, assumptions and ideas that, correctly or incorrectly, is linked to the secondary subject and can be derived from it." An "explicit secondary predicate" specifies "those associations crucial for a given simile's (or metaphor's) construal."[128]

Even without the explanatory clause "in abundance," Hushai's listeners likely would have understood the implication of the simile, for this expression occurs fifteen times in the Bible, a degree of frequency unusual in this literary corpus.[129] As a result, such similes have been labeled "traditional,"[130] "proverbial,"[131] "cliche,"[132] and a "stock hyperbole."[133] In ten of the fifteen verses, the simile includes

---

[127] Alter, *The David Story*, 298. Alter adds that such a conscription would be time-consuming, thus benefiting David and his forces.

[128] Darr, 40. Many of the similes catalogued in Samuel Noah Kramer's article, "Sumerian Similes: A Panaramic View of Some of Man's Oldest Literary Images," *JAOS* 89 (1969) 1–10, contain such "explicit secondary predicates," such as in the description of Nippur "as lofty as heaven" (3) or "the oft-repeated simile 'as numerous as ewes' " (7).

[129] Similes with the phrase כחול אשר על שפת הים, כחול הים, or a similar formulation with כחול appear in Gen 22:17; 32:13; 41:49; Josh 11:4; Judg 7:12; 1 Sam 13:5; 2 Sam 17:11; 1 Kgs 4:20; 1 Kgs 5:9; Isa 10:22; 48:19; Hos 2:1; Hab 1:9; Ps 78:27; Job 29:18. Comparisons with מחול or מחול ימים appear in Jer 15:8; Ps 139:18; Job 6:3.

[130] Alter, *The David Story*, 298.

[131] Mordechai Cogan, *1 Kings* (New York: Doubleday, 2000), 211 (comment on 1 Kgs 4:20).

[132] Francis I. Andersen, *Habakkuk* (New York: Doubleday, 2001), 202 (comment on Hab 1:9).

[133] Lundbom, 728 (comment on Jer 15:8, מחול ימים).

a verb, adjective, or other clause that specifies that the comparison centers on the abundance of sand, the hypothetical situation, and the large quantity of the item in the actual situation. For instance, God promises to "greatly multiply (וְהַרְבָּה אַרְבֶּה)" Abraham's seed so that his descendants are "like the stars in the heavens and like the sand on the shore of the sea" (Gen 22:17). Further on, God assures Jacob that his seed will be "like the sand of the sea which cannot be counted for its abundance (כְּחוֹל הַיָּם אֲשֶׁר לֹא יִסָּפֵר מֵרֹב)" (Gen 32:13).[134] Joshua 11:4 emphasizes the point by repeating the adjective רב ("abundant") twice and adding the phrase לָרֹב ("in abundance") in the description of the forces mustered by the Canaanite kings: "And they went out, they and all their troops with them, an abundant army like the sand on the shore of the sea in abundance, and horses and chariots in great abundance."[135] Although this simile is used elsewhere in the Tanakh to characterize an array of objects, including grain (Gen 41:49), camels (Judg 7:12), and Solomon's wisdom (1 Kgs 5:9), it is most famously associated with God's promise to the patriarchs (Gen 22:17; 32:13). By invoking this vow, Hushai subtly legitimates Absalom's fantasy of himself as the rightful ruler of Israel, thereby further enhancing the would-be-king's exalted self-image.

In his analysis of Hushai's speech, Bar-Efrat praises "Hushai's psychological percipience," which he claims is demonstrated by his repeated use of widely-used phrases. He recognizes that our limited knowledge of the language of the biblical period makes it difficult to assess the originality or banality of Hushai's language. Nevertheless, he asserts that when an expression appears in several biblical books belonging to different genres, then "this indicates with a reasonable degree of certainty that it was a widely used term."[136] For instance, he notes that the simile "as the sand by the sea" is found, with slight changes, in Genesis, in each of the Early Prophets, in the Later Prophets, and in the Writings. The simile, "like a bear bereaved" appears in Joshua, Samuel, and Proverbs. The metaphor of the melting heart occurs ten times in Deuteronomy, Joshua, Samuel, Isaiah, Ezekiel and Nahum.[137] Bar-Efrat posits that such familiar utterances produce a clear rhetorical effect:

---

[134] Similarly, see Gen 41:49; Judg 7:12; Hos 2:1; cf. Jer 33:22.

[135] לָרֹב also appears in Judg 7:12; 1 Sam 13:5; 1 Kgs 4:20.

[136] Bar-Efrat, *Narrative Art in the Bible*, 234.

[137] Bar-Efrat, *Narrative Art in the Bible*, 233–234. He also notes that the term "from Dan to Beersheba" appears seven times, five times in Samuel and once each in

By using well-known expressions Hushai creates the impression that
what he says is based on widely-known and acknowledged facts. A
claim based on something which has long been known to its hearer
and accepted by him as a true and undisputed fact, is able to convince
him more readily; he will nod his head in agreement and fail to realize
that the subject really deserves more thought. This accounts for the
considerable persuasive power of commonly used sayings and idioms.[138]

E. *2 Samuel 17:12*—ונחנו עליו כאשר יפל הטל על האדמה
("and we will alight upon him like the dew falls upon the ground")

As Hushai develops his plan, he details how the battle will unfold:
"And we shall come upon him in one of the places where he may
be found, and we shall alight upon him like the dew falls upon the
ground, and there will not be left to him or to all the men who are
with him even one" (17:12). In contrast to the frequency with which
the prior simile occurs, commentators characterize this simile as
"more innovative"[139] and "original."[140] Similes involving dew appear
throughout the Tanakh to describe a variety of referents, including
Moses' speech (Deut 32:2), a king's favor (Prov 19:12), or God's
beneficence toward Israel (Hos 14:6);[141] yet only here is the simile
applied to a military maneuver. What, precisely, does the comparison suggest about the way Absalom and his men will confront David's
forces? Does Hushai intend to imply that the troops will attack
swiftly? Does he mean that they will cover the entire area, suffusing
the battleground as the vast army spreads out? Or does he propose
that the troops will attack covertly, appearing suddenly without being
detected by David's men? Several sources of information can help
to resolve these questions, namely, the immediate narrative context,
other relevant biblical passages, and basic data about dew.

Judges and Kings, with the expression reversed ("from Beersheba to Dan") twice
in Chronicles (233).

[138] Bar-Efrat, *Narrative Art in the Bible*, 234. A number of expressions employed by
Ahtiophel also are attested repeatedly, with citations distributed throughout the
Tanakh. The verb באש is used in a manner similar to 2 Sam 16:21 three other
times in Samuel, as well as in Genesis, Exodus, Proverbs, and Chronicles. References
to the strengthening of the hands and drooping hands appear with even greater
frequency, mainly in the Prophets and Writings. If Bar-Efrat is correct about the
persuasive power of widely-used expressions, this factor may contribute to the success of Ahitophel's first piece of advice.

[139] Alter, *The David Story*, 298.

[140] J. P. Fokkelman, *Narrative Art and Poetry in the Books of Samuel*, vol. 1 (Assen:
Van Gorcum, 1981), 218.

[141] Also see Isa 18:4; 26:19; Hos 6:4; 13:3; Mic 5:6; Ps 110:3; 133:3.

Bar-Efrat labels this simile an "open comparison" because "the point of correspondence between the compared objects is not noted (in contrast to the simile 'as the sand by the sea *for multitude*')."[142] But, in fact, the surrounding narrative context does contain certain hints about the point of the analogy. Had Hushai simply said, "And we will be like dew," the simile would have been far more open-ended and ambiguous. On the other hand, had he inserted an adjective or other grammatical element, like "and we will alight upon him *swiftly*" or "and we will alight upon him like the dew falls upon the ground *during the night*," he would have clarified the intended associated commonplaces.[143] As the verse stands, several elements provide subtle interpretive clues.

In the phrase preceding the simile, ונחנו עליו, the first word can be identified in two different ways. Most translators of this verse concur about the sense of this statement, rendering it as a *qal*, perfect, first common plural form of the root נ.ו.ח., meaning "light upon" (Alter, Fox, *KJV*, *NRS*) or "descend" upon (*JPS*, McCarter). In contrast, several biblical dictionaries treat this attestation of the lexeme נחנו as a first common plural pronoun, which when combined with the prepositional phrase creates a nominal sentence meaning, "and we will be upon him."[144] Two factors support the verbal reading. First, several passages use the verb נוח in a somewhat similar manner, to describe the how various winged creatures—birds, locusts, flies, bees—descend in flight and settle upon an area or object.[145] In the verse at hand, Hushai envisions Absalom and his forces descending upon David's troops and decimating them in their hiding places. Secondly, the wording of the simile signals that the focus of the comparison rests on the action, not the subjects. By placing the verb in

---

[142] Bar-Efrat, *Narrative Art in the Bible*, 235.

[143] Compare Hos 6:4, where the prophet articulates the commonality between Israel's loyalty and dew, the "explicit secondary predicate," to use Darr's terminology: "And your loyalty is like morning clouds and like dew *that goes away early* (וכטל משכים הלך)." Hillers cites an Akkadian "Fire Incantation" that contains the simile, "scatter like fog, disperse like dew" (translation by W. G. Lambert; quoted in Hillers, 182).

[144] *DCH* labels נחנו in 2 Sam 17:12 as a first common plural pronoun, which it translates as "we shall be upon him," as does Koehler-Baumgartner (s.v. נחנו). In the נחנו entry in *BDB*, a parenthetical comment states that in 2 Sam 17:12 נחנו is a first plural perfect *qal* from נוח; however, the verbal entry נוח does not cite ונחנו as an attested form of the verb, nor does it mention 2 Sam 17:12.

[145] Exod 10:14; 2 Sam 21:10; Isa 7:19.

front of the subject (כאשר יפל הטל) the speaker calls attention to the
movement of the dew, which resembles the movement of Absalom's
men. Thus the two verbs ונחנו and יפל together with the prepositional phrase על האדמה ("on the ground"), narrow the number of
possible connections between the actual and hypothetical situations,
shifting the emphasis to the manner in which the troops attack.[146]

Even after resolving this issue, uncovering the exact nuance of the
comparison requires further information and explication. Whereas
the average ancient Israelite presumably would have been familiar
with the properties of dew, contemporary readers may need to rely
on knowledge gleaned from the Bible as well as empirical studies or
observations. As Tigay notes, the Hebrew word טל "can refer to rain
or dew, both of which were thought to fall from the sky,"[147] even
though dew actually condenses from the atmosphere on a cool surface. Nahum Sarna explains the significance of dew in ancient Israel:

> Throughout most of the rainless summer months, dew provides a major
> source of irrigation for crops in many places in the Land of Israel.
> The westerly and north-westerly winds that blow in from the Mediter-
> ranean Sea carry moisture overland. When the air is saturated with
> water vapor, the cool night temperatures cause the vapor to condense
> into a heavy mist. This is particularly true of the western Negeb, the
> central coastal plain, the western slopes of the hills of Judea and
> Samaria, on Mount Carmel, and in Gilead.[148]

In his commentary on 2 Sam 17:12, Fokkelman lists several facts
about dew: "Dew falls at night and is encountered plentifully in the
morning by the peasant in Palestine. Dew is heavy and yet light. It
falls silently, gradually and inimitably and is a blessing to the plants
of the field."[149] This information shapes his reading of Hushai's
remarks, as he uses similar language to explicate the simile: "Absalom's

---

[146] Note that Col. J. C. Coleman, chief of staff for the First Marine Expeditionary
Force in Iraq, used a related simile to describe the original plan for the marines
to enter the city of Falluja in a low-key manner. He stated: "We were going to
roll in there all quiet like the fog" (*New York Times*, April 2, 2004). In this case, the
modifying statement "all quiet" clarifies the associated commonplace.

[147] Tigay, 300 (comment to Deut 32:2).

[148] Nahum Sarna, *Genesis* (Philadelphia: Jewish Publication Society, 1989), 192
(comment on Gen 27:28). Also see Oestreich, 157–160.

[149] Fokkelman, 218. Otzen provides a similar account in his *TDOT* article on
"טל *tal*": "It falls during the night . . . and vanishes quickly in the morning . . . The
dew 'lies' on the ground . . . and appears in large concentrations on uneven surfaces" (323–324).

army is to steal in and 'descend upon' . . . David equally vastly, ubiq-
uitously and inimitably."[150] Likewise, Alter bases his understanding
of the simile upon his knowledge of dew: "The dew falls silently,
effortlessly, and this is how this huge army will 'light upon' David's
forces."[151] Bar-Efrat views the intersection between the hypothetical
situation, the way dew "falls," and the actual situation, the way
Absalom's forces will descend upon David's troops, somewhat differently. Linking the simile in v. 12 with the one in v. 11, he focuses
more on size and less on stealth when he asserts that the comparison "can be understood not only as an illustration of vast numbers
but also as intimating that the action will extend to and include
everyone, and that no one will be able to oppose it."[152]

F. *Reflections on Simile and Metaphor in 2 Samuel 17*

The simile in 2 Sam 17:12 displays the type of ambiguity and interpretive potential that raises questions about the notion of a simile
as necessarily "weaker" than metaphor.[153] Such an example contains
"ambience and suggestiveness," thus challenging Black's assertion that
an explicit comparison gives up "the distinctive power and effectiveness
of a good metaphor."[154] In a recent book on metaphor and the
Psalms, William Brown weighs in on the question of the degree of
substantial difference between metaphor and simile. He asserts that
"the difference between metaphor and simile may be anything but
negligible," due to the following factors:

> With the simple addition of the term of comparison (e.g., 'like' or 'as'),
> one referent is subordinated to the other. Some contend that whereas
> immediacy, spontaneity, and vividness characterize the metaphor, the
> simile designates a secondary level of abstraction that diffuses, in effect,
> the tension between the actual elements of comparison, the source and
> target domains.[155]

---

[150] Fokkelman, 218.

[151] Alter, *The David Story*, 298.

[152] Bar-Efrat, *Narrative Art in the Bible*, 235.

[153] For examples of those who consider simile weaker than metaphor, see Black,
"More About Metaphor," 30; Leech, 156–157; Sam Glucksberg and Boaz Keysar,
"How Metaphors Work," in *Metaphor and Thought*, 2nd edition, ed. Andrew Ortony
(Cambridge: Cambridge University Press, 1993), 406.

[154] Black, 31.

[155] William P. Brown, *Seeing the Psalms: A Theology of Metaphor* (Louisville: Westminster
John Knox Press, 2002), 7.

Insisting that "such a global claim . . . needs to be judged on an individual basis,"[156] he cites an example from the Song of Songs in which
two parallel lines contain an analogy: the first presents a metaphor
and the second a simile, with "no appreciable difference" between
the two comparisons.[157] Brown contrasts this case with the reference
in Psalms to God as "my rock and my redeemer" (Ps 19:15). He
argues that "something is lost in the more prosaic statement 'my
God is *like* a rock' or, worse yet, 'God is like my rock.' "[158] What
distinguishes these two examples? Why does the presence of an
explicit term of comparison diminish the power of the utterance in
one instance but not another? Brown concludes:

> At the very least, the simile represents a form of analogical language
> that *may* relieve the ambiguity and narrow the interpretive possibilities
> provoked by the metaphor, but not necessarily. By comparison, the
> metaphor *may* convey a more evocative level of literary artistry by virtue
> of the tension it generates for the reader. Given its heuristic nature,
> the metaphor can initiate the process of imaginative reflection, or dis-
> cernment and synthesis, that a simile may not match.[159]

The research presented so far shows the wisdom of Brown's advice
to judge each simile on a case-by-case basis. As Soskice and White
point out, because metaphors and similes vary widely in artistry and
depth, the conclusions drawn about either trope will be influenced
by the examples cited. A metaphor like "they were a wall around
us" (1 Sam 25:16) or a simile such as "like the sand that is by the
sea in abundance" (2 Sam 17:11) may not contain the same degree
of complexity as a metaphor like "he swooped down on them" (1
Sam 25:14) or a simile such as "and we will alight upon him like
the dew falls on the ground" (2 Sam 17:12). The difference depends
on a variety of factors, some of which involve the nature of the analogy itself and others concern the placement of the comparison within
a larger narrative context: How do the actual and hypothetical situations correspond? Is the connection obvious or familiar, unexpected or puzzling? Has the speaker specified the grounds of the

---

[156] Brown, 7.
[157] Brown presents the following example from Song 4:1: "How beautiful you
are, my love, how very beautiful! / Your eyes are doves behind your veil; your
hair is *like* a flock of goats, / moving down the slopes of Gilead" (7).
[158] Brown, 7.
[159] Brown, 7.

comparison, or must the interpreter decipher the intended associated commonplaces based on clues in the text and background information? How well does the comparison fit in its narrative context? Does it illuminate or obfuscate the matter at hand? These questions apply to metaphor and simile alike, and the answers determine the power and effectiveness of either trope.

G. *A Different Type of Comparison*

A different type of comparison appears in an earlier segment of this narrative unit, when, after reporting that Absalom slept with David's concubines, the narrator adds: "And Ahitophel's advice which he advised in those days was like one would inquire of a word of God; thus was Ahitophel's advice for David and also for Absalom" (16:23). The narrator's statement differs from the similes spoken by Hushai in a number of respects. First, the statement is more syntactically convoluted than the straightforward comparisons analyzed above, in part because the narrator avoids directly comparing Ahitophel's and God's counsel. Instead of setting up a more direct equivalence between the two sources of insight, perhaps by stating, "Ahitophel's advice was like God's advice (עצת אחיתפל כעצת האלהים)," the narrator places the emphasis on the perception of the person seeking the counsel: "Ahitophel's advice . . . was like one would inquire of a word of God (ועצת אחיתפל . . . כאשר ישאל בדבר האלהים)" (16:23). Polzin suggests that the wording of this verse reflects the narrator's desire to distinguish his perspective from the characters' point of view when he writes:

> What leaps out from these words is the sheer audacity of the comparison, a figure so striking that the narrator is at pains in verse 23b to make it clear that the startling comparison itself represents how David and Absalom see things, rather than how the narrator does.[160]

Beyond the syntactic structure, this verse differs from the prior similes in terms of the relationship between the two elements involved in the comparison. Hushai's similes create a connection between two distinct entities, such as a human being and a bear or troops and sand on the seashore. In this case, however, the statement associates two types of advice: the insight requested from an individual and

---

[160] Polzin, 172–173.

the wisdom received from God. The contrast between the similes in
2 Sam 17:8–12 and the comparison in 2 Sam 16:23 shows why
scholars have attempted to differentiate between various types of
comparisons. Polzin might argue that this comparison "lack[s] the
graphic imaging that belongs to a simile as a figure of speech."[161]
Others might take a cognitive approach and distinguish between "literal" and "nonliteral" comparisons or between "inner-categorical"
and "cross-categorical comparisons."

A similar example appears in a comment by the narrator found
in the earlier episode of Abigail and Nabal. While setting the stage
for the final confrontation between husband and wife, the narrator
remarks: "And, look, he was having a feast in his house like a king's
feast (והנה לו משתה בביתו כמשתה המלך)" (1 Sam 25:36). Just as the
utterance in 2 Sam 16:23 compares two types of advice, this statement compares two types of banquets. Both verses fit within Long's
notion of "inner-categorical comparisons," as opposed to a "cross-
categorical comparison" created by equating a feast to a distinct
semantic entity, such as a circus.

If a person unfamiliar with medical equipment asks, "What is a
scalpel?" someone might answer by equating the unknown with the
known: "A scalpel is like a razor." In Long's example, as in Ortony's
illustration, "Encyclopedias are like dictionaries," similitude functions
as a means of providing information. However, when the narrator
in Samuel compares Nabal's feast to a king's feast or Ahitophel's
counsel to an oracle from God, the intent is not merely to convey
expository data, but to influence the audience's impression of the
characters and understanding of the evolving plot. For instance, the
comment that Nabal's sheep shearing celebration resembles a royal
banquet supplements the introductory depiction of Nabal as a rich
man (1 Sam 25:2) and contributes to the overall negative portrayal
of Nabal. Nabal is prosperous enough to throw a party fit for a king,
but he is unwilling to part with a portion of his wealth as requested
by the future king, a foolish, and ultimately deadly, decision. In addition, the narrator's remark heightens the dissonance between Nabal's
insular world and the events around him: he hosts an elaborate party,
oblivious to the massacre averted by his wife. Likewise, the "daring
comparison"[162] in 2 Sam 16:23 also produces various narrative effects.

---

[161] Polzin, 172.
[162] Polzin, 173.

Not only does the comment justify Absalom's egregious, but politically astute, actions, but it also enhances the ensuing drama. The audience wonders: Given the authority Absalom invests in Ahitophel, how can Hushai possibly contend with him? What will Hushai have to do in order to overcome the allegiance and reverence reserved for Ahitophel?[163]

While these two comparisons differ in some respects from the four similes found in 2 Samuel 17, is it accurate to label them "literal" or "nonfigurative," or to assume that they do not involve "graphic" or "pictorial" images? One issue to consider is the degree of similitude implied in the comparison. Second Samuel 16:23 may involve two types of advice, but, as Polzin points out, "Ahitophel's counsel is certainly not equal to God's word."[164] Another factor includes the rhetorical potential of such comparisons. These two examples may differ from the type of cross-categorical comparison usually defined as a "simile," but they are not devoid of the suggestiveness and effectiveness created by metaphor and other tropes.

IV. Concluding Observations on Hyperbole and Tropic Effect

This chapter has concentrated primarily on three rhetorical devices: metaphor, metonymy, and simile. However, to maximize the persuasive potential and rhetorical impact of an address, speakers utilize a variety of tropes. In the discourse of Ahitophel and Hushai, just as in the speeches of Abigail and Nabal's servant, tropes appear in clusters. In Hushai's speech, in particular, a number of tropes "operate together, reinforcing one another,"[165] resulting in a speech that "is full to overflowing with rhetorical devices and appeals to his audience's emotions."[166] Most notably, the element of hyperbole in this section deserves greater attention. Standard definitions of hyperbole focus on the element of "exaggeration or overstatement that

---

[163] Polzin sees other implications for the reader: "Whereas the story line in chapters 15–17 asks us, as it does Absalom, to compare Ahitophel's individual counsel to Hushai's (is one piece of advice better than the other?), 16:23 specifically invites the reader to compare, as David and Absalom did in their day, the *practice* of counseling the king and that of inquiring of God" (175).

[164] Polzin, 173.

[165] Bar-Efrat, *Narrative Art in the Bible*, 233. See, especially, 2 Sam 17:10–11.

[166] Bar-Efrat, *Narrative Art in the Bible*, 237.

exceeds the truth and reality of things"[167] and is used to "emphasize feelings and intensify rhetorical effect."[168]

One example of hyperbole can be seen in Hushai's promise that
after Absalom attacks David and his men, "not a single one will be
left of all the men who are with him" (17:12). Just in case such an
assurance does not entice Absalom, Hushai adds a fanciful contin-
gency plan. He proposes that should David manage to escape to a
nearby town, "all Israel" will converge upon the town with ropes in
hand and haul away the stones of the outer wall "until there cannot be found there a stone" (17:13). Both remarks contain an element of absoluteness, conveyed through the noun כֹל ("all" the men
with David will be killed and "all" Israel will help carry away the
stones) and the negative particle לֹא (not one soldier will be left and
not a stone will be found). While, in theory, Hushai's proposal to
descend upon David and his forces with a much larger army may
be militarily sound, his suggestion that the men dismantle the town's
fortification wall seems rather impractical. If the goal was to develop
a sensible plan, and not to impress and persuade the audience, surely
Hushai could have devised a more efficient, less labor-intensive way
of capturing the run-away king. Bar-Efrat offers the following explanation of what motivates Hushai to make such a claim:

> The speech, which is coloured throughout by a plethora of images
> and figurative language reaches its apogee in this respect at its close.
> In order to conceal the weakness of his plan, Hushai appeals to his
> audience's emotions, using fantastic descriptions in order to inflame its
> imagination. Excitement suppresses rational consideration. Hushai's use
> of exaggeration, which has featured earlier in his speech ('sand', 'dew',
> 'not one') reaches a pinnacle here: 'until there be not one small stone
> found there.'[169]

As Bar-Efrat points out, similes can exhibit an element of exaggeration as well. Most notably, Hushai compares the number of soldiers in Absalom's imagined army to the innumerable granules of
sand on the sea shore (17:11). This simile contains an element of
imbalance and impracticality as it purports to equate these two dis-

---

[167] Henrich Plett, "Hyperbole," *Encyclopedia of Rhetoric*, ed. Thomas Sloane (Oxford: Oxford University Press, 2001), 364.

[168] Elizabeth Patnoe, "Hyperbole," *Encyclopedia of Rhetoric and Composition*, ed. Theresa Enos (New York: Garland Publishing, Inc., 1996), 344.

[169] Bar-Efrat, *Narrative Art in the Bible*, 236–237.

similar quantities. The first two similes examined above also display a hyperbolic quality, for they compare human beings to wild animals with legendary characteristics, as do the comparisons in 1 Sam 25:36 and 2 Sam 16:23. While both of these verses liken two items of the same semantic category, the objects are of unequal rank: human versus divine counsel and a feast by a commoner versus royalty. The equation of something of a lower status to a higher status creates a sense of exaggeration. Likewise, metaphor and metonymy commonly contain an element of overstatement and incredibility that marks hyperbole, as in the statement that Absalom's face will walk into battle (17:11), or the description of the melting warrior (17:10). As these examples demonstrate, hyperbole can either stand as a distinct trope or appear as part of other figurative devices.

Common to all the tropes discussed in this chapter is the attempt to produce an interactional effect. Bar-Efrat astutely and repeatedly highlights the rhetorical power of Hushai's language. For instance, he claims that the simile of the bereaved bear allows Hushai to depict David's soldiers in a "vividly impressive way" and to arouse "fear and apprehension in [Hushai's] audience."[170] Further on, he compares the bear and lion similes to the sand and dew similes, discerning patterns in the sources for the hypothetical situations, the main points of the comparisons, and their rhetorical effects. He perceptively observes:

> The images in the first part of the speech are taken from the world of beasts, illustrating quality and designed to engender fear in the audience, whilst those in the second part are taken from the world of inanimate nature, illustrating quantity and designed to create confidence in the audience.[171]

The effectiveness of the diverse rhetorical devices employed by Hushai is proven by the fact that Absalom is persuaded to favor Hushai's advice over Ahitophel's more sensible military strategy. In spite of Ahitophel's stature and the sagacity of his military strategy, Absalom decides: "The counsel of Hushai the Archite is better than the counsel of Ahitophel" (2 Sam 17:14).

Bar-Efrat's comments on the rhetorical language in 2 Sam 16:16–17:14 concentrate on the impact of one character's words on the

---

[170] Bar-Efrat, *Narrative Art in the Bible*, 227.
[171] Bar-Efrat, *Narrative Art in the Bible*, 232.

other characters in the narrative. As discussed in chapter four, the tropes that pervade this story produce interactional effects for the reader as well. In this passage, as in 1 Samuel 25, tropes can create a sense of narrative cohesion. For instance, the four similes in Hushai's speech function as a structuring device that unifies his remarks. In addition, the references to the bereaved bear and abundant sand establish connections between this story and other episodes in the Tanakh, links that enrich the audience's understanding of the characters and the significance of the events. The tropes studied in this chapter also establish relationships of equivalence and contrast, as seen in Hushai's advice, where the repetition of the word "hand" sets up a contrast between the predicted strength of Absalom's supporters and the projected weakness of David and his men. These sorts of tropic connections and contrasts help to communicate the main themes of the story and to direct the audience's attention to the complexities of character and plot that distinguish biblical narrative.

CHAPTER SIX

A REEVALUATION OF THE CONCEPT
OF "DEAD" METAPHORS

I. The Debate about Translating So-Called "Dead" Metaphors

The preceding analysis of 1 Samuel 25 and 2 Samuel 16–17 has demonstrated a tendency among certain biblical translators to transform the concrete, figurative language found in biblical narrative into abstract expressions. Alter explores this phenomenon in the introduction to his translation and commentary on the book of Genesis. He charges nearly all the modern English versions of the Bible with committing "the heresy of explanation,"[1] meaning that translators pass off "explanation under the guise of translation."[2] As Alter explains, this trend is particularly pronounced in the treatment of figurative language:

> One of the most salient characteristics of biblical Hebrew is its extra-ordinary concreteness, manifested in a fondness for images rooted in the human body. The general predisposition of modern translators is to convert most of this concrete language into more abstract terms that have the purported advantage of clarity but turn the pungency of the original into stale paraphrase.[3]

Alter exemplifies his point by examining the Hebrew noun זֶרַע, meaning "seed," which applies to agriculture as well as human beings. Used in connection with human beings, the term for semen also functions as the word designating the children produced from human "seed." For instance, God's covenant with Abraham states: "I will greatly bless you and will greatly multiply your seed, as the stars in the heavens and as the sands on the shore of the sea" (Gen 22:17). Alter claims that the visual, physical properties shared by agricultural

---

[1] Alter, *Genesis*, xvi.
[2] Alter, *Genesis*, xiv.
[3] Alter, *Genesis*, xii.

seeds, semen, stars, and sand enhance the power of the promise. He
asserts:

> To substitute offspring for seed here may not fundamentally alter the
> meaning but it diminishes the vividness of the statement, making it
> just a little harder for readers to sense why these ancient texts have
> been so compelling down through the ages.[4]

Alter recognizes that "a good deal of this concrete biblical language
based on the body is what a linguist would call lexicalized metaphor—
imagery . . . that is made to stand for some general concept as a fixed
item in the vocabulary of the language."[5] He insists, however, that
the label "dead" or "lexicalized" does not diminish the potential
power of an utterance or justify its transformation into an abstract
expression. Alter argues that dead metaphors "are the one persuasive instance of the resurrection of the dead—for at least the ghosts
of the old concrete meanings float over the supposedly abstract accep-
tations of the terms."[6]

A fair number of biblical scholars and translators would vigor-
ously challenge Alter's assertions. Those who advocate a more idiomatic
style of translation might label Alter's treatment of זרע in Gen 22:17
as "mechanical,"[7] "archaic,"[8] or "obscure."[9] These contrasting view-
points can be seen in two translations of Gen 37:27. Alter preserves
the concrete sense of the word יד ("hand") in Genesis 37 because
the repeated references to the hand in this chapter function as "a
focusing device that both defines and complicates the moral themes
of the story."[10] Thus, he renders Judah's advice to his brothers concerning the fate of Joseph: "Come, let us sell him to the Ishmaelites
and our hand will not be against him" (Gen 37:27). In contrast,

---

[4] Alter, *Genesis*, xiv.
[5] Alter, *Genesis*, xii.
[6] Alter, *Genesis*, xiii.
[7] Harry M. Orlinsky, ed., *Notes on the New Translation of the Torah* (Philadelphia:
The Jewish Publication Society, 1970), 13 and *passim*.
[8] Gerald Hammond, citing the perspective of many contemporary English versions ("English Translations of the Bible," in *The Literary Guide to the Bible*, ed. Robert
Alter and Frank Kermode [Cambridge: The Belknap Press of Harvard University
Press, 1987], 655).
[9] Jan de Waard and Eugene A. Nida, *From One Language to Another: Functional
Equivalence in Bible Translating* (Nashville: Thomas Nelson Publishers, 1986), 9.
[10] Alter, *Genesis*, xv.

Harry Orlinsky insists on an "idiomatic, and correct,"[11] translation that "bring[s] out the nuance" of the phrase in its particular context[12] and displays a "rigorous fidelity to the meaning of the original, expressed in simple and intelligible language."[13] As a result, the *JPS* version of this verse reads: "Come, let us sell him to the Ishmaelites, but let us not do away with him ourselves."

Jan de Waard and Eugene Nida recognize that "probably the most serious problems for translators occur in attempts to do justice to figurative expressions,"[14] particularly what might be termed "a dead figure of speech."[15] To what extent can the present study of figurative language contribute to the ongoing debate between those who advocate a more literal mode of translation and the proponents of a more idiomatic style? Before addressing this question, the notion of "dead" metaphors requires a thorough investigation.

II. An Examination of the Notion of "Dead" and "Living" Metaphors

The notion of "dead" metaphors surfaces frequently in the literature on this topic. In an attempt to differentiate varying types of metaphors, scholars have concocted a host of classifications. As David Cooper notes, "a favourite game has been to devise scales or spectra on which dead metaphors are placed at, or near, one end, with the liveliest, neonate ones at the other."[16] For instance, intent on replacing the "trite opposition" between "dead" and "live" metaphors with "a set of finer discriminations," Black distinguishes between "extinct," "dormant," and "active" metaphors.[17] Macky creates a more detailed

---

[11] Orlinsky, 29.

[12] Orlinsky, 28.

[13] Orlinksy, 9, quoting the aims of the Episcopal Committee of the Confraternity of Christian Doctrine in producing a new translation for the Catholic Biblical Association, which was published in 1969. This statement echoes Orlinsky's goal, which was to create a new Jewish version of the Bible featuring two main elements: "(1) intelligibility in diction and (2) the fuller use both of the older commentaries . . . and the recently discovered extrabiblical materials" (17). Orlinsky served as the editor-in-chief of the *JPS* translation of the Torah, which was first published in 1962.

[14] De Waard and Nida, 112.

[15] De Waard and Nida, 111.

[16] David E. Cooper, *Metaphor* (Oxford: Basil Blackwell, 1986), 119.

[17] Black, "More About Metaphor," 25.

system, which ranges from "novel," to "familiar," "standard," "hidden," and "retired" metaphors.[18] J. Hobbs utilizes somewhat similar terminology as he traces the phases in the life-cycle of a metaphor, from "creative and alive," to "familiar," then "tired," and finally "dead."[19] Others differentiate between "fresh" and "stored" metaphors[20] or between "fresh," "frozen," or "dead" metaphors.[21]

Behind these different schemas stands a shared desire to discriminate innovative metaphors from more familiar metaphors and, especially, metaphors scarcely recognizable as such because they have become part of the accepted understanding of a particular word or expression. Researchers strive to distinguish well-worn phrases, like "leg of a table" and "foot of a mountain," from more novel utterances, like "Life's but a walking shadow"[22] or "My dream's suspended bridge is shattered."[23] In addition, they endeavor to explain how words like "pedigree" and "grasp" fit into the discussion, words whose etymologies or definitions suggest a metaphorical origin.[24] Scholars debate whether a "dead" metaphor is still a metaphor.[25] They confront issues surrounding the metaphorical extension of language, like the way metaphor relates to polysemy and catachresis. They operate with differing definitions of terms like "literal," "conventional," and "idiom";

---

[18] Macky, 73–80.

[19] J. Hobbs, "Metaphor, Metaphor Schemata and Selective Inferencing," *Technical Note No. 204 SRI International* (1979), cited in Cacciari, 32.

[20] Jerry L. Morgan, "Observations on the Pragmatics of Metaphor," in *Metaphor and Thought*, ed. Andrew Ortony (Cambridge: Cambridge University Press, 1979), 129–130.

[21] Nicholas Burbules, Gregory Schraw, and Woodrow Trathen, "Metaphor, Idiom, and Figuration," *Metaphor and Symbolic Activity* 4 (1989) 106.

[22] Example from Geoffrey Leech, *A Linguistic Guide to English Poetry* (London: Longman Group Limited, 1969), 153.

[23] Line from a Japanese poem by Fujiwara Teika, in Richard Monaco and John Briggs, *The Logic of Poetry* (New York: McGraw-Hill Book Company, 1974), 21.

[24] Examples from Lakoff and Turner, 129. They note that "pedigree" originates from the Old French "pied de grue," meaning "foot of a crane," a shape resembling a family diagram. They explain that we use the word "grasp" to mean understand because "there is a live conceptual metaphor in which UNDERSTANDING IS GRASPING."

[25] Black, for instance, argues that "a so-called dead metaphor is not a metaphor at all, but merely an expression that no longer has a pregnant metaphorical use" ("More About Metaphor," 25). Others, like Soskice (74) and Kittay (89), take the opposing viewpoint and insist that "no mater how 'dead,' or conventionalized, metaphors are metaphors none the less" (Kittay, 89). Also see Cooper, 118–139.

and they disagree on the dividing line or intersection between these terms and "metaphor."

The lack of consensus on these matters and the plethora of proposed systems to classify various stages of "dead" and "live" metaphors testify to the intractability, if not the futility, of this enterprise. Early in the modern study of metaphor, Richards recognized the shortcomings of this nomenclature and called for a reconsideration of the topic. He wrote:

> This favourite old distinction between dead and living metaphors (itself a two-fold metaphor) is, indeed, a device which is very often a hindrance to the play of sagacity and discernment throughout the subject. For serious purposes it needs drastic re-examination.[26]

For all that has been written on metaphor since the 1936 publication of Richard's lectures, no one has succeeded in solving the problems inherent in the concept of a "dead" metaphor and developing a viable alternative.

One sign of the unsatisfactory nature of the notion of a "dead" metaphor is the frequent mention of the "revival" of such metaphors. As Richards points out, although "the leg of a table," which he labels as the "simplest, most familiar" metaphor, may be called "dead," "it comes to life very readily."[27] Richard Monaco and John Briggs echo this sentiment when they write: "In a strong poem even a thoroughly dead metaphor like the 'mouth of a jar' or the 'ship of state' might revive itself as other levels and possibilities emerged."[28] Kittay illustrates how this process of revitalization takes place. Her argument that "no matter how 'dead,' or conventionalized, metaphors are metaphors none the less," rests in part on her observation about "the ease with which their metaphorical origins may be called forth."[29] She explains:

> Few metaphors seem as dead and worn-out to us as the 'leg of a table.' Yet, reputedly, within the purview of Victorian sexual prudery

---

[26] Richards, 102.

[27] Richards, "The Command of Metaphor" (Lecture VI), 117.

[28] Monaco and Briggs, 6. Likewise, Winfried Nöth speaks about "the poetic device of remetaphorization or resurrection of a dead metaphor," a process which "shows that the dead metaphor retains a potential, revivable image which goes unnoticed in our everyday use of language" ("Semiotic Aspects of Metaphor," in *The Ubiquity of Metaphor*, ed. R. Dirven and W. Paprotte [Amsterdam: John Benjamins, 1985], 6). Also see Soskice, who comments on "the phenomenon of dead metaphors 'coming to life' and surprising us by their implications" (74).

[29] Kittay, 89.

this phrase was revivified, replete with salacious meaning: Victorians
regarded it as necessary to cover tables with long table-cloths to avoid
the indecency of viewing exposed 'limbs.'[30]

Kittay also shows how another frequently cited example of a "dead"
metaphor, "foot of a mountain," can be revitalized. She notes:

> In Baudelaire's poem 'La Géante', the poet says he would love to have
> lived near a young giantess, 'as a voluptuous cat at the feet of a queen'.
> He speaks of her in terms appropriate to a mountain—for example,
> 'climb on the slope of her huge knees'. . . . In the poem, we begin at
> the 'feet of a queen' (*aux pieds d'une reine*), climb up her immense body
> as we would climb a mountain, and return to 'the foot', this time 'the
> foot of the mountain' (*au pied d'une montagne*), a catachresis which here
> facilitates and even seals the metaphorical juxtaposing and eventual
> identification of giantess and mountain. Moreover, the catachresis is
> returned to its metaphorical origin so that we see the mountain as
> being with corporal parts like our own.[31]

As these examples demonstrate, though use and age may diminish
the potency of a metaphor, "given the proper context, the metaphor
may be revived."[32]

Similarly, a number of biblical scholars comment on the potential
"resurrection" of so-called "dead" metaphors and reflect on how this
process occurs. For instance, Bar-Efrat observes that certain Hebrew
phrases, such as "the head of the bed" (Gen 47:31) and "the house
of Israel" (Exod 16:31), "have become stale and worn-out with use."
He adds, however, that such "fossilized expressions can be revived
by hinting at their original meaning—as is sometimes done in literature—thus restoring their full stylistic value to them."[33] He cites
several narrative passages that exemplify his point:

> Thus, in Judg. 9.36, the expression 'mountain tops' ('heads' in Hebrew)
> contrasts with 'the centre of the land' ('navel' in Hebrew) in the
> following verse, and the term 'head' or 'heads' (in the sense of a group
> or company of soldiers) often occurs in this context. In 2 Samuel 7
> the word 'house' is used both in the sense of a dynasty (nine times)

---

[30] Kittay, 89.

[31] Kittay, 297, note 17.

[32] Kittay, 299. She notes that one way this sort of metaphoric revival occurs is
when "terms from the original semantic field of the vehicle [are] present in the linguistic environment" (299). In Baudelaire's poem, this means using other words connected with mountains, like "climb on the slope," to describe the giantess.

[33] Bar-Efrat, *Narrative Art in the Bible*, 207.

and a building (six times): David wishes to build a house for the Lord, and the Lord promises to make him a house.[34]

Greenberg observes a similar phenomenon in the book of Ezekiel, where commonplace, stock phrases and figures of speech "are vivified, literalized, or skewed in a dramatic manner."[35] If so many scholars agree that even the most moribund metaphors can remain vital and effective in certain contexts, why retain a label that contradicts this reality?

In the introduction to his research on the understanding of metaphors in literature, Steen articulates another flaw in the attempt to categorize metaphors as somewhere on a scale from "live" to "dead." Lost in nearly all discussions of "dead" metaphors is an acknowledgement of the individuality involved in the perception and interpretation of figurative language. When scholars speak about words or phrases progressing along some sort of spectrum, who determines when an utterance reaches a particular stage? When and for whom does a metaphor become "familiar" or "trite" as opposed to "fresh" or "active"? In *Understanding Metaphor in Literature*, Steen repeatedly empha- sizes the role of the individual in the comprehension of language. Whereas other cognitive linguists deal with conceptual metaphors "located at the supra-individual level of language and culture as systems," Steen focuses on the "individual language user," not "the *idealized* native speaker."[36] He cautions that cultural and linguistic knowledge "is bound to have highly variable cognitive representations and effects at the level of individual minds."[37] Thus, the same utterance might be perceived as novel by one person but labeled a cliche by another, depending on a number of factors, including each individual's

---

[34] Bar-Efrat, *Narrative Art in the Bible*, 207.

[35] Greenberg, 78. In his commentary on Ezek 1:28–3:15, Greenberg highlights a few examples: "The commonplace 'sons [*bᵉne*] of Israel' is peculiarly literalized in the context of the theme of hereditary sinfulness. The iterated variations on the conventional notion 'brazen-faced [*panim*]' injects life into the nominal complement of the stock phrase 'do not be dismayed by them [*pᵉnehem*]'—lit. 'by their faces'" (78–79). Also see Oestreich, who proposes three ways in which "dead metaphors can be revived": "by a word in the same context or an elaboration of the metaphor or by a new metaphor of the same image field which brings to mind the seman- tic field to which the term originally belonged" (39).

[36] Steen, 17.

[37] Steen, 20.

linguistic sophistication and literary background, as well as the context
of the expression.

Gibbs points out another defect in the notion of the "dead"
metaphor as he analyzes the phrase "fork in the road." He notes
that one reasonably could imagine that at some early stage in the
history of the lexeme "fork," the word was applied exclusively to the
eating and cooking utensil. Later, recognizing an analogy between
the shape of this implement and a divided pathway, people started
using the metaphoric expression, "a fork in the road." Since most
people today "do not necessarily make use of this earlier metaphorical
mapping between eating implements and divided pathways when
understanding *fork in the road*," many would consider the phrase a
"dead" metaphor. Gibbs warns, however, that one problem with this
analysis, "as well as with many of our intuitions about the historical
development of idioms, is that it happens to be wrong."[38] He explains:

> As it turns out, the original meaning of *fork* (from the Old English
> *forca* and Latin *furca*) is not the eating or cooking implement. This is
> a later sense, first recorded in the 15th century. The original sense
> seems to be the agricultural implement (pitchfork), and this developed
> in Middle English into a more general sense: anything that forks,
> bifurcates, or divides into branches. Thus, *fork in the road* is not really
> a dead metaphor because it did not develop as a metaphoric extension
> of *eating fork* or of *pitchfork* for that matter. Rather, both *fork in the road*
> and *kitchen fork* are specific tokens of the general sense "anything that
> forks," which is a concept that is very much alive in our conceptual
> systems.[39]

As this example demonstrates, the average language user lacks the
linguistic knowledge needed to reconstruct a lexeme's diachronic
development. Without accurate etymological information, it becomes
difficult to establish the evolutionary stages of a particular word or
expression. Furthermore, even when such information is available,
questions arise about its utility. To what extent does the history of
a word or a label such as "standard" or "dormant" affect the interpretation of a metaphor embedded a specific context?

Additional evidence of the problematic nature of the "dead"
metaphor concept comes from recent research on idioms. In an article on "The Place of Idioms in a Literal and Metaphorical World,"

---

[38] Gibbs, 59.
[39] Gibbs, 59.

Cristina Cacciari contrasts the established view of idioms with the findings of a new wave of studies. She notes that for years an idiom was defined "as an expression whose meaning is not formed by the composition of the meanings of the constituent words, according to the morpho-syntactic rules of the language." Traditionally, idioms have been characterized as complex lexical units that must be retrieved from lexical memory.[40] Chitra Fernando summarizes the three most frequently cited features of idioms:

1 *Compositeness*: idioms are commonly accepted as a type of multiword expression (*red herring, make up, smell a rat, the coast is clear*, etc.) . . .
2 *Institutionalization*: idioms are conventionalized expressions, conventionalization being the end result of initially ad hoc, and in this sense novel, expressions.
3 *Semantic opacity*: the meaning of an idiom is not the sum of its constituents.[41]

Gibbs adds another facet to the standard perception of idioms:

Compared to metaphors, which are thought to be "alive" and creative, idioms traditionally have been viewed as dead metaphors or expressions that were once metaphorical, but that have lost their metaphoricity over time. Scholars generally have assumed that idioms exist as frozen, semantic units within speakers' mental lexicon . . . [I]dioms presumably are understood through the retrieval of the stipulated meanings from the lexicon.[42]

A number of studies published since the late 1980's have challenged the noncompositional notion of idioms. According to Cacciari, recent evidence refutes the traditional idea that idioms lost their metaphoricity over time and evolved into fixed expressions "directly stipulated in the lexicon with no possible use of the semantics of the words composing them." This research shows that for most idioms, the meanings of the constituent words and their internal structure still are influential in their analysis. As a result, Cacciari considers certain idioms "motivated string of words"; she concludes that such motivation,

---

[40] Cristina Cacciari, "The Place of Idioms in a Literal and Metaphorical World," in *Idioms: Processing, Structure, and Interpretation*, ed. Cristina Cacciari and Patrizia Tabossi (Hillsdale, NJ: Lawrence Erlbaum Associates, 1993), 33.
[41] Chitra Fernando, *Idioms and Idiomaticity* (Oxford: Oxford University Press, 1996), 3.
[42] Gibbs, 57. Gibbs rejects this view as he asserts: "My purpose in this chapter is to show that the dead metaphor view of idiomaticity is dead wrong" (57).

"far from being a simple etymological fancy, is available and usable in comprehension and interpretation."[43]

Gibbs demonstrates how individuals might utilize the separate elements of an idiom to understand an expression:

> The results of linguistic analyses and various experimental work in psycholinguistics have shown that American speakers know that *spill the beans* is analyzable because beans refers to an idea or secret and *spilling* refers to the act of revealing the secret. Similarly, in the phrase *pop the question*, it is easy to discern that the noun *question* refers to a marriage proposal when the verb *pop* is used to refer to the act of uttering it.[44]

Gibbs calls such idioms "decomposable," because "each of their components obviously contributes to their overall figurative interpretations."[45] These findings suggest that when a person encounters a supposedly "dead" metaphor, like "the leg of a table" or "mouth of a jar," the constituent parts of the utterance may be "available and usable," and not irrelevant. Rather than ignoring the concrete, figurative language, an individual language user may envision the evoked image or ponder the underlying analogy.[46] Likewise, a skilled writer or speaker may exploit the potential in even the most familiar metaphor.

All of these factors support Richard's contention that the distinction between "dead" and "living" metaphors is "a device which is very often a hindrance to the play of sagacity and discernment."[47] When studying metaphors in the Bible, the problems discussed above become even more acute. Researchers like Gibbs and Steen enhance our understanding of metaphor by conducting empirical studies of how people actually process figurative language. For biblical Hebrew,

---

[43] Cacciari, 32. Gibbs echoes this point when he writes: "I argue that many idioms are very much alive metaphorically, and that speakers make sense of idioms because of the metaphorical knowledge that motivates these phrases' figurative meanings" (57).

[44] Gibbs, 62.

[45] Gibbs, 62. Gibbs differentiates "decomposable" idioms from "nondecomposable" idioms like "kick the bucket" and "shoot the breeze," which people have difficulty deciphering by breaking down their component parts (62).

[46] For an example of the type of empirical research that attempts to verify suppositions about how people process idioms, see Gibbs' summary of the 1990 study he conducted with J. O'Brien, entitled "Idioms and Mental Imagery: The Metaphorical Motivations for Idiom Processing" (67–69).

[47] Richards, 102.

no informants exist to testify as to how ancient Israelites conceived of figurative words and phrases. One can count the number of times an expression appears in the Tanakh and thus gauge frequency of usage. However, this type of data does not indicate whether an individual Israelite would have disregarded the concrete imagery and directly translated "seed" as "descendant" or whether the figurative language would have "impose[d] itself visually on the retina of the imagination."[48] Given the number of problems inherent in the general notion of a "dead" metaphor, along with the additional complications involved in studying biblical Hebrew, those interested in figurative language would be better off abandoning the attempt to classify metaphors. Instead, greater insight may be gleaned from the analysis of how metaphors and other tropes operate in specific literary contexts.

III. 1 Samuel 24: A Case Study

A close reading of 1 Samuel 24 reveals how figurative language, no matter how customary and common, can be employed effectively in biblical narrative. In this chapter, the tables are turned in the relationship between David and Saul and the pursuer unwittingly becomes the pursued. Informed of David's latest whereabouts, Saul sets out with three thousand men, intent on finally capturing his nemesis.

---

[48] Alter, *Genesis*, xiv. Long and Oestreich unsuccessfully attempt to establish criteria to indicate how biblical metaphors were understood in ancient Israel. Long proposes that if a metaphoric expression "has parallels in other ancient Near Eastern cultures and/or in other passages of the Hebrew Bible, and it does not offer a substantially meaningful difference from its parallels," then the biblical writer likely would understood the expression directly as a "dead" metaphor. If the metaphoric expression differs substantially from its parallels, then it is likely to have been processed figuratively as a "live" metaphor (524–525). The biblical and extra-biblical data remain too sparse to draw such conclusions. Oestreich adds another criterion, asserting that a metaphor should be considered conventional "if the metaphor is introduced in such a way that the audience is given no hint of a figurative understanding but is expected to be able to understand the expression instantaneously as a metaphor." Yet Oestreich himself acknowledges one of the shortcomings of such rules when he admits: "Because of the limited data at our disposal we may still incorrectly evaluate metaphors as novel ones which are actually conventionalized. We may even understand dead metaphors as novel or active" (39).

Along the way, he slips alone into a cave, unaware that David and his men are ensconced in the rear of the cave. Although David's men urge him to kill the vulnerable king, David refuses to harm God's anointed. Instead, he furtively cuts off a corner of Saul's cloak, and a dramatic confrontation then ensues between David and Saul. This narrative episode contains a number of noteworthy instances of figurative language that highlight several issues discussed above.

A. *1 Samuel 24:4*—ויבא שאול להסך את רגליו
("And Saul went to cover his feet")

As the story begins, the narrator reports that Saul entered the cave "to cover his feet" (1 Sam 24:4). What does this expression mean? The Targum delicately translates the phrase as "Saul went to take care of his needs." Similarly, most modern translations state that Saul went "to relieve himself."[49] Commentators characterize this utterance as a euphemism, for an offensive or crude expression has been replaced by something more agreeable and refined. The expression exhibits the defining features of an idiom, since it constitutes a fixed, multiword phrase with a conventional meaning that differs from the decontextualized sense of the components. But how does this expression operate? How does one get from the decontextualized meaning of the words to the text-in-context construal?

In this verse, as in several other biblical passages, the "leg" (רגל) euphemistically and metonymically stands for the penis.[50] Bar-Efrat explains that the verb "to cover" functions in a manner similar to the biblical verses that substitute the verb "to bless" for the verb "to curse."[51] For instance, in order to avoid saying that Job will curse God, the text states: "He will bless You to Your face" (Job 1:11). Those familiar with this convention understand that they must mentally switch the written, sanitized text with the intended, theologically problematic verb. In the case of 1 Sam 24:4, after exchanging "to cover" with its opposite and "leg" with its less discreet referent, the phrase is understood to mean: "And Saul went to uncover his penis."[52]

---

[49] See, for instance, Alter, McCarter, *JPS*, and *NRS*.

[50] The identical expression occurs in Judg 3:24; other examples of the euphemistic use of "leg" include Exod 4:25 and Isa 7:20.

[51] Bar-Efrat, *1 Samuel*, 303.

[52] Others interpret the sentence in a different, less compelling manner. Babut explains that in a society in which men wore long tunics, a man would cover his

Still, arriving at the precise meaning of the expression involves an additional exegetical step. Saul enters the cave in order to urinate, an act preceded by the "uncovering of the penis." According this analysis, the expression would be considered a "noncompositional" or "nondecomposable" idiom, meaning that it is difficult to decipher the utterance based solely on the decontextualized definitions of the individual words and the grammatical structure of the sentence. Interpreting the verse requires knowledge of these two conventional substitutions, as well as an understanding of the metonymic link between disrobing and urinating.

B. *1 Samuel 24:5b, 12—כנף המעיל ("wing/edge of the cloak")*

With Saul preoccupied, David cuts off a piece of his cloak. This piece of clothing provides David with physical evidence to prove that he had access to the king and the potential to kill him, but restrained himself from doing so. Symbolically, the cloak "has already been linked emblematically with kingship in the final estrangement between Samuel and Saul, and so David is in symbolic effect 'cutting away' Saul's kingship."[53] Fokkelman stands out from other commentators in that he calls attention to the figurative origins of this phrase: "The text uses a metaphor for the corner of the cloak: it is a 'wing' (*kanaf*) of the cloak."[54] Translators tend to render the expression nonmetaphorically as the "skirt" (Alter, McCarter, *KJV*), "corner" (Fox, *JPS, NRS*), "end" (*NAB*), or "border" (*NJB*) of Saul's garment. Most likely, they would label this a "lexicalized" or "dead" metaphor.

---

feet with his tunic when he crouched down to defecate. He argues that the idiomatic expression consists of a series of double metonymies in which the effect (hidden feet) represents the cause (crouching down) (17). McCarter, like Rashi, agrees that the expression means "to defecate" (383), as does *BDB* (s.v. סבך). Such a reading understands the expression as a reference to a literal covering of the feet by the garments when the individual bends to relieve himself. Not only does this interpretation ignore the convention of using the word רגל to denote the penis, but, as Bar-Efrat points out, the norm would have been to lift up the robe, not let it drop to the feet (*I Samuel*, 303).

[53] Alter, *The David Story*, 148. Alter refers to the scene in which Saul grasps Samuel's cloak and Samuel then declares: "YHWH has torn away the kingship of Israel from you this day and given it to your fellowman, who is better than you" (1 Sam 15:28). Cf. 1 Sam 18:4 and 1 Kgs 11:29–32.

[54] Fokkelman, *Narrative Art and Poetry in the Books of Samuel*, vol. 2, 472.

Kittay might consider this an example of catachresis. She explains:

> Catachresis is, literally, a misuse of language. It is sometimes taken to
> refer to those cases of metaphor which arise out of a need to name
> some unnamed entity ... or it is sometimes said to be an *abuse* of
> language.[55]

When used in the former sense, "catachresis" designates instances in
which a term is extended to fill a lexical gap and then becomes an
established part of the language. Kittay cites two examples in which
a particular object or set of objects needs a label, and the label is
chosen from a related object or set of objects in a metonymic fashion:
the use of the verb "dialing" to speak about operating a push-button
telephone and the name "lead pencils" for graphite pencils.[56] In the
case at hand, one might speculate that the word כָּנָף, denoting the
outermost portion of birds or other flying creatures, was applied
metaphorically to the extremity of a garment. In the absence of an
alternative lexeme to name the hem of a cloak or skirt, כָּנָף became
the established term.[57]

Others might regard כָּנָף ("wing") used in connection with an article of clothing as an instance of polysemy: a single lexeme with multiple, related meanings. The argument might be made that in spite
of its metaphorical origins, כָּנָף eventually became the standard, literal
term for the edge of a garment. Steen explains the phenomenon this
way:

> To the individual language user, the metaphorical meaning of some
> words and phrases has become just as directly accessible as their literal
> meaning. The analogical mapping originally motivating or maintain-
> ing the figurative connection between the two meanings may thus have
> lost its use in the mental lexicon of individual language users.[58]

---

[55] Kittay, 296.

[56] Kittay, 296.

[57] Outside of 1 Samuel 24, כָּנָף ("wing") is used in connection with a garment
in about a dozen passages, including Num 15:38; 1 Sam 15:27 (כְּנַף מְעִילוֹ); Ruth
3:9. The noun is combined with the word אֶרֶץ to refer to the "end(s) of the earth"
(Isa 24:16; Job 37:3; 38:13) or "the four corners of the earth" (Isa 11:12; Ezek 7:2).

[58] Steen, 17–18.

As E. Leise demonstrates, clarifying the relationship between metaphor and polysemy remains a difficult task. He writes:

> The word *foot* can be defined as 'lowest portion of a human or ani-mal leg (on which the creature stands)'. In this case *foot of the mountain* is a metaphor. But it is not impossible to define *foot* from the very beginning as 'lowest portion on which someone or something stands'. In this case *foot of the mountain* would not be a metaphor. Depending on the definition of a word's normal meaning a given usage will appear as within it or outside it. Even when we clearly have two meanings before us, it may remain open, whether the case counts as metaphor or not. English *eye* means (1) 'organ of sight' and (2) 'hole in a tool'. Is the second meaning a metaphor? Certainly the first use of the word *crane* for a machine with a lifting arm was metaphoric, but its status today is disputable.[59]

Instead of debating how to label the phrase כְּנַף הַמְּעִיל, a more pro-ductive line of questioning would be: Does the expression produce a tropic effect in this particular context? Does the author appear to activate the metaphorical element in any way? In this instance, neither the surrounding narrative in chapter 24 nor the larger story of Saul and David contains obvious links to the underlying analogy. Therefore, a translation like "edge of the cloak" seems appropriate.

In theory, how might a writer call attention to and play with the metaphorical aspect of "wing of the cloak"? Imagine that at an ear-lier point in the narrative the biblical author wanted to emphasize Saul's fickle nature, the way he vacillates between affection and hatred toward David. One way to do this would be to compare Saul to a bird fluttering from one place to another, using either a simile or metaphor. Given such a context, the choice of the phrase "wing of the cloak" would take on greater significance, for the standard term for the extremity of a garment would become a clever allusion to the prior depiction of Saul. In light of the imagined characterization of Saul as a bird, the scene of David cutting Saul's "wing" would not only foreshadow the transference of the kingship, but also convey an implicit message about the negative effect that David has on Saul as a person, the way that David's prowess diminishes Saul's persona.

---

[59] E. Leise, *Praxis der englischen Semantik* (Heidelberg: Winter, 1973), 174–175; trans-lated by Nöth, 7. For other discussions of metaphor and polysemy, see Cooper, 123–136 and Kittay, 109–113.

C. *1 Samuel 24:6*—אתו ויך לב דוד *("And David's heart struck him")*

Even though David merely cuts off a piece of the king's cloak instead of taking his life, David nevertheless condemns himself for this deed. The narrator states: "And it happened afterwards that David's heart struck him because he had cut off an edge that was Saul's" (24:6). With the exception of Fox, most modern biblical translators, including Alter, provide an exegetical gloss instead of a literal translation of this verse. Some translators retain the sense of the Hebrew verb, while adjusting the role and nuance of the noun "heart." For instance, Alter writes: "David was smitten with remorse," while McCarter translates the expression: "David was conscience-stricken." Others treat the utterance more liberally: "David reproached himself" (*JPS*) and "David regretted" (*NAB*) his actions.[60]

How does the example of personification in this passage function? One way to understand the utterance is to consider it a description of the physical sensation experienced by David after cutting Saul's cloak. The writer assigns agency to the organ in which the emotion manifests itself, for the sentence conceives of the heart as the forceful cause of the quickening of the heart presumably felt by David. An alternative rendering of the expression interprets the subject, "David's heart," metonymically as an instance in which a part of the body stands for the person as a whole. In this case, one might construe the phrase to mean that "David beat himself up," implying not that David inflicted upon himself physical harm, but that he suffered emotionally from the reproach and guilt triggered by his deed. As observed in the previous chapter, determining conclusively how a figurative expression operates sometimes can prove a challenging task.

D. *1 Samuel 24:8*—בדברים אנשיו את דוד וישסע
("And David tore apart his men with words")

When David's men discover that Saul has entered the cave alone and unaware of their presence, their instinct is to murder the man

---

[60] Both Alter and *JPS* provide a literal translation in a footnote. Fox translates the expression literally, as does the *KJV*, but he feels obligated to add an explanatory note in parentheses: "David's heart struck him (with remorse)." The *NRS* version transfers the original subject into a prepositional phrase, "David was stricken to the heart," as does the Targum. The expression in 1 Sam 24:6 appears again in 2 Sam 24:10, describing David's reaction after ordering a census of the people.

who fervently seeks their leader's life. By encouraging David to "do what is good in [his] eyes" (24:5), they imply that he should kill Saul, yet they carefully avoid a direct charge to assassinate the king. David does, in fact, "do what is good in [his] eyes," but his perception of the prudent course of action does not comport with the counsel of his men. After making a decision to spare Saul, David declares: "YHWH forbid me that I should have done this thing to my lord, to YHWH's anointed, to reach out my hand against him, for YHWH's anointed is he" (24:7). Next, the narrator reports that David somehow prevents his men from rising up against Saul: וישסע דוד את אנשיו בדברים (24:8). Although the meaning of the verb שסע is clear elsewhere in the Tanakh, commentators have struggled to ascertain the sense of the verb in this particular context.

In Leviticus and Deuteronomy, the *qal* form of the root is used to designate animals with or without cleft hoofs (Lev 11:7, 26; Deut 14:6). Twice, the *pi'el* verb refers to the ripping apart of animals: Leviticus 1:17 instructs the priests to tear open a bird by its wings without severing it, and Judg 14:6 describes how Samson tears open a lion with his bare hands "as one might tear open a kid." These few verses establish enough of a pattern of usage to distinguish 1 Sam 24:8 as anomalous, for here the *pi'el* verb appears with a human object, as opposed to an animal, and it is used in conjunction with the prepositional phrase "with words."

What does it mean to "tear apart his men with words"? One interpretation maintains that David "tore into" his men, or attacked them verbally for proposing to harm the king. A number of translators convey this nuance when they render the Hebrew with the English verb, "rebuke."[61] But note that David does not chastise his men in his recorded speech in the prior verse. In his remarks in v. 7, David focuses on the first, not the third, person[62] as he explains why it would be inconceivable for him to kill Saul; but he does not criticize his men for suggesting he do so. Another approach reads the utterance as if it said that David tore apart his men from Saul with his words, meaning that his remarks proved persuasive enough to cause his men either to distance themselves physically from Saul or to back down from their urge to kill him. Several translators

---

[61] Fox, *JPS*, *REB*; *NRS* uses the translation "scolded."
[62] He refers to the first person four times: לי, אעשה, לאדני, ידי.

imply this interpretation when they state that "David restrained his
men with words."[63] Alter expresses a similar sentiment when he
explains that David used his words "to interpose a kind of barrier
between them and the king": "And David held back his men with
words."[64]

Is the problem with this verse philological or exegetical? Has a
faulty reading of the verb crept into the text? Or does the limited
number of attestations of this root prevent a fuller understanding of
its semantic range? To what extent do scholars simply shy away
from the concrete, metaphoric nature of the utterance? McCarter
comments that though the verb "ought to mean 'tore to pieces,'"
this definition "seems too strong even if taken figuratively."[65] *BDB*
objects that "1 Sam 24:8 gives too violent a meaning" and concludes
that the word is probably a corrupt version of some word meaning
"restrain."[66] As noted above, the verb does connote a degree of vir-
ulence not evident in David's response in v. 7. However, perhaps
the narrator intends to imply through such a strong verb that the
men exhibited a forceful resolve to do away with Saul, a will that
required David to select his words wisely and effectively in order to
save Saul from danger. The tone of the verb, along with uncertainties
about what it means and how it fits in this context, prompts the
search for alternate readings. Another factor contributing to the
ambiguity of this utterance is its novelty. While scholars tend to
denigrate the repeated usage of an expression and celebrate innovative
metaphors, in this case, the uniqueness of the collocation leads to
questions about its correctness and decisions to abandon any hint of
the possible underlying analogy in favor of greater exegetical clarity.

---

[63] McCarter, *NAB, NJB; KJV* renders the sentence: "David stayed his servants
with these words."

[64] Alter, *The David Story*, 148. Similarly, Bar-Efrat suggest that the intention of
the utterance is that David separate between Saul and his men (*Narrative Art in the
Bible*, 304).

[65] McCarter, 381.

[66] *BDB*, s.v. שסע. McCarter surveys a range of proposed solutions, none of which
he deems convincing. He notes that the Septuagint *kai epeisen* ("and he per-
suaded/prevailed upon") "is little help" and perhaps "a guess from context."

E. *1 Samuel 24:15*— אַחֲרֵי מִי יָצָא מֶלֶךְ יִשְׂרָאֵל אַחֲרֵי מִי אַתָּה רֹדֵף אַחֲרֵי
כֶּלֶב מֵת אַחֲרֵי פַּרְעֹשׁ אֶחָד ("*After whom has the king of Israel come forth?*
After whom are you chasing? After a dead dog? After a single flea?")

After the incident in the cave, David confronts Saul, asserting his
innocence and challenging Saul about his unjustified pursuit. Toward
the conclusion of his speech, he asks: "After whom has the king of
Israel come forth? After whom are you chasing? After a dead dog?
After a single flea?" (24:15). The preposition אַחֲרֵי recurs four times,
linking together the four parts of this artfully constructed verse. The
first two lines begin with the identical preposition and interrogative,
establishing a degree of equivalence that is offset by the semantic
and grammatical contrasts in the remainder of these lines. In the
first line, David addresses Saul in the third person, referring to him
more formally as the "king of Israel"; in the second, he uses a more
intimate, second person pronoun, "you." Whereas the nouns decrease
in formality, the verbs increase in intensity and specificity: from יָצָא
("come forth") in the perfect, to the chiastically arranged participle,
רֹדֵף ("chase"). In the latter half of the verse, David introduces two
rather different metaphors, both united by the repetition of אַחֲרֵי.
Although an interrogative pronoun is not used in these lines, they
also are read as rhetorical questions.

When David refers to himself, with a sense of ridicule and incredulity,
as a "dead dog," he invokes a familiar metaphor. In a prior contest
with a supposed superior, he provoked Goliath with a related rhetorical question: "Am I a dog that you come against me with sticks?"
(1 Sam 17:43). Further on in the book of Samuel, Mephibosheth
prostrates himself before David and says, self-effacingly: "What is
your servant, that you should have turned to a dead dog like me?"
(2 Sam 9:8). Later, Abishai, referring to Shimei, tells David: "Why
should this dead dog curse my lord the king?" (2 Sam 16:9).[67]

---

[67] In addition, in 2 Sam 3:8, Abner angrily announces to Ish-bosheth: "Am I a
dog's head attached to Judah?" In 2 Kgs 8:13, Hazel says to Elisha: "What is your
servant, the dog, that he should do this great thing?" George Coats identifies 2
Kgs 8:13 and 2 Sam 9:8 as examples of stereotypical self-abasement and insult formulas, which generally involve two parts: first, "a nominal sentence, introduced by
an interrogative particle . . . and followed by a personal pronoun, a proper name,
or a noun" and then, a verbal sentence usually connected to the initial question
by a כִּי (George Coats, "Self-Abasement and Insult Formulas," *JBL* 89 [1970] 14).

As these passages demonstrate, "to identify oneself as a dog is to draw attention to one's miserable condition as an inconsequential creature" and "to refer to another human as a dog is to insult the other as among the lowest in the social scale."[68] In addition to these biblical citations, several Lachish ostraca preserve examples in which the dog metaphor, paired with the term "servant" and couched in a rhetorical question, is employed as a form of self-abasement. For instance, a correspondent writes to his superior: "Who is your servant (but) a dog that you should have sent to your servant these letters?"[69] The dog metaphor is attested even more often in the Amarna letters. For example, a city ruler, Artamanya, says to the Egyptian king: "As you have written to me to make preparations before the arrival of the archers, who am I, a mere dog, that I should not go?"[70] Similarly, another vassal writes: "Whatever the king, my lord, has written me, I have listened to very carefully. Who is the dog that would not obey the orders of the king, his lord, the son of the Sun?"[71] José Galán argues that in the Amarna letters, the "dog" reference does not function as an invective, but as a way to stress "someone's status as inferior, subordinate and dependant."[72]

The subsequent metaphor in David's speech occurs with considerably less frequency. Only here and in the parallel episode in 1 Samuel 26 does a person invoke the metaphor of a flea. After David again relinquishes an opportunity to kill the man who stalks him, David warns Saul: "And now, do not let my blood fall to the ground, away from YHWH's presence, for the king of Israel has come forth to seek a single flea, as he would chase a partridge in the hills" (1 Sam 26:20). In these two passages, what does David imply when he equates

---

[68] *Dictionary of Biblical Imagery*, s.v. "Dog," 214.

[69] Lachish Ostracon 5:4, translated by Dennis Pardee in *Context of Scripture*, vol. III, ed. William W. Hallo (Leiden: Brill, 2002), 80. Lachish Ostraca 2:4 and 6:3 also state: "Who is your servant (but) a dog . . ."

[70] *EA* 201:9–16, from José M. Galán, "What Is He, The Dog," *Ugarit-Forschungen* 25 (1993) 176.

[71] *EA* 320:16–25, from Galán, 176.

[72] Galán, 175, 179. Galán cites several occasions in which the dog reference occurs in conjunction with the designation of one's status as "servant" (*ardu*), like *EA* 71:16–19: "What is Abdi-Ashirta, servant and dog, that he takes the land of the king for himself" (174).

the actual situation, Saul in pursuit of David, with the hypothetical situation, the king in pursuit of a flea? In both contexts, the metaphor operates on two levels: not only does David implicitly or explicitly compare a flea to another animal, but he implies that Saul misguidedly perceives an analogy between David and a flea.

In chapter 24, the parallel structure of the lines suggests a certain correspondence between a dog and a flea. What do the two have in common? If a dog was seen as a "pariah at the bottom of the social scale,"[73] a flea presumably was considered an even more lowly pest.[74] Alter observes:

> A dead dog was proverbial in ancient Israel as a contemptible, worthless thing, but David goes the idiom one better by saying he is scarcely more important than a single flea on the dead dog's carcass—a brilliant adaptation to prose of the logic of intensification of biblical poetry, in which a term introduced in the first part of the line is raised to the second power semantically in the parallel second half.[75]

As noted with regard to the first two lines of v. 15, the utterance becomes more dynamic because of the interplay of equivalence and contrast. While a dog and flea share the trait of a lowly status, the creatures differ in various respects, including the fact that, unlike a dead dog, a flea is difficult to capture. Thus, through this cleverly crafted utterance, David criticizes Saul for two misconceptions: belittling David's personal status and underestimating his military prowess. If Saul thought that David would be as easy to capture as a dead dog, the king has learned that apprehending David can be as baffling as catching a rapidly leaping flea. Earlier, Saul referred to David as a dead man, a בן מות (literally a "son of death") (20:31); achieving that end proves more challenging than initially anticipated, since David does not behave like a כלב מת, a "dead dog."

This subtle nuance about the wily nature of the flea becomes more apparent in chapter 26, when the flea metaphor is followed by a simile involving a partridge: "the king of Israel has come forth to seek a single flea, as he would chase a partridge in the hills" (1 Sam

---

[73] *Dictionary of Biblical Imagery*, s.v. "Dog," 214.

[74] With the exception of these two verses, no other biblical passages provide additional clues about attitudes toward fleas in ancient Israel.

[75] Alter, *The David Story*, 150.

26:20). Jack Lundbom provides some background information about the partridge:

> In 1 Sam 26:20 it is said to be hunted in the mountains, which fits the sand partridge (*ammoperdix heyi*), who is known to inhabit desert and semidesert areas of Jordan, Israel, and Sinai, also areas around the Dead Sea. . . . [W]hen disturbed, it will be observed running with agility up steep, rocky slopes.[76]

His comment indicates that, like the flea, the partridge resists easy capture. Another aspect of the metaphors emphasized in chapter 26 is the imbalance in power between David and Saul. The more simplified wording of the utterance in 26:20 juxtaposes, in closer proximity, the "king of Israel" and "a single flea," creating a comical image of the mighty ruler pursing a tiny insect with the same equipment and entourage that would be used for a royal partridge hunt. Through this contrast, David alludes to the imbalance in military forces, with Saul at the helm of three thousand soldiers (24:3) and David in charge of about six hundred men (23:13). Ironically, even with a large army, Saul cannot catch David; twice, "the flea" catches the "king of Israel" and magnanimously spares his life.

The utterances in 1 Sam 26:20 and 24:15 exhibit a notable degree of complexity, due in part to the overlapping analogies and multi-faceted messages. The use of repetition, parallelism, and rhetorical questions in 24:15 further enhances the artistry and sophistication of the verse. As noted above, in contrast to the rarity of the flea metaphor, figurative references to dogs are found a number of times in the Tanakh, primarily in the David story. Does the fact that the dog metaphor appears elsewhere in the Bible and extra-biblical sources diminish its effectiveness in this particular context? One might label the flea metaphor "novel" and the dog metaphor "conventional" or "cliche," but do such titles illuminate the way these metaphors operate in this specific passage? A survey of other references to dogs in the Tanakh and ancient Near Eastern texts reveals a generally negative

---

[76] Lundbom, 791 (comment on Jer 17:11). A number of commentators have noted the word play inherent in the Hebrew word for partridge (קֹרֵא), since Abner earlier says to David: "Who are you, that you have called out (קָרֵאתָ) to the king?" (26:14). Alter comments about this "witty pun": "Partridge (*qor'e*) is a homonym for 'he who calls out' . . . a caller out on the mountain, a partridge pursued on the mountains" (166).

attitude towards dogs and a repeated use of the dog metaphor to
abase the self or others. However, understanding and appreciating
the metaphors in this verse requires a close reading of the language
and structure of the utterance, an analysis of the analogies, and a
consideration of how the verse fits in the surrounding narrative. The
dynamics of the immediate and broader contexts, not frequency of
usage, determine the potency of the metaphor.

F. *Common Expressions Involving Hands and Eyes in 1 Samuel 24*

A prominent feature of 1 Samuel 24 is the repetition of the word
יד ("hand"), eleven times in twenty-three verses: once in the advice
of David's men (v. 5), once in David's reply to his men (v. 7), seven
times in David's speech to Saul (vv. 11–16), and twice in Saul's
response (vv. 19, 21). Most of the seven different expressions with
the word יד ("hand") operate in a figurative manner; only once does
a speaker refer literally to a person's actual hand. The passage also
contains two fairly common metonymic phrases that mention eyes.
Should such routine expressions be dismissed as "dead" metaphors
or idioms and rendered in a nonfigurative manner? Or, given the
proper circumstances, do these expressions prove capable of producing
a tropic effect, a factor that justifies a more literal translation?

1. *1 Samuel 24:5a*—הנה אנכי נתן את איביך בידך *("Here, I give your
enemy into your hand")*
1 Samuel 24:11a—נתנך יי היום בידי במערה *("YHWH has given you
today into my hand in the cave")*
After David's men discover that Saul has slipped into the cave, they
announce with confidence: "Here is the day about which YHWH
said to you: 'Here, I give your enemy into your hand'" (24:5). Later,
David declares to Saul: "Here, this day your eyes have seen that
YHWH has given you today into my hand in the cave." The phrase
נתן ביד ("give into the hand") occurs quite often in the Tanakh,
approximately one hundred and fifteen times. On a few occasions,
the expression operates on a literal level as a human subject puts
some sort of concrete object into the hand of another person.[77] In

---

[77] Rebecca places food into Jacob's hand (Gen 27:17), the cup bearer places a
cup in Pharaoh's hand (Gen 40:13), and Ahimelech, the priest of Nob, places loaves
of bread in David's hand (1 Sam 21:4).

contrast, the vast majority of verses using this expression contain a divine subject and an object comprised of either an individual, a collective body of people, a city, or some other locale.[78] In such passages, as in the above quotations from 1 Sam 24:5 and 11, God's decision to "give" the adversary "into the hand" of the opposing party signals the first, and requisite, stage of victory. The phrase operates metonymically, with "hand" referring to power or control. Those who prefer abstract language to the physicality of the Hebrew often translate the verb נתן in such contexts as "deliver." Some retain the word "hand," while others provide a metonymic substitution, as in the following translation of 1 Sam 24:5: "I am going to deliver your enemy into your power."[79]

2. *1 Samuel 24:19*—סנרני יי בידך *("YHWH shut me into your hand")*
Saul uses a somewhat similar expression when he acknowledges that David has dealt kindly with him: "YHWH shut me into your hand, yet you did not kill me" (24:19). The expression "shut into the hand," formulated in the *piʿel* as סנר ביד or in the semantically equivalent *hipʿil*, הסניר ביד, appears far less often than נתן ביד ("give into the hand"). Four out of the ten occurrences possess a divine subject and human object, as in 1 Sam 24:19 and David's boastful exclamation to Goliath: "This day YHWH has shut you into my hand. And I will strike you down and cut off your head" (1 Sam 17:46).[80] The remaining six citations contain a human subject and human object, as when David asks God whether or not the men of Keilah will surrender him over to Saul: "Will [they] shut me into his hand?" (1 Sam 23:11, 12).[81] In the *qal* and the *nipʿal* forms, the verb סנך refers

---

[78] For instance, reassuring the Israelites about the destruction of the Canaanites, Moses predicts: "[YHWH your God] will give their kings into your hand, and you shall blot out their name from under the heavens; no one shall stand up to you, until you have devastated them" (Deut 7:24). In another, smaller category of cases, the phrase נתן ביד is used with a human subject and a human object. For instance, Deut 19:12 describes the surrender of a murderer: "And the elders of his town . . . shall give him into the hand of the blood-avenger to be put to death"; additional examples include Judg 15:13; 2 Sam 10:10; 21:9.

[79] McCarter; compare *JPS*: "I will deliver your enemy into your hands."

[80] Also see 1 Sam 26:8 and Ps 31:9; cf. 2 Sam 18:28, which lacks the prepositional phrase.

[81] Also see Josh 20:5; 1 Sam 23:20; 30:15; cf. Obad 1:14, which lacks the prepositional phrase, and Amos 1:6, 9.

to objects like gates or doors that are closed[82] or to people shut out of or into a house, town, or camp.[83]

The general sense of this expression is that God has given over control of the opponent, thus enabling the person to defeat the enemy. Some treat this expression as synonymous with נתן ביד ("give into the hand") and translate it as "delivered."[84] Others render the verb differently, either retaining the word "hands" or opting for a metonymic translation. For instance, Fox writes: "YHWH turned me over to your hand," where as McCarter translates: "Yahweh handed me over to you," and *NJB* reads: "Yahweh has put me in your power."

3. *1 Samuel 24:7*—חלילה לי מיי אם אעשה את הדבר הזה לאדני למשיח *יי לשלח ידי בו* ("YHWH forbid me that I should have done this thing to my lord, YHWH's anointed, to reach out my hand against him")
1 Samuel 24:11b—ואמר לא אשלח ידי באדני ("and I say: 'I will not reach out my hand against my lord'")

Once David realizes that he has been given the opportunity to eliminate Saul, he must determine whether to follow his men's advice or to spare the king. As he declares twice, he refuses to "reach out his hand against" the anointed leader. The phrase שלח יד ("reach out the hand") appears approximately sixty times in the Tanakh. In about one quarter of the citations, the verb is used with a human subject and either an inanimate, concrete indirect object, like fruit or a sword, or a animate indirect object, like a snake or a person.[85] The verbs that often follow שלח יד, such as לקח ("to take"), אחז ("to grasp"), and החזיק ("to seize"), clarify that the phrase describes the first step of a two-part process: a person reaches out his or her hand in order to then physically take hold of something.[86]

---

[82] For example, Gen 19:10 or 2 Kgs 6:32.

[83] Ezek 3:24; 1 Sam 23:7; Num 12:14, 15.

[84] For example, Alter and *JPS*.

[85] Gen 3:22; Judg 3:21; Ex 4:4; Gen 19:10, respectively. For example, Gen 8:9 tells how Noah "reached out his hand and took (וישלח ידו ויקחה)" the dove after it found no resting place on land. First Chronicles 13:9 describes how Uzzah "reached out his hand to grasp (וישלח עזא את ידו לאחז)" the ark.

[86] Another quarter of the citations include miscellaneous cases. For example, in Exodus "reaching out a hand against" property specifically refers to robbery (Exod 22:8, 11); in Ps 138:7 and 144:7, where the expression parallels the verbs הושיע

In nearly half of the sixty occurrences, the formulation שלח יד
("reach out the hand") occurs exclusively with human indirect objects.
In these cases, the expression conveys a sense of harm inflicted by
the human or divine subject on an individual or collective body of
people. For example, the narrator reports that "the king's servants
were unwilling to reach out a hand to strike (לשלח את ידם לפגע) the
priest of YHWH" (1 Sam 22:17). Further on, David challenges the
Amalekite who helps put an end to Saul's life: "How were you not
afraid to reach out your hand to destroy (לשלח ידך לשחת) YHWH's
anointed?" (2 Sam 1:14). In these verses, the infinitive verbs that follow שלח יד specify the purpose of reaching out the hand: to fatally
injure another person. In other instances, as in 1 Sam 24:7 and 11,
the larger narrative context makes the text-in-context construal obvious. When David asserts that he did not reach out his hand against
Saul, he means that he did not stab or otherwise harm the king.
He leaves no doubt about what might have happened had he done
so when he reminds Saul: "When I cut off the edge of your cloak,
I did not kill you" (24:12). In the metonymic expression under discussion, a preliminary act comes to refer to the subsequent action
or, more generally, to the end result: the inflicting of injury or death.[87]

4. *1 Samuel 24:13, 14*—וידי לא תהיה בך *("And my hand will not be
upon you")*
As part of his assertion of innocence and accusation of injustice, David
quotes a proverb to Saul: "From the wicked, wickedness goes forth"
(24:14). Immediately before and after this proverb, David reiterates:
"And my hand will not be upon you" (24:13, 14). This expression
functions similarly to the one examined above: an initial act points
to the succeeding injury that may result from that act. The notion
of laying hands upon a person serves as a way to refer to causing a
person harm, be it by the hands or by some other means. The utterance encompasses any potential threat of violence, whether or not it
actually involves the placement of one's hands on the victim's body.

("to save") and הציל ("to deliver"), respectively, the phrase connotes salvation. Edward
Greenstein discusses this expression in his article on "Trans-semitic Idiomatic
Equivalency and the Derivation of Hebrew *ml'kh*," *UF* 11 (1979), see 333–336.
    [87] The translations surveyed stick fairly closely to the wording of the Hebrew,
many preferring a reading that transfers easily into English: "I will not raise my
hand against my lord" (24:11); see, for instance, *JPS, NRS*, McCarter.

5. *1 Samuel 24:12a*—וְאָבִי רְאֵה גַּם רְאֵה אֶת כְּנַף מְעִילְךָ בְּיָדִי ("*And, my father, see, yes, see the edge of your cloak in my hand.*")

1 Samuel 24:12b—דַּע וּרְאֵה כִּי אֵין בְּיָדִי רָעָה וָפֶשַׁע ("*Know and see that there is no wickedness or transgression in my hand.*")

David cleverly employs the prepositional phrase בְּיָד ("in the hand") twice in v. 12, in a way that juxtaposes literal and figurative references to this part of the body. First, he calls attention to the cloak he manually holds in his possession as physical, visible proof that he could have, but did not, slay the king. Next, he emphasizes what he does not possess "in his hand," or, here, in his psyche as manifested in his deeds: "wickedness or transgression." The statements surrounding these two assertions reinforce the comparison between the negative and the positive, for they set up an opposition between what David elects not to do—kill Saul—and what Saul insists on doing—trying to murder David: "And, my father, see, yes, see the edge of your cloak in my hand, for when I cut off the edge of your cloak, I did not kill you. Know and see that there is no wickedness or rebellion in my hand and I did not sin against you, yet you stalk my life, to take it" (24:12).

6. *1 Samuel 24:16*—וּשְׁפָטַנִי מִיָּדֶךָ ("*and judge me from your hand*")

Convinced of his righteousness, David calls upon God to judge between him and Saul (יִשְׁפֹּט יי בֵּינִי וּבֵינֶךָ) (24:13). At the conclusion of his discourse, he repeats this sentiment when he asserts: "YHWH will be arbiter and judge between me and you (וְהָיָה יי לְדַיָּן וְשָׁפַט בֵּינִי וּבֵינֶךָ), that He may see and plead my case, and judge me from your hand (וּשְׁפָטַנִי מִיָּדֶךָ)" (24:16). Alter translates the final phrase in v. 16 as "judge me against you," which he explains means "judge me favorably and rescue me from your hand."[88] The prepositional phrase מִיָּד ("from the hand") appears with the verb שָׁפַט ("to judge") on only two other occasions, when various characters state that God has vindicated someone "from the hand" of an enemy (2 Sam 18:19, 31). In contrast to expressions like שְׁלַח יָד ("reach out the hand"), סָגַר בְּיָד ("shut into the hand"), and נָתַן בְּיָד ("give into the hand"),

---

[88] Alter, *The David Story*, 150. Other translations vary, from Fox's more literal translation, "and exact-justice from your hand," to metonymic treatments of יָד like those seen in McCarter ("and set me free from your power") and *JPS* ("and vindicate me against you").

which are used with varying degrees of frequency in the Bible, this
anomalous syntactic combination, like the one discussed below, stands
out as rather distinctive.

7. 1 Samuel 24:21—וקמה בידך מלכת ישראל ("and the kingship of Israel will arise/stand in your hand")

After hearing David's words and seeing the torn edge of his cloak,
Saul not only acknowledges the upright and unprecedented nature
of David's actions, but he concedes that one day David will sit upon
the throne: "And now, here, I know that you will surely be king
and the kingship of Israel will arise/stand in your hand"[89] (24:21).
What is the precise nuance of the verb לקום ("to arise or stand") in
this utterance? Does the second statement semantically echo the first,
with both statements recognizing that David will become king, or
does a greater degree of contrast separate the two? According to the
first possibility, the utterance carries the meaning of לקום as "to
arise," a sense reflected in the translations of v. 21 with the English
term, "to be established."[90] In line with the second proposal, a degree
of semantic contrast distinguishes the two statements, with the second half of the sentence meaning that after David becomes king, he
will stay in power. Whereas the kingship was torn away from Saul,
the kingdom of Israel will "remain" or "stay" in David's control and
result in the Davidic dynasty.[91]

   The collocation of the verb לקום ("to arise or stand") and the
prepositional phrase ביד ("in the hand") is unique in the Bible. Why
use such an unusual formulation? Perhaps two literary factors drive
this choice of words. First, by using the verb לקום, along with the
noun ממלכת ("kingship"), the writer creates a linguistic link to Samuel's
earlier prediction to Saul: "Your kingship shall not stand (ועתה ממלכתך
לא תקום)" (1 Sam 13:14). This allusion suggests that Saul accepts
both the inevitability future and the indubitability of the past. Secondly,

---

[89] Berlin suggests the possibility of reading the prepositional phrase, "by your
hand" (personal correspondence).

[90] See, for instance, Fox, McCarter, or *NRS*; the *NAB* translation emphasizes this
nuance and metonymically treats יד: "sovereignty over Israel shall come into your
possession."

[91] Translations by *JPS* and Alter, respectively, both of which retain the word
"hand"; *REB* conveys this general sense with a more exegetical translation: "the
kingdom of Israel will flourish under your rule."

the phrase קָמָה בְיָדֶךָ ("arise/stand in the hand") reinforces the *Leitwort* of this chapter, the word יָד ("hand"). In order to accomplish these two aims, the writer may have been willing to pay the price of a small degree of semantic uncertainty or syntactic awkwardness.

8. *1 Samuel 24:5a—*וְעָשִׂיתָ לּוֹ כַּאֲשֶׁר יִטַב בְּעֵינֶיךָ *("and you may do to him whatever is good in your eyes")*

Whereas the expressions surveyed above repeat the word "hand," two figurative phrases in this chapter contain a different body part, the eyes. As David's men urge him to take action against Saul, they cite a divine promise not mentioned in the prior narrative: "Here, I am placing your enemy into your hand, and you may do to him whatever is good in your eyes" (24:5). In this familiar biblical expression,[92] one segment of the body metonymically signals the person as a whole, as reflected in translations like: "and you shall do to him as it seems good to you."[93] Another approach to this expression interprets the mention of the eyes as a reference to the function performed by that part of the body, "do what seems good in your sight," or the more general mental function, "do what seems good in your opinion."[94]

9. *1 Samuel 24:11a—*הִנֵּה הַיּוֹם הַזֶּה רָאוּ עֵינֶיךָ אֵת אֲשֶׁר נְתָנְךָ יי הַיּוֹם בְּיָדִי בַּמְּעָרָה *("Here, this day your eyes have seen that YHWH has given you today into my hand in the cave")*

Further on in chapter 24, David challenges Saul to recognize the implications of the events that transpired in the cave. After asking Saul why he listens to those who tell him that David seeks to do him harm (24:10), David urges him to trust his eyes, not his ears: "Here, this day your eyes have seen that YHWH has given you today into my hand in the cave" (24:11). Similar to the expression above, the eye metonymically refers to the larger individual. Therefore, many translators again eliminate any mention of the eyes and, here,

---

[92] The phrase יִטַב בְּעֵינַיִם occurs sixteen times in the Tanakh, with four citations located in the book of Samuel; various forms of the synonymous phrase טוֹב בְּעֵינַיִם appear approximately thirty-seven times, with fifteen citations found in Samuel.

[93] *NRS*, which is similar to McCarter, *JPS*, and others. Of the translations surveyed, only Alter and Fox retain the word "eyes."

[94] See *DCH*, s.v. יטב and טוב, respectively.

emphasize the second person pronoun: "You can see for yourself."[95]
This formulation is found in nine verses, including when Moses
reminds Joshua that he has seen for himself what God did to Kings
Sihon and Og; as a result, given his first-hand knowledge of God's
power, he should not fear the other kingdoms he will encounter
(Deut 3:21).[96] The placement of the noun עינים ("eyes") as the subject of the verb ראה ("to see") enables to the speaker to stress that
the person has witnessed something with his or her own eyes.

G. *Criteria and Implications*

Is there anything remarkable about the presence of the above
expressions in 1 Samuel 24? Is the author simply utilizing standard
biblical idioms, or has the writer selected these phrases in order to
produce a tropic effect? Some might consider expressions like נתן ביד
("give into the hand") and שלח יד ("reach out the hand") as "dead"
metaphors or stock figures of speech, phrases that "exist as frozen,
semantic units within speakers' mental lexicon."[97] Assuming that such
sayings represent the normative way to express the concepts of deliverance and harm in biblical Hebrew, many translate the Hebrew
into the more abstract concepts supposedly retrieved from lexical
memory. But can the concrete, figurative language be so easily dismissed?

Certain criteria can be established to help determine when an
author appears to tap into the tropic potential of standard biblical
expressions. Reviewing the analysis of the word יד ("hand") in
1 Samuel 24, one can identify a number of factors that suggest that
the writer deliberately calls attention to the figurative elements in
the language in order to achieve certain rhetorical purposes:

(1) Repetition establishes a given lexeme as a key word in the current
    narrative context. Whereas the word עינים ("eyes") only appears
    twice in 1 Samuel 24, יד ("hand") is used eleven times. In the
    latter case, a certain amount of repetition may simply testify to
    the prevalence of expressions involving body parts in the biblical

---

[95] *JPS*, which resembles McCarter and others; Alter, Fox, and *NRS* preserve the
reference to the eyes.
[96] Also see Deut 4:3; 11:7; Jos 24:7; Isa 6:5; 30:20; Jer 32:4; 42:2.
[97] Gibbs, 57.

corpus; however, the relatively large number of occurrences in a concentrated passage, in conjunction with the other factors discussed below, signals the creation of a key word.

(2) Placement of the vocabulary within a given unit influences its effectiveness, for a high frequency of a particular word within a compact literary unit highlights the repetition. In chapter 24, seven of the eleven occurrences of the noun "hand" are clustered in David's speech to Saul (24:10–16). In contrast, this same noun is found six times in 1 Samuel 26, but the citations are spread throughout the chapter: once in Abishai's comment to David (v. 8), twice in David's remarks to his men (vv. 9–11), and three times in David's speech to Saul (vv. 18, 23).[98] The fewer times the word is repeated and the more diffuse its appearance, the weaker the impact.

(3) The presence of a variety of different expressions containing the same word also highlights the particular lexeme. In 1 Samuel 24, seven separate phrases contain the word יד ("hand"): קם ביד, בידי, שפט מיד, ידי לא תהיה בך, שלח יד, סגר ביד, נתן ביד.[99]

(4) Unusual syntactic formulations further draw attention to the key word, as seen in the cases of שפט מיד and קם ביד.[100]

(5) Combining figurative and literal uses of the same word produces a similar effect. Just as 1 Sam 24:12 juxtaposes what literally is and figuratively is not in David's hand, 1 Samuel 23 plays with different formulations of the verb סגר. Because David "has shut himself in (נסגר) by entering a town with gates and bars," Saul thinks: "God has transferred him into my hand (נכר אתו כידי אלהים)" (23:7).[101] David avoids this fate, however, since he inquires

---

[98] שלח יד appears three times (26:9, 11, 23); the following expressions occur once: סגר ביד (26:8), נתן ביד (26:23), and ומה בידי רעה (26:18).

[99] Similarly, this noun recurs eight times in 1 Samuel 23, in five different expressions: נתן ביד (v. 4, 14), הסניר ביד (vv. 11, 12, 20), נכר ביד (v. 7), חזק את היד (v. 16), מצא יד (v. 17).

[100] Likewise, נכר ביד in 1 Sam 23:7 stands out as distinctive, though commentators question the correctness of the Masoretic text. In place of נכר, "to make a stranger," some prefer the Septuagint reading which reflects מכר, meaning "sold." McCarter proposes another solution: "The context suggest that the original was *skr*. The expression *sikkar beyad*, 'shut up in the hand of,' is a rare (only here and in Isa 19:4) equivalent of *siggar beyad*, 'enclose in the hand of'" (369–370).

[101] As mentioned above, the reading of נכר ביד in 1 Sam 23:7 remains uncertain. This translation is influenced by a note to Fox's translation, "God alienated

of God and learns that the men of Keilah intend to "shut him into Saul's hand" (הסניר ביד) (23:11, 12).[102]

(6) An allusion or echo to another literary passage can reinforce the physical language prominent in biblical Hebrew. For instance, commenting on David's insistence that his hand will not be upon Saul (24:13, 14), Alter writes:

> The words that the writer attributes to David ironically echo the words of Saul's first murderous plot against David, conveyed in the interior monologue, when Saul said, 'Let not my hand be against him but let the hand of the Philistines be against him' (18:17).[103]

Fokkelman finds significance in the connections between Saul's choice of words in 24:19, "YHWH shut me into your hand (בידך סנרני יי)," and the recurrence of this verb in chapter 23. He observes:

> [Saul] does not use *ntn but *sgr, the delivering word which was characteristic of the Keilah scene. Thus he indicates that the reality (himself in David's hands) is diametrically opposite his illusions (David in the trap).[104]

These factors bolster the argument that the author has not simply cited standard biblical expressions, but has selected the wording in 1 Samuel 24 carefully, with an awareness of the potential power in even a common metonymic phrase like נתן ביד ("give into the hand"). When these criteria are applied to the expressions involving eyes in this chapter, the utterances discussed above do not initially display the types of traits that strongly suggest an attempted play upon their figurative potential. The word "eyes" only occurs twice, in separate

---

him into my hand"; he explains that this means "transferred, as in 'alienating property,'" an insight he attributes to Edward Greenstein in a written communication (114). Cf. *CAD*, s.v. nakāru 11a, which lists citations in which nukkuru means "to transfer, reassign persons, to move someone to another location."

[102] Other examples have been cited earlier in this chapter, in Alter's comments on the interplay of the figurative and concrete senses of the term "hand" in Genesis 39 (*Genesis*, xv) and Bar-Efrat's observations about the use of the word "house" to refer to both a dynasty and a building in 2 Samuel 7 (*Narrative Art in the Bible*, 207).

[103] Saul's desire for David to fall at the hand of the Philistines is repeated in 18:21, 25. In this earlier episode, the word יד is emphasized by the contrast between David, who "was playing [a lyre] with his hand (ודוד מנגן בידו)" and Saul, who had a spear in his hand (והחנית ביד שאול) (18:10).

[104] Fokkelman, 470.

scenes: in the comments of David's men (v. 5) and in David's address to Saul (v. 11). Both expressions appear elsewhere in the Tanakh, though ראו עינים ("the eyes see") is not as well attested as the commonplace ייטב/טוב בעינים ("it is good in the eyes"). However, several additional elements in the chapter influence the perception of these two phrases and prompt a reconsideration of this impression. First, the related verb, ראה ("to see"), repeats five times in David's seven-verse speech to Saul (vv. 11, 12, 16), including three times in v. 12 alone. In this verse, David utilizes the verb in two ways, as he first calls upon Saul to look at the cloak and then pleads with Saul to acknowledge his innocence: "And, my father, see, yes, see (ראה גם ראה) the edge of your cloak in my hand. . . . Know and see (דע וראה) that there is no wickedness or transgression in my hand" (24:12). Furthermore, David begins his address by asking Saul: "Why do you listen to the words of the people, saying: 'Here, David is seeking your evil'" (24:10). In the following verse, he sets up a contrast between hearing and seeing, between rumors and visible proof of David's motives: "Here, this day your eyes have seen (ראו עיניך) that YHWH has given you today into my hand in the cave" (24:11). These supplemental considerations support the contention that here, as well, metonymic references to a body part contribute to the message and its artistry.

H. *Conclusion*

The concrete, figurative language that pervades biblical Hebrew provides a skilled storyteller with a valuable tool for forming meaningful links within a narrative and between separate episodes, developing and focusing attention on key themes, creating contrast, and producing other effects. Since the meanings of the constituent words may be available to the individual language user, common figurative expressions cannot be dismissed as "dead" metaphors. The language and imagery evoked by these words "still play a role in understanding and interpreting"[105] the smaller semantic units and their larger narrative contexts. As a result, a full appreciation of the meaning and power of biblical Hebrew and biblical narrative demands a serious consideration of metaphors, metonyms, and other tropes.

---

[105] Cacciari, 32.

CHAPTER SEVEN

CONCLUSION

I. Figurative Language and Biblical Translation

In the previous chapter the question was raised regarding the implications of the study of figurative language in biblical prose for the longstanding debate about biblical translation. Edward Greenstein provides a number of angles from which to view the "oversimplified" split between "literal" and "idiomatic" translations. He proposes using the term "literary" to characterize the former approach, the method of translation practiced by those who consider literature "as the art of using words."[1] He contrasts the "literary" mode of translation with what he labels a "philological" approach:

> The philological approach understands a text primarily as a medium of information, and it seeks to transmit that information through an accurate, contemporary equivalent in the language of the translation . . . . In the 'literary' view it is perhaps more crucial to convey the rhetorical features of the text and the manifold connotations of its words than it is to convey the denoted or ideational message of the text.[2]

Greenstein further distinguishes these two schools of thought by their conception of the relationship between form and content. "Literary" translators prove more "form-oriented," for they emphasize the "inseparability of form and content," whereas the "content-oriented" translators "see a dichotomy between form and content."[3] He also classifies the former approach as "author-oriented" and the latter as

---

[1] Edward Greenstein, "Theories of Modern Bible Translation," in *Essays on Biblical Method and Translation* (Atlanta: Scholars Press, 1989), 86.

[2] Greenstein, 93. Anticipating his critics, he writes: "There are those who would argue the reverse: the most literal method produces the least literary translation— using 'literary' to refer to a translation that itself amounts to literature" (94).

[3] Greenstein, 88–89.

"audience-oriented," based on a well-known quotation by Friedrich Schleiermacher:

> Either the translator leaves the author in peace, as much as possible, and moves the reader towards him; or he leaves the reader in peace, as much as possible, and moves the author towards him.[4]

Scholars who advocate a more literal style of translation support their position by pointing to the negative ramifications that result from altering the wording and syntax of the Hebrew text. The most frequent critique concerns the propensity to eliminate repetition, a prominent stylistic feature of idiomatic translations driven by the desire to avoid redundancies and language that is perceived as sounding archaic.[5] To cite one example, Gerald Hammond charges that "the modern translators' insistence upon a clear, readable style . . . masks the techniques of repetition which are so basic to the literary effects of the Bible."[6] After discussing the "diminishments consequent upon tinkering with the original syntax,"[7] Hammond addresses the fact that "many modern versions eschew anything which smacks of imagery and metaphor."[8] As a result of these factors, he posits: "For the doubtful gain in semantic precision, the literary loss is large,"[9] both in terms of aesthetics and meaning.[10] Hammond's observations echo Alter's scathing conclusions about the way many contemporary biblical translators "turn the pungency of the original into stale paraphrase"[11] through their mishandling of figurative language and their neglect of other aspects of "the magic of biblical style"[12] such as syntax and diction. Alter insists that by substituting abstract terms for the concrete language that pervades biblical Hebrew, modern translators

---

[4] Greenstein, 96, quoting Friedrich Schleiermacher's essay, "On the Different Methods of Translation."

[5] Hammond, 655. Orlinsky labels this an attempt to achieve "intelligibility in diction" (17).

[6] Hammond, 654. Also see Greenstein, 87 and Alter, *Genesis*, ix–xxxix. In addition, Tigay writes about the "troublesome" way that the *JPS* translation's avoidance of literalism "can obscure significant and possibly intentional word plays in the text" ("On Translating the Torah," *Conservative Judaism* 26/2 [1972] 18).

[7] Hammond, 660.

[8] Hammond, 663.

[9] Hammond, 652.

[10] Hammond, 663.

[11] Alter, *Genesis*, xii.

[12] Alter, *Genesis*, xxxvi.

end up "subverting the literary integrity of the story."[13] He contends: "Such substitutions offer explanations and interpretations instead of translations and thus betray the original."[14]

The study of metaphors and common metonymical expressions employed in 1 Samuel 24 provides compelling support for those who promote a more literal, "literary" approach to translation. Here and in the other selections from Samuel examined above, the rhetorical effects generated by metaphor and other tropes are muted or altogether eliminated by converting figurative utterances into abstract statements. To say that Nabal "spurned" instead of "swooped down on" David's messengers[15] or that the soldier will "grow faint with fear"[16] instead of "melt" diminishes some of the potential power, complexity, and artistry of the narrative. To remove the mention of hands and render the promise to Absalom as "all your partisans will take courage" and the assessment of David's condition as "discouraged"[17] robs the storyteller of an important device for conveying meaning and evoking interactional effects. In addition, these more idiomatic translations introduce a degree of specificity of meaning not necessarily present in the Hebrew text.

II. METAPHOR AND AMBIGUITY

Even though de Waard and Nida are proponents of a "functional equivalence" method of translation aligned in many ways with the idiomatic approach, they recognize that "there is a tendency for some translators to avoid figurative meanings."[18] They write:

> One should, however, avoid the tendency to delete or de-metaphorize figurative expressions, for figures of speech add insights, contribute impact, provide aesthetic enhancement, and can be very important in contributing in-group identification.[19]

---

[13] Alter, *Genesis*, xv.
[14] Alter, *Genesis*, xvi.
[15] *JPS* translation of 1 Sam 25:14.
[16] McCarter's translation of 2 Sam 17:10.
[17] *NAB* translations of 2 Sam 16:21 and 17:2.
[18] De Waard and Nida, 155.
[19] De Waard and Nida, 155.

Nevertheless, they maintain that literal renderings of figurative expressions often prove "quite meaningless," "lead to distortions of meaning," or "produce very negative associative meanings."[20] As a result, they advise that "unless the figurative significance of an expression is rather obvious from the context," the translator should change the form of the utterance in order to make the text meaningful in the receptor language.[21]

An important issue separating the two basic approaches to biblical translation concerns the tolerance for ambiguity. Reflecting on the merits of the early seventeenth century Authorized or King James Version of the Bible, Hammond observes:

> It seems to have been an important principle that its renderings be capable of embracing differing, even apparently incompatible, interpretations . . . A translation which could admit ambiguity was nearly always to be preferred to a narrowly interpretive one—a practice completely opposed to the aims of most modern translators, and one which has significant literary consequences.[22]

Compare the Authorized Version's attitude toward ambiguity to the stance of de Waard and Nida, who argue:

> Rather than incorporate obscure, ambiguous, and potentially misleading expressions into the text of a translation, it is far better to provide receptors with a meaningful equivalent in the text and possible alternatives in the margin.[23]

A number of scholars highlight the connection between metaphor and ambiguity. For instance, Exum prefaces her study of the extended similes in Isaiah with the following remarks:

> The meaning of an image cannot be reduced to what it signifies. One reason for this irreducibility lies in the nature of words and images to be connotative rather than simply denotative. Figurative language embraces ambiguity. In fact, much of its power derives from its plurisignificance, from its ability to be suggestive of multiple meanings.[24]

White dedicates a chapter of his book to what he describes as the largely ignored phenomenon of metaphoric ambiguity.[25] After illus-

---

[20] De Waard and Nida, 157–158.
[21] De Waard and Nida, 112.
[22] Hammond, 661.
[23] De Waard and Nida, 34.
[24] Exum, 333.
[25] White, 37.

trating how a single metaphoric utterance can be construed in several different ways, he encourages his readers to value and explore the multiplicity of meaning inherent in metaphor. He emphasizes that "understanding the metaphor is not merely deciding which of these many readings is *the* correct one, but of accepting them all, and realising how each of them corresponds to different" aspects of the subject at hand.[26] The title of Aaron's book, *Biblical Ambiguities: Metaphor, Semantics, and Divine Imagery*, reflects the importance he attaches to this topic. He establishes at the outset that "most figurative, rhetorical devices thrive on ambiguity," particularly metaphor.[27]

The in-depth analysis of the metaphors and other tropes in 1 Samuel 24–25 and 2 Samuel 16:16–17:14 reveals that ambiguity can arise from a variety of factors. In a number cases, like פוקה (1 Sam 25:31), ויעט בהם (1 Sam 25:14), or וישסע דוד את אנשיו בדברים (1 Sam 24:8), uncertainty of meaning results from questions concerning the denotation of a given lexeme or the import of a particular syntactic construction. In other instances, interpretive indecision is caused by a lack of knowledge about biblical customs and concepts, like the "bundle of the living" (1 Sam 25:29). Both sorts of ambiguity stem from deficiencies in the exegete's understanding of the words of the Bible or the world portrayed in this ancient text. In such cases, what remains obscure to a twenty-first century reader may have been perfectly clear to the average Israelite long ago. Compensating for such lacunae requires an array of resources, mainly contextual clues, studies of patterns of usage, and extrabiblical resources.

At other times, metaphoric ambiguity is generated by the underlying analogy: the comparison itself, the way the analogy is formulated, or how it fits in the embedded narrative context. As White explores "how it is that the way of combining words that we find in metaphor can generate . . . radically different readings,"[28] he observes: "The most obvious source of ambiguity is that if I compare *A* with *B*, there may be a wide variety of different properties of *B*, each of which could give a point to the comparison."[29] When the speaker or writer does not specify the intended associated commonplaces, the interpreter must determine which potential points of intersection

---

[26] White, 42.
[27] Aaron, 1.
[28] White, 38.
[29] White, 38.

between the actual and hypothetical situations drive the particular
metaphor. What does a raptor swooping down on its prey have in
common with Nabal's treatment of David's messengers? In what
ways does dew falling on ground resemble the arrival of Absalom's
forces? The biblical texts examined above show that interpretive
uncertainty and multiplicity of meaning can develop from tensions
between the actual and hypothetical situations, as well as from an
uneasy fit between the metaphor and the surrounding text. Does the
depiction of David's men as a wall accurately reflect the actions they
performed in the wilderness? How does the juxtaposition of the dog
and flea metaphors influence the understanding of the two utterances and the implied messages about David and Saul?

White contends that "in practice, the possible ambiguity will in
most cases be instantly resolved by the fact that contextual considerations only permit one of the alternative readings of the metaphor."[30]
In the case of biblical narrative, however, alternative interpretations
often are not so easily resolved, and many metaphors remain somewhat indeterminate. The narrative as a whole is enriched by the
resultant interplay of variant potential meanings. Identifying and
interpreting metaphor does not necessarily resolve the ambiguities of
biblical narrative. For instance, in 1 Samuel 25, does the servant's
statement that David's men "were a wall" around the shepherds
indicate that David's request for a share of Nabal's bounty is well-
intentioned and well-deserved, and not some form of extortion? Does
Abigail employ an abundance of metaphors when speaking to David
merely to save her husband, or does she anticipate an opportunity
to impress the future king and possibly improve her own position?
The interpretive process succeeds in raising valuable questions, but
it does not always yield definitive answers.

Aaron cites another facet of metaphoric uncertainty when he writes
that there often exists "a lingering ambiguity as to whether something is even meant to be understood metaphorically."[31] While the
majority of utterances studied in the prior chapters can be assigned to

---

[30] White, 40–41.
[31] Aaron, 1. In addition, he discusses an "internal" ambiguity that "results from
uncertainty as to how the first part of a nonliteral expression is to be understood
in terms of its second, or implied, part" (1).

established tropic categories, several examples resist easy classification. Does the description of Nabal as a "hard" man constitute a literal or figurative usage of language? Should the statement, "You have made yourself stink to your father" be termed a metaphor or metonymy? What type of metonymic relationship best accounts for the connection between the decontextualized meaning and the text-in-context construal of the sentence, "And the hands of all who are with you will be strengthened"? As noted in chapter five, the creative, artful use of language sometimes defies the taxonomical attempt to categorize forms of figurative language. More important than the label given to an utterance is the investigation of how the utterance operates in a specific literary context and the exegetical outcomes of that interpretive process.

III. Figurative Language and Narrative Exegesis

In order to explore the mechanics of metaphor and other tropes, various theoretical approaches and heuristic devices have been applied to selected narratives in the book of Samuel. As has been acknowledged, these analytical tools do not always work flawlessly, in part because of inherent methodological imperfections as well as the challenges involved in the study of a restricted literary corpus written in an ancient language. Critics have raised legitimate objections to aspects of the theory of componential semantics, the concept of selection restriction violations, and assumptions about basic, context-free meanings of words. Likewise, White's interpretive technique cannot be applied with equal success to all biblical metaphors. Nevertheless, the results of this study demonstrate that the benefits outweigh the weaknesses.

By its very nature, biblical narrative places a considerable exegetical burden on its audience. Marked by terseness and lacunae, reluctant to reveal motives and feelings, sparing in physical details, the style of biblical narrative necessitates close reading. Reflecting on the demands placed on the reader by "a multi-dimensional narrative," Berlin writes:

> The resulting narrative is one with depth and sophistication; one in which conflicting viewpoints may vie for validity. It is this that gives biblical narrative interest and ambiguity. The reader of such narrative

is not a passive recipient of a story, but an active participant in trying
to understand it. Because he is given different points of view, sees
things from different perspectives, he must struggle to establish his
own.[32]

The text-based approach to figurative language employed in this
study enhances the reader's ability to participate in this interpretive
process. The methods introduced to identify and interpret metaphor
and other tropes help the exegete to pay close attention to how
language is used and to the rhetorical effects produced by the
anomalous collocation of lexemes in a given utterance. An in-depth
analysis of the figurative language in Samuel results in a richer, more
nuanced reading of the story, its characters, and its language. A better understanding of the "internal drama performed by the actual
words of the metaphor"[33] and other tropes contributes to a better
understanding of figurative language in general and the compelling,
artfully-crafted dramas that unfold in Bible.

---

[32] Berlin, *Poetics and Interpretation of Biblical Narrative*, 82.
[33] White, 115.

BIBLIOGRAPHY

Aaron, David. *Biblical Ambiguities: Metaphor, Semantics and Divine Imagery*. Leiden: Brill Academic Publishers, Inc., 2001.

Abū Dīb, Kamāl. *Al-Jurjānī's Theory of Poetic Imagery*. Warminster: Aris and Phillips, 1979.

Adler, Elaine. *Background for the Metaphor of Covenant as Marriage in the Hebrew Bible*. Ph.D. diss., University of California at Berkeley, 1990.

Agha, Asif. "Tropic Aggression in the Clinton-Dole Presidential Debate." *Pragmatics* 7 (1996) 461–497.

Alonso Schökel, Luis. *A Manual of Hebrew Poetics*. Rome: Pontifical Biblical Institute, 1988.

Alter, Robert. *The Art of Biblical Literature*. New York: Basic Books, Inc., 1981.

———. *The David Story*. New York: W. W. Norton & Company, 1999.

———. *The Five Books of Moses*. New York: W. W. Norton & Company, 2004.

———. *Genesis*. New York: W. W. Norton & Company, 1996.

Andersen, Francis I. *Habakkuk*. New York: Doubleday, 2001.

Andersen, Francis and David Noel Freedman. *Hosea*. New York: Doubleday, 1980.

Aristotle. *The Art of Rhetoric*. Translated by H. C. Lawson-Tracred. New York: Penguin Books, 1991.

———. *The Poetics*. Translated by Stephen Halliwell. London: Gerald Duckworth and Co. Ltd., 1987.

Babut, Jean-Marc. *Idiomatic Expressions of the Hebrew Bible: Their Meaning and Translation through Componential Analysis*. Translated by Sarah E. Lind. North Richland Hills, Texas: BIBAL Press, 1999.

Bar-Efrat, Shimon. *1 and 2 Samuel: With Introduction and Commentary* (in Hebrew). Tel Aviv: Am Oved; Jerusalem: Magnes Press, 1996.

———. *Narrative Art in the Bible*. Sheffield: Sheffield Academic Press, 1989.

Barcelona, Antonio. "Introduction: The Cognitive Theory of Metaphor and Metonymy." In *Metaphor and Metonymy at the Crossroads: A Cognitive Perspective*, ed. Antonio Barcelona, 1–30. Berlin: Mouton de Gruyter, 2000.

———, ed. *Metaphor and Metonymy at the Crossroads: A Cognitive Perspective*. Berlin: Mouton de Gruyter, 2000.

Barnstone, Willis. *The Poetics of Translation: History, Theory, Practice*. New Haven: Yale University Press, 1993.

Barr, James. "Scope and Problems in the Semantics of Classical Hebrew." *ZAH* 6 (1993) 3–14.

Beardsley, M. C. *Aesthetics: Problems in the Philosophy of Criticism*. 2d ed. Indianapolis: Hackett Publishing Company, Inc., 1981.

Berlin, Adele. *Dynamics of Biblical Parallelism*. Bloomington: Indiana University Press, 1985.

———. "Introduction to Hebrew Poetry." In *The New Interpreter's Bible*, vol. IV, 301–315. Nashville: Abingdon Press, 1996.

———. "On Reading Biblical Poetry: The Role of Metaphor." *Congress Volume, Cambridge 1995*, ed. J. A. Emerton, 25–36. Leiden: Brill, 1997.

———. *Poetics and Interpretation of Biblical Narrative*. Sheffield: Almond Press, 1983.

Biddle, Mark E. "Ancestral Motifs in 1 Samuel 25: Intertextuality and Characterization." *JBL* 121 (2002) 617–638.

Bird, P. "To Play the Harlot: An Inquiry into an Old Testament Metaphor." In *Gender and Difference in Ancient Israel*, ed. Peggy Day, 75–94. Minneapolis: Fortress Press, 1989.

Black, Max. "Metaphor." In *Philosophical Perspectives on Metaphor*, ed. Mark Johnson, 63–82. Minneapolis: University of Minnesota Press, 1981; reprint *Proceedings from the Aristotelian Society*. N.S. 55 (1954–55) 273–294.

———. "More about Metaphor." In *Metaphor and Thought*, ed. Andrew Ortony, 19–41. Cambridge: Cambridge University Press, 1979.

Blenkinsopp, Joseph. *Ezra-Nehemiah*. Philadelphia: The Westminster Press, 1988.

———. *Isaiah 1–39*. New York: Doubleday, 2000.

Blois, Kees de. "Metaphor in Common Language Translations of Joel." *Bible Translator* 36 (1985) 208–216.

Bohn, W. "Jakobson's Theory of Metaphor and Metonymy, An Annotated Bibliography." *Style* 18 (1984) 534–550.

Booth, Wayne C. "Metaphor as Rhetoric: The Problem of Evaluation." In *On Metaphor*, ed. Sheldon Sacks, 47–70. Chicago: University or Chicago Press, 1979.

Borowski, Oded. *Every Living Thing: Daily Use of Animals in Ancient Israel*. Walnut Creek, CA: Altamira Press, 1998.

Botterweck, G. J. and H. Riggren. *Theological Dictionary of the Old Testament*. 12 vols. Grand Rapids: Eerdmans, 1974–2003.

Bourguet, Daniel. *Des métaphores de Jérémie*. Paris: J. Gabalda, 1987.

Braaten, Laurie J. "Parent-Child Imagery in Hosea." Ph.D. Dissertation, Boston University, 1987.

Bredin, H. "Metonymy." *Poetics Today* 5 (1984) 45–58.

Brenner, Athalya and Jan Willem van Henten, eds. *Bible Translation on the Threshold of the Twenty-First Century: Authority, Reception, Culture and Religion*. Sheffield: Sheffield Academic Press, 2002.

Brensinger, Terry Lee. *Simile and Prophetic Language in the Old Testament*. Lewiston, NY: The Edwin Mellen Press, 1996.

Brettler, Marc Zvi. *God Is King: Understanding an Israelite Metaphor*. Sheffield: Sheffield Academic Press, 1989.

———. "Incompatible Metaphors for YHWH in Isaiah 40–66." *JSOT* 78 (1998) 97–120.

———. "The Metaphorical Mapping of God in the Hebrew Bible." In *Metaphor, Canon and Community: Jewish, Christian and Islamic Approaches*, ed. Ralph Bisschops and James Francis, 219–232. Oxford: Peter Lang, 1999.

Brooke-Rose, Christine. *A Grammar of Metaphor*. London: Secker & Warburg, 1958.

Brown, F., S. R. Driver, and Charles A. Briggs. *A Hebrew and English Lexicon of the Old Testament*. Oxford: Clarendon Press, 1951.

Brown, Leslie. *Birds of Prey: Their Biology and Ecology*. New York: A & W Publishers, Inc, 1977.

Brown, William P. *Seeing the Psalms: A Theology of Metaphor*. Louisville: Westminster John Knox Press, 2002.

Buber, Martin and Franz Rosenzweig. *Scripture and Translation*. Translated by Lawrence Rosenwald with Everett Fox. Bloomington: Indiana University Press, 1994.

Buccellati, Giorgio. "Towards a Formal Typology of Akkadian Similes." In *Cuneiform Studies in Honor of Samuel Noah Kramer*, ed. Barry Eichler et al., 59–70. Kevelaer: Butzon and Bercker, 1976.

Burbules, Nicholas, Gregory Schraw, and Woodrow Trathen. "Metaphor, Idiom, and Figuration." *Metaphor and Symbolic Activity* 4 (1989) 93–110.

Burk, Kenneth. "Four Master Tropes." In *A Grammar of Motives*. Berkeley: University of California Press, 1945.

Cacciari, Cristina. "The Place of Idioms in a Literal and Metaphorical World." In *Idioms: Processing, Structure, and Interpretation*, ed. Cristina Cacciari and Patrizia Tabossi, 27–55. Hillsdale, NJ: Lawrence Erlbaum Associates, 1993.

Caird, G. B. *The Language and Imagery of the Bible*. Grand Rapids, MI: William B. Eerdmans Publishing Company, 1997.

Camp, Claudia V. "Metaphor in Feminist Biblical Interpretation: Theoretical Perspectives." In *Women, War, and Metaphor: Language and Society in the Study of the Hebrew Bible*, ed. Claudia V. Camp and Carole R. Fontaine, 3–36. Semeia, 61. Atlanta: Scholars Press, 1993.

————. "Woman Wisdom as Root Metaphor: A Theological Consideration." In *The Listening Heart*, ed. K. Hoglund, et al., 45–76. Sheffield: JSOT Press, 1987.

Childs, Brevard. *Isaiah*. Louisville: Westminster John Knox Press, 2001.

Cicero. *Oratory and Orators*. Translated by J. S. Watson. Carbondale: Southern Illinois University Press, 1986.

Clark, David J. "Sex-related Imagery in the Prophets." *Bible Translator* 33 (1982) 409–13.

Clines, David, ed. *The Dictionary of Classical Hebrew*. 5 vols. Sheffield: Sheffield Academic Press, 1993–2001.

Coats, George W. "Self-Abasement and Insult Formulas." *JBL* 89 (1970) 14–26.

Cogan, Mordechai. *I Kings*. New York: Doubleday, 2000.

Cogan, Mordechai and Hayim Tadmor. *II Kings*. New York: Doubleday, 1988.

Cohen, L. Jonathan. "The Semantics of Metaphor." In *Metaphor and Thought*, ed. Andrew Ortony, 64–77. 2d ed. Cambridge: Cambridge University Press, 1993.

Cohen, Mordechai. "Moses Ibn Ezra vs. Maimonides: Argument for a Poetic Definition of Metaphor (*Istiʿāra*)." *Edebiyât: Journal of Middle Eastern and Comparative Literature* 11 (2000) 1–28.

————. *Three Approaches to Biblical Metaphor: From Ibn Ezra and Maimonides to David Kimhi*. Leiden: Brill, 2003.

Cohen, Ted. "Metaphor and the Cultivation of Intimacy." In *On Metaphor*, ed. Sheldon Sacks, 1–10. Chicago: University of Chicago Press, 1979.

Cooper, D. *Metaphor*. Oxford: Basil Blackwell, 1986.

Corro, Anicia del. "The Use of Figurative Language." *The Bible Translator* 42 (1991) 114–127.

Croft, William. "The Role of Domains in The Interpretation of Metaphors and Metonymies." In *Metaphor and Metonymy in Comparison and Contrast*, ed. René Dirven and Ralf Pörings, 161–205. Berlin: Mouton de Gruyter, 2002.

Crystal, David. *The Cambridge Encyclopedia of Language*. 2d ed. Cambridge: Cambridge University Press, 1997.

Culler, Jonathan. "The Turns of Metaphor." In *The Pursuit of Signs: Semiotics, Literature, Deconstruction*, 188–209. Ithaca: Cornell University Press, 1981.

Dahood, M. J. "Congruity of Metaphors." In *Hebräische Wortforschung*, 40–49. Leiden: E. J. Brill, 1967.

Darr, Katheryn Pfisterer. *Isaiah's Vision and the Family of God*. Louisville, KY: Westminster/John Knox Press, 1994.

————. "Two Unifying Female Images in the Book of Isaiah." In *Uncovering Ancient Stones: Essays in Memory of H. Neil Richardson*, ed. Lewis M. Hopfe. Winona Lake, IN: Eisenbrauns, 1994.

Davidson, Donald. "What Metaphors Mean." In *On Metaphor*, ed. Sheldon Sacks, 29–45. Chicago: University of Chicago Press, 1979.

Day, Peggy. "Adulterous Jerusalem's Imagined Demise: Death of a Metaphor in Ezekiel XVI." *VT* 50 (2000) 285–309.

Dhorme, E. *L'emploi metaphorique des noms de parties du corps en hébreu et en akkadien*. Paris: 1923.

Dick, M. B. "The Legal Metaphor in Job 31." *CBQ* 41 (1979) 37–50.

Dijk-Hemmes, Fokkelien van. "The Metaphorization of Woman in Prophetic Speech: An Analysis of Ezekiel XXIII." *VT* 43 (1993) 162–70.

Dirven, René. "Metonymy and Metaphor: Different Mental Strategies of Conceptual-
     isation." In *Metaphor and Metonymy in Comparison and Contrast*, ed. René Dirven
     and Ralf Pörings, 75–111. Berlin: Mouton de Gruyter, 2002.
———. "Metaphor as a Basic Means for Extending the Lexicon." In *The Ubiquity
     of Metaphor*, ed. R. Dirven and W. Paprotte, 85–119. Amsterdam: John Benjamins,
     1985.
Dirven, René and Ralf Pörings, eds. *Metaphor and Metonymy in Comparison and Contrast*.
     Berlin: Mouton de Gruyter, 2002.
Driver, G. R. "Birds in the Old Testament, I. Birds in Law." *Palestine Exploration
     Quarterly* (1955), 5–20.
———. "Birds in the Old Testament, II. Birds in Life." *Palestine Exploration Quarterly*
     (1955), 129–140.
Driver, S. R. *Notes on the Hebrew Text of the Books of Samuel*. Oxford: Clarendon Press,
     1913.
Dubois, Jacques, et al. *Rhétorique générale*. Paris: Larousse, 1970.
Eco, Umberto. "Sémantique de la métaphore." *Tel Quel* 55 (1973) 25–46.
Eissfeldt, O. "Der Beutel der Lebendigen, alttestamentliche Erzahlungs und Dich-
     tungsmotive in Lichte neuer Nuzi-texte," *Berichte uber die Verhandlungen der Sachsischen
     Akademie der Wissenschaften zu Leipzig*, Philologisch-historische Klasse, Band 105,
     Heft 6. Berlin, 1960.
Empson, William. *The Structure of Complex Words*. New York: New Directions, 1951.
Exum, J. Cheryl. "Of Broken Pots, Fluttering Birds and Visions in the Night:
     Extended Simile and Poetic Technique in Isaiah." *CBQ* 43 (1981) 331–352.
Fensham, F. C. "The Marriage Metaphor in Hosea for the Covenant Relationship
     between the Lord and His People (Hos. 1:2–9)." *JNSL* 12 (1984) 71–78.
Fernando, Chitra. *Idioms and Idiomaticity*. Oxford: Oxford University Press, 1996.
Feyaerts, Kurt, ed. *The Bible through Metaphor and Translation: A Cognitive Semantic
     Perspective*. Oxford: Peter Lang, 2003.
Fields, Weston. "The Translation of Biblical Live and Dead Metaphors and Similes
     and Other Idioms." *Grace Theological Journal* (1981) 191–204.
Fisch, Harold. "The Analogy of Nature, a Note on the Structure of Old Testament
     Imagery." *Journal of Theological Studies* NS, 6 (1955) 161–173.
Fokkelman, J. P. *Narrative Art and Poetry in the Books of Samuel*. 4 vols. Assen: Van
     Gorcum, 1981–1993.
Forsman, Dick. *The Raptors of Europe and The Middle East*. London: T & AD Poyser,
     1999.
Fox, Everett. *The Five Books of Moses*. New York: Schocken Books, 1995.
———. *Give Us a King*. New York: Schocken Books, 1999.
Franzmann, Majella. "The City as Woman: The Case of Babylon in Isaiah 47."
     Australian Biblical Review 43 (1995) 1–9.
Fronzaroli, Pelio. "Componential Analysis." *ZAH* 6 (1993) 79–91.
Frye, Northrop. *The Great Code: The Bible and Literature*. San Diego: Harcourt, Brace,
     Jovanovich, 1983.
Galambush, Julie. *Jerusalem in the Book of Ezekiel: The City as Yahweh's Wife*. Atlanta:
     Scholars Press, 1992.
Galán, José M. "What Is He, The Dog." *UF* 25 (1993) 173–180.
Garsiel, Moshe. *The First Book of Samuel: A Literary Study of Comparative Structures, Analogies
     and Parallels*. Tel Aviv: Revivim Publishing Houses, 1985.
———. "Wit, Words, and a Woman: 1 Samuel 25." In *On Humour and the Comic in
     the Hebrew Bible*, ed. Yehuda Radday and Athalya Brenner, 161–168. Sheffield:
     The Almond Press, 1990.
Gaster, Theodor. *Myth, Legend, and Custom in the Old Testament*. New York: Harper
     & Row, Publishers, 1969.

Genette, Gérard. "La Rhétorique restreinte." In *Figures III*, 21–40. Paris: Edtitions du Seuil, 1972.

Gibbs, Raymond W., Jr. *The Poetics of Mind: Figurative Thought, Language and Understanding.* Cambridge: Cambridge University Press, 1994.

———. "Process and Products in Making Sense of Tropes." In *Metaphor and Thought*, ed. Andrew Ortony, 252–276. 2d ed. Cambridge: Cambridge University Press, 1993.

———. "The Process of Understanding Literary Metaphor." *Journal of Literary Semantics* 19 (1990) 65–79.

———. "Skating on Thin Ice: Literal Meaning and Understanding Idioms in Conversation." *Disclosure Processes* 9 (1986) 17–30.

———. "Speaking and Thinking with Metonymy." In *Metonymy in Language and Thought*, ed. Klaus-Uwe Panther and Günter Radden, 61–76. Amsterdam/Philadelphia: John Benjamins Publishing Company, 1999.

———. "Why Idioms Are Not Dead Metaphors." In *Idioms: Processing, Structure, and Interpretation*, ed. Cristina Cacciari and Patrizia Tabossi, 57–77. Hillsdale, NJ: Lawrence Erlbaum Associates, 1993.

Gibson, J. C. L. *Language and Imagery in the Old Testament.* Peabody, MA: Hendrickson Publishers, Inc., 1998.

Ginsberg, H. L. "Heart." Page 8 in vol. 8 of *Encyclopaedia Judaica.* Jerusalem: Encyclopaedia Judaica, 1971–72.

Gitay, Yehoshua. "Why Metaphors: A Study of the Texture of Isaiah." *Writing and Reading the Scroll of Isaiah: Studies of an Interpretive Tradition*, ed. Craig C. Broyles and Craig A. Evans, 57–65. Leiden: Brill, 1997.

Glucksberg, Sam. "Idiom Meanings and Allusional Content." In *Idioms: Processing, Structure, and Interpretation*, ed. Cristina Cacciari and Patrizia Tabossi, 3–26. Hillsdale, NJ: Lawrence Erlbaum Associates, 1993.

Glucksberg, Sam and Boaz Keysar. "How Metaphors Work." In *Metaphor and Thought*, ed. Andrew Ortony, 401–424. 2d ed. Cambridge: Cambridge University Press, 1993.

———. "Understanding Metaphorical Comparisons: Beyond Similarity." *Psychology Review* 97 (1990) 3–18.

Good, E. M. "Ezekiel's Ship: Some Extended Metaphors in the Old Testament." *Semitics* 7 (1970) 79–103.

Goossens, Louis. "From Three Respectable Horses' Mouths: Metonymy and Conventionalization in a Diachronically Differentiated Data Base." In *By Word of Mouth: Metaphor, Metonymy and Linguistic Action in a Cognitive Perspective*, Louis Goossens, et al., 175–204. Amsterdam/Philadelphia: John Benjamins Publishing Company, 1995.

———. "Metaphtonymy: The Interaction of Metaphor and Metonymy in Figurative Expressions for Linguistic Action." In *By Word of Mouth: Metaphor, Metonymy and Linguistic Action in a Cognitive Perspective*, Louis Goossens, et al., 159–174. Amsterdam/Philadelphia: John Benjamins Publishing Company, 1995.

Goossens, Louis et al. *By Word of Mouth: Metaphor, Metonymy and Linguistic Action in a Cognitive Perspective.* Amsterdam/Philadelphia: John Benjamins Publishing Company, 1995.

Gordon, Robert. "David's Rise and Saul's Demise: Narrative Analogy in 1 Samuel 24–26." *Tyndale Bulletin* 31 (1980) 37–64.

Gray, J. "A Metaphor from Building in Zephaniah II 1." *VT* 3 (1953) 404–407.

Green, Barbara. *Like a Tree Planted: An Exploration of Psalms and Parables through Metaphor.* Collegeville, MN: The Liturgical Press, 1997.

Greenberg, Moshe. *Ezekiel 1–20.* New York: Doubleday, 1983.

———. *Ezekiel 21–37.* New York: Doubleday, 1997.

Greenstein, Edward. "Trans-semitic Idiomatic Equivalency and the Derivation of Hebrew *ml'kh*," *UF* 11 (1979) 329–336.

———. "Theories of Modern Bible Translation." Chap. in *Essays on Biblical Method and Translation*, 85–118. Atlanta: Scholars Press, 1989.

Gruber, Mayer I. *Aspects of Nonverbal Communication*. Rome: Biblical Institute Press, 1980.

Gunn, David. *The Fate of King Saul*. Sheffield: Almond Press, 1980.

Gunn, David and Danna Nolan Fewell. *Narrative in the Hebrew Bible*. Oxford: Oxford University Press, 1993.

Hall, Gary. "Origin of the Marriage Metaphor." *Hebrew Studies* 23 (1983) 167–171.

Hallo, William W., ed. *Context of Scripture*. Vol. III. Leiden: Brill, 2002.

Hammond, Gerald. "English Translations of the Bible." In *The Literary Guide to the Bible*, ed. Robert Alter and Frank Kermode, 647–666. Cambridge: The Belknap Press of Harvard University Press, 1987.

Harris, Wendell V. *Dictionary of Concepts in Literary Criticism and Theory*. Westport, CN: Greenwood Press, 1992.

Harvey, Warren Zvi. "The Pupil, the Harlot and the Fringe Benefits: Midrashic Interpretation of Metaphor, Num. 15:37–41." *Prooftexts* 6 (1986) 259–264.

Hawke, Terence. *Metaphor*. London: Methuen, 1984.

Hillers, D. R. "A Convention in Hebrew Literature: The Reaction to Bad News." *ZAW* 77 (1965) 86–90.

———. "The Effective Simile in Biblical Literature." *JAOS* 103 (1983) 181–185.

Hospers, Johannes Hendrik. "Polysemy and Homonymy." *ZAH* 6 (1993) 114–123.

Irwin, William H. "The Metaphor in Prov. 11:30." *Biblica* 65 (1984) 97–100.

Jackendoff, Ray and David Aaron. Review of *More Than Cool Reason*, by George Lakoff and Mark Turner. In *Language* 67 (1991) 320–338.

Jakobson, Roman. "Linguistics and Poetics." In *Style and Language*, ed. T. A. Sebeok. Cambridge: MIT Press, 1960.

———. "Two Aspects of Language and Two Types of Aphasic Disturbances." In *Language in Literature*, ed. Krystyna Pomorska and Stephen Rudy, 95–114. Cambridge: Belknap Press of Harvard University Press, 1987.

Jenni, E. and C. Westermann, eds. *Theological Lexicon of the Old Testament*. 3 vols. Translated by Mark Biddle. Peabody, MA: Hendrickson Publishers, 1997.

Johnson, Mark. "Introduction: Metaphor in the Philosophical Tradition." In *Philosophical Perspectives on Metaphor*, ed. Mark Johnson, 3–47. Minneapolis: University of Minnesota Press, 1981.

Jorgensen, E. Jordt. *Encyclopedia of Bible Creatures*. Philadelphia: Fortress Press, 1965.

Joüon, Paul. *A Grammar of Biblical Hebrew*. Translated by T. Muraoka. Rome: Pontifical Biblical Institute, 1993.

Katz, Jerrold J. and Jerry A. Fodor. "The Structure of Semantic Theory." *Language* 39 (1963) 170–210.

Keel, O. *Symbolism of the Biblical World: Ancient Near Eastern Iconography and the Book of Psalms*. Translated by Timothy J. Hallett. New York: Seabury Press, 1978.

King James Version of the Holy Bible. New York: New American Library, Inc., 1974.

Kittay, Eva. *Metaphor: Its Cognitive Force and Linguistic Structure*. Oxford: Clarendon Press, 1987.

Kleven, Terence. "The Cows of Bashan: A Single Metaphor at Amos 4:1–3." *CBQ* 58 (1996) 215–227.

Knorina, Lida. "The Range of Biblical Metaphors in smikhut." Unpublished paper, 1994.

Koehler, Ludwig and Walter Baumgartner. *Hebräisches und aramäisches Lexikon zum Alten Testament*. 4 vols. Leiden: E. J. Brill, 1967–1990.

Korpel, Marjo C. A. "Metaphors in Isaiah LV." *VT* 46 (1996) 43–55.

———. *A Rift in the Clouds: Ugaritic and Hebrew Descriptions of the Divine*. Munster: UGARIT-Verlag, 1990.

Kovecses, Zoltan and Peter Szabo. "Idioms: A View from Cognitive Semantics." *Applied Linguistics* 17 (1996) 326–355.

Kramer, Samuel Noah. "Sumerian Similes: A Panoramic View of Some of Man's Oldest Literary Images." *JAOS* 89 (1969) 1–10.

Kronfeld, Chana. "Novel and Conventional Metaphors: A Matter of Methodology." *Poetics Today* 2 (1980/81) 13–24.

Kruger, P. A. "Prophetic Imagery: On Metaphors and Similes in the Book of Hosea." *JNSL* 14 (1988) 143–151.

Lakoff, George. "The Contemporary Theory of Metaphor." In *Metaphor and Thought*, ed. Andrew Ortony, 202–251. 2d ed. Cambridge: Cambridge University Press, 1993.

———. "The Meanings of Literal." *Metaphor and Symbolic Activity* 1 (1986) 291–296.

Lakoff, George and Mark Johnson. *Metaphors We Live By*. Chicago: University of Chicago Press, 1980.

Lakoff, George and Mark Turner. *More Than Cool Reason: A Field Guide to Poetic Metaphor*. Chicago: University of Chicago Press, 1989.

Leech, Geoffrey. *A Linguistic Guide to English Poetry*. London: Longman Group Limited, 1969.

Levenson, Jon D. "1 Samuel 25 as Literature and History." *CBQ* 40 (1978) 11–28.

Levin, Samuel R. "Language, Concepts, and Words: Three Domains of Metaphor." In *Metaphor and Thought*, ed. Andrew Ortony, 112–123. 2d ed. Cambridge: Cambridge University Press, 1993.

Lodge, David. *The Modes of Modern Writing*. Ithaca, NY: Cornell University Press, 1977.

Loewenberg, Ina. "Identifying Metaphors." *Foundations of Language* 12 (1975) 315–338.

Long, Gary Alan. "Dead or Alive?: Literality and God Metaphors in the Hebrew Bible." *JAAR* 62 (1994) 509–537.

Lowth, Robert. *Lectures on the Sacred Poetry of the Hebrews (1787)*. Vol. 1. Hildesheim: Georg Olms Verlag, 1969.

Lundbom, Jack. *Jeremiah 1–20*. New York: Doubleday, 1999.

Lyons, John. *Introduction to Theoretical Linguistics*. Cambridge: Cambridge University Press, 1968.

———. *Language and Linguistics*. Cambridge: Cambridge University Press, 1981.

———. *Linguistic Semantics*. Cambridge: Cambridge University Press, 1995.

MacCormac, Earl R. *A Cognitive Theory of Metaphor*. Cambridge: The MIT Press, 1985.

Machinist, Peter. "Assyria and Its Image in the First Isaiah." *JAOS* 103 (1983) 719–737.

Macky, Peter W. *Centrality of Metaphors to Biblical Thought: A Method for Interpreting the Bible*. Lewiston, NY: The Edwin Mellen Press, 1990.

Malul, Meir. "Adoption of Foundlings in the Bible and Mesopotamian Documents: A Study of Some Legal Metaphors in Ezekiel 16:1–7." *JSOT* 46 (1990) 97–126.

Martin, Wallace. "Metaphor." In *The New Princeton Encyclopedia of Poetry and Poetics*, ed. Alex Preminger and T. V. F. Brogan, 760–768. Princeton: Princeton University Press, 1993.

Matthews, Robert J. "Concerning a 'Linguistic Theory' of Metaphor." *Foundations of Language* 7 (1971) 413–425.

McCarter, P. Kyle. *1 and 2 Samuel*. 2 vols. New York: Doubleday, 1980, 1984.

McFague, Sallie. *Metaphorical Theology: Models of God in Religious Language*. Philadelphia: Fortress Press, 1982.

Merrel, Floyd. "Of Metaphor and Metonymy." *Semiotica* 31 (1980) 289–307.

———. "Metaphor and Metonymy: A Key to Narrative Structure." *Language and Style* 11 (1978) 146–163.

Metzger, Bruce M. *The Bible in Translation: Ancient and English Versions*. Grand Rapids: Baker Academic, 2001.

Mikre-Sellassie, G. Ammanuel. "Metonymy in the Book of Psalms." *The Bible Translator* 44 (1993) 418–425.

Miller, P. D. "Meter, Parallelism, and Tropes: The Search for Poetic Style." *JSOT* 28 (1984) 99–106.

Miscall, Peter. *1 Samuel: A Literary Reading*. Bloomington: Indiana University Press, 1986.

Monaco, Richards and John Briggs. *The Logic of Poetry*. New York: McGraw-Hill, 1990.

Moran, William. *The Amarna Letters*. Baltimore: The John Hopkins University Press, 1992.

Morgan, J. L. "Observations on the Pragmatics of Metaphor." In *Metaphor and Thought*, ed. Andrew Ortony, 124–134. 2d ed. Cambridge: Cambridge University Press, 1993.

Nach, S. and M. P. Weitzman. "*Tiros*—Wine or Grape? A Case of Metonymy." *VT* 44 (1994) 115–120.

Netzer, Ehud. "Massive Structures: Processes in Construction and Deterioration." In *The Architecture of Ancient Israel*, ed. Aharon Kempinski and Ronny Reich, 17–27. Jerusalem: Israel Exploration Society, 1992.

New American Bible. Washington, D.C.: Confraternity of Christian Doctrine, 1986.

New Jerusalem Bible. New York: Darton, Longman & Todd, Ltd and Doubleday, 1985.

New Revised Standard Version Bible. New York: National Council of the Churches of Christ in the U.S.A., 1989.

Newmark, Peter. "The Translation of Metaphor." In *The Ubiquity of Metaphor*, ed. R. Dirven and W. Paprotte, 295–326. Amsterdam: John Benjamins, 1985.

Newsom, Carol. "A Maker of Metaphors—Ezekiel's Oracles Against Tyre." *Interpretation* 38 (1984) 151–64.

Nida, Eugene A. *Componential Analysis of Meaning*. The Hague: Mouton, 1975.

Nida, Eugene A. and Charles R. Taylor. *The Theory and Practice of Translation*. Leiden: E. J. Brill, 1982.

Nielsen, Kirsten. "Old Testament Metaphors in the New Testament." In *New Directions in Biblical Theology*, ed. Sigfred Pedersen. Leiden: E. J. Brill, 1994.

———. *There is Hope for a Tree. The Tree as Metaphor in Isaiah*. Sheffield: JSOT Press, 1989.

Noppen, J. P. van, ed. *Metaphor: A Bibliography of Post-1970 Publications*. Amsterdam/Philadelphia: John Benjamins Publishing Company, 1985.

Noppen, J. P. van and Edith Hols, eds. *Metaphor II: A Classified Bibliography of Publications 1985 to 1990*. Amsterdam/Philadelphia: John Benjamins Publishing Company, 1990.

Nöth, W. "Semiotic Aspects of Metaphor." In *The Ubiquity of Metaphor*, ed. R. Dirven and W. Paprotte, 1–15. Amsterdam: John Benjamins, 1985.

Oestreich, Bernhard. *Metaphors and Similes for Yahweh in Hoseah 14:2–9*. Frankfurt am Main: Peter Lang, 1998.

Orlinsky, Harry M. ed. *Notes on the New Translation of the Torah*. Philadelphia: The Jewish Publication Society, 1970.

Ortony, Andrew. "Metaphor, Language, and Thought." In *Metaphor and Thought*, ed. Andrew Ortony. 2d ed. Cambridge: Cambridge University Press, 1993.

———, ed. *Metaphor and Thought*. 2d ed. Cambridge: Cambridge University Press, 1993.

Owen, Stephen and Walter Reed. "A Motive for Metaphor." *Criticism* 21 (1979) 287–306.

Panther, Klaus-Uwe and Günter Radden, eds. *Metonymy in Language and Thought*. Amsterdam/Philadelphia: John Benjamins Publishing Company, 1999.

Paprotte, Wolf and René Dirven, eds. *The Ubiquity of Metaphor*. Amsterdam: John Benjamins Publishing Company, 1985.

Pardee, Dennis, S. David Sperling, J. David Whitehead, Paul E. Dion. *Handbook of Ancient Hebrew Letters*. Chico: Scholars Press, 1982.

Parker, Margaret. "Exploring Four Persistent Prophetic Images," *Bible Review* 6 (1990) 38–45.

Patnoe, Elizabeth. "Hyperbole." In *Encyclopedia of Rhetoric and Composition*, ed. Theresa Enos, 334–335. New York: Garland Publishing, Inc., 1996.

Paul, Shalom. "Heavenly Tablets and the Book of Life." *JANES* 5 (1973) 345–353.

Pauwels, Paul and Anne-Marie Simon-Vandenbergen. "Body Parts in Linguistic Action: Underlying Schemata and Value Judgements." In *By Word of Mouth: Metaphor, Metonymy and Linguistic Action in a Cognitive Perspective*, Louis Goossens, et al., 35–69. Amsterdam/Philadelphia: John Benjamins Publishing Company, 1995.

Perdue, Leo G. *Wisdom in Revolt: Metaphorical Theology in the Book of Job*. Sheffield: The Almond Press, 1991.

Pinney, Roy. *The Animals in the Bible: The Identity and Natural History of All the Animals Mentioned in the Bible*. Philadelphia: Chilton Books, 1964.

Plett, Henrich. "Hyperbole." In *Encyclopedia of Rhetoric*, ed. Thomas Sloane, 364. Oxford: Oxford University Press, 2001.

Polzin, Robert. *David and the Deuteronomist*. Bloomington: Indiana University Press, 1993.

———. *Samuel and the Deuteronomist*. Bloomington: Indiana University Press, 1989.

Pope, Marvin. *Job*. New York: Doubleday & Company, Inc., 1973.

Porter, Paul. *Metaphors and Monsters: A Literary Critical Study of Daniel 7 and 8*. Lund: CWK Gleerup, 1983.

Porter, Stanley F. and Richard S. Hess, eds. *Translating the Bible: Problems and Prospects*. Sheffield Academic Press, 1999.

Priestly, Joseph. *Lectures on Oratory and Criticism*, ed. V. M. Bevilacqua and R. Murphy. Carbondale: Southern Illinois University Press, 1965.

Propp, William. *Exodus 1–18*. New York: Doubleday, 1998.

Quinn, Arthur. *Figures of Speech*. Davis, CA: Hermagoras Press, 1993.

Quintilian. *Institutio Oratoria*. 4 vols. Translated by H. E. Butler. London: William Heinemann, 1921.

Radden, Günter and Zoltan Kovecses. "Towards a Theory of Metonymy." In *Metonymy in Language and Thought*, ed. Klaus-Uwe Panther and Günter Radden, 17–59. Amsterdam/Philadelphia: John Benjamins Publishing Company, 1999.

Reddy, Michael J. "A Semantic Approach to Metaphor." In *Papers from the Fifth Regional Meeting, Chicago Linguistics Society*, 240–251. Chicago: University of Chicago Department of Linguistics, 1969.

Reich, Ronny. "Building Materials and Architectural Elements in Ancient Israel." In *The Architecture of Ancient Israel*, ed. Aharon Kempinski and Ronny Reich, 1–16. Jerusalem: Israel Exploration Society, 1992.

Reinhart, T. "On Understanding Poetic Metaphor." *Poetics* 5 (1976) 383–402.

Revised English Bible. Oxford: Oxford University Press and Cambridge University Press, 1989.

Rhetorica Ad Herennium. Translated by Harry Caplan. Cambridge: Harvard University Press, 1954.

Richards, I. A. *The Philosophy of Rhetoric*. Oxford: Oxford University Press, 1936.

Ricoeur, Paul. "Metaphor and the Main Problem of Hermeneutics." *New Literary History* 6 (1974–75) 95–110.

———. *The Rule of Metaphor*. Translated by R. Czerny. Toronto: University of Toronto Press, 1977.

Roberts, J. J. M. "Job's Summons to Yahweh: The Exploitation of a Legal Metaphor." *Restoration Quarterly* 16 (1973) 159–165.

Rofé, Alexander. "Biblical Antecedents of the Targumic Solution of Metaphors (Ps 89:41–42; Ezek 22:25–28; Gen 49:8–9, 14–15)." *The Interpretation on the Bible* (1998) 333–338.

Rollinson, Phillip. *Classical Theories of Allegory and Christian Culture*. Pittsburgh: Duquesne University Press, 1981.

Ruegg, Maria. "Metaphor and Metonymy: The Logic of Structuralist Rhetoric." *Glyph* 6 (1979) 141–157.

Rumelhart, David E. "Some Problems with the Notion of Literal Meanings." In *Metaphor and Thought*, ed. Andrew Ortony, 70–82. 2d ed. Cambridge: Cambridge University Press, 1993.

Ryken, Leland. "Metaphor in the Psalms." *Christianity and Literature* (1982) 9–29.

Ryken, Leland, James Wilhoit, and Tremper Longman III, eds. *Dictionary of Biblical Imagery*. Dowmers Grove, IL: InterVarsity Press, 1998.

Sacks, Sheldon, ed. *On Metaphor*. Chicago: University of Chicago, 1979.

Sadock, Jerrold M. "Figurative Speech and Linguistics." In *Metaphor and Thought*, ed. Andrew Ortony, 42–57. 2d ed. Cambridge: Cambridge University Press, 1993.

Sarna, Nahum. *Genesis*. Philadelphia: Jewish Publication Society, 1989.

Schofer, Peter and Donald Rice. "Metaphor, Metonymy, and Synecdoche Revis(it)ed." *Semiotica* 21 (1977) 121–49.

Searle, John. "Metaphor." In *Metaphor and Thought*, ed. Andrew Ortony, 83–111. 2d ed. Cambridge: Cambridge University Press, 1993.

Segal, M. H. *Studies in the Books of Samuel*. Part II. Philadelphia: Dropsie College for Hebrew and Cognate Learning, 1917. Reprinted in *JQR* 8 (1917–18), 75–100.

Seto, Ken-ichi. "Distinguishing Metonymy from Synecdoche." In *Metonymy in Language and Thought*, ed. Klaus-Uwe Panther and Günter Radden, 91–120. Amsterdam/Philadelphia: John Benjamins Publishing Company, 1999.

Sharon-Zisser, Shirley. "A Distinction No Longer of Use: Evolutionary Discourse and the Disappearance of the Trope/Figure Binarism." *Rhetorica* 11 (1993) 321–342.

Shibles, Warren. *Metaphor: An Annotated Bibliography and History*. Whitewater, WI: Language Press, 1971.

Silverstein, Michael. "Metapragmatic Discourse and Metapragmatic Function." In *Reflexive Language*, ed. John Lucy, 33–58. Cambridge: Cambridge University Press, 1993.

Simian-Yofre, H. "La métaphore d'Ezechiel 15" in *Ezekiel: His Book*, ed. J. Lust. Leuven: Leuven University Press, 1986.

Smith, H. P. *A Critical and Exegetical Commentary on the Books of Samuel*. New York: Scribner, 1899.

Soskice, Janet Martin. *Metaphor and Religious Language*. Oxford: Oxford University Press, 1985.

Steen, Gerard. *Understanding Metaphor in Literature*. London: Longman Group Limited, 1994.

Stern, Josef. *Metaphor in Context*. Cambridge: The MIT Press, 2000.

Sternberg, Meir. *Poetics of Biblical Narrative*. Bloomington: Indiana University Press, 1985.

Stienstra, Nelly. *YHWH Is the Husband of His People: Analysis of a Biblical Metaphor with Special Reference to Translation*. Kampen: Kok Pharos, 1993.

Syreeni, Kari. "Metaphorical Appropriation: (Post) Modern Biblical Hermeneutic and the Theology of Metaphor." *Literature and Theology* 9 (1995) 321–338.

Tanakh: The Traditional Hebrew Text and The New JPS Translation. 2d ed. Philadelphia: Jewish Publication Society, 1999.

Taverniers, Miriam. *Metaphor and Metaphorology: A Selective Genealogy of Philosophical and Linguistic Conceptions of Metaphor from Aristotle to the 1990s*. Ghent: Academia Press, 2002.

Tigay, Jeffrey. *Deuteronomy*. Philadelphia: Jewish Publication Society, 1996.

———. "On Translating the Torah." *Conservative Judaism* 26 (1972) 14–30.

Toolan, Michael. *Total Speech: An Integrational Linguistic Approach to Language*. Durham: Duke University Press, 1996.

Tourageau, R. and L. Ripps. "Interpreting and Evaluating Metaphors." *Journal of Memory and Language* 30 (1991) 245 68.

Traugott, Elizabeth Closs. "'Conventional' and 'Dead' Metaphors Revisited." In *The Ubiquity of Metaphor*, ed. R. Dirven and W. Paprotte, 17–56. Amsterdam: John Benjamins, 1985.

Trudinger, Paul. "Biblical Metaphors and Symbols: Handle with Care." *Faith and Freedom* 46 (1993) 45–49.

Tuggy, David. "The Literal-Idiomatic Bible Translation Debate from the Perspective of Cognitive Grammar." In *The Bible Through Metaphor and Translation: A Cognitive Semantic Perspective*, ed. Kurt Feyaerts. Oxford: Peter Lang, 2003.

Tur Sinai, N. H. *The Book of Job: A New Commentary*. Rev. ed. Jerusalem: Kiryath Sepher, 1967.

Viberg, Ake. "Waking a Sleeping Metaphor: A New Interpretation of Malachi 1:1." *Tyndale Bulletin* 45 (1994) 297–319.

Waard, Jan de. "Biblical Metaphors and Their Translation." *Bible Translator* 25 (1974) 107–116.

Waard, Jan de and Eugene A. Nida. *From One Language to Another: Functional Equivalence in Bible Translating*. Nashville: Thomas Nelson Publishers, 1986.

Ward, Graham. "Biblical Narrative and the Theology of Metonymy." *Modern Theology* 7 (1991) 335–349.

Watson, Wilfred G. E. *Classical Hebrew Poetry*. Sheffield: JSOT Press, 1995.

———. "The Metáphor in Job 10:17." *Biblica* 63 (1982) 255–57.

Weinreich, U. "Explorations in Semantic Theory." In *Theoretical Foundations*, ed. T. A. Sebeok, 395–477. The Hague: Mouton, 1966.

Weisberg, David B. "Loyalty and Death: Some Ancient Near Eastern Metaphors." *Maarav* 7 (1991) 253–267.

Weiss, Meir. *The Bible From Within: The Method of Total Interpretation*. Jerusalem: The Magnes Press, 1984.

West, Gerald. "The Effect and Power of Discourse: A Case Study of a Metaphor in Hosea." *Scriptura* 57 (1996) 201–212.

Wheelwright, Philip. *Metaphor and Reality*. Bloomington, Indiana University Press, 1962.

White, Roger M. *The Structure of Metaphor*. Oxford: Blackwell Publishers, 1996.

Wilson, Robert. "The Hardening of Pharaoh's Heart." *CBQ* 41 (1979) 18–36.

Wolff, Hans Walter. *Hosea*. Philadelphia: Fortress Press, 1974.

Zatelli, Ida. "Pragmalinguistics and Speech-Act Theory as Applied to Classical Hebrew." *ZAH* 6 (1993) 60–74.

Zehnder, Markus Philipp. *Wegmetaphorik im Alten Testament: Eine semantische Untersuchung der alttestamentlichen und altorientalischen Weg-Lexeme mit besonderer Berücksichtigung ihrer metaphorischen Verwendung*. Berlin: Walter de Gruyter, 1999.

INDEX OF SCRIPTURES

INDEX OF SUBJECTS

INDEX OF AUTHORS